INFORMATION
TECHNOLOGY IN ACTION
TRENDS AND PERSPECTIVES

Selected titles from the YOURDON PRESS COMPUTING SERIES

Ed Yourdon, Advisor

Andrews and Leventhal: Fusion: Integrating IE, Case, and JAD
August: Joint Application Design
Baudin: Manufacturing Systems Analysis with Application to Production Scheduling
Bellin and Suchman: Structured Systems Development Manual
Block: The Politics of Projects
Boddie: Crunch Mode: Building Effective Systems on a Tight Schedule
Bouldin: Agents of Change: Managing the Introduction of Automated Tools
Brill: Building Controls into Structured Systems
Brill: Techniques of EDP Project Management: A Book of Readings
Chang: Principles of Visual Programming Systems
Coad and Nicole: Object-Oriented Programming
Coad and Yourdon: Object-Oriented Design
Coad and Yourdon: Object-Oriented Analysis, 2/E
Connell and Shafer: Structured Rapid Prototyping
Constantine and Yourdon: Structured Design
DeGrace and Stahl: Wicked Problems, Righteous Solutions
DeMarco: Controlling Software Projects
DeMarco: Structured Analysis and System Specification
Embley, Kurtz, and Woodfield: Object-Oriented Systems Analysis
Flavin: Fundamental Concepts in Information Modeling
Follman: Business Applications with Microcomputers
Fournier: Practical Guide to Structured System Development and Maintenance
Glass: Software Conflict
Grochow: SAA: A Guide to Implementing IBM's Systems Application Architecture
King: Current Practices in Software Development: A Guide to Successful Systems
King: Project Management Made Simple
Larson: Interactive Software: Tools for Building Interactive User Interfaces
Martin: Transaction Processing Facility: A Guide for Application Programmers
McMenamin and Palmer: Essential System Design
Mellor and Shlaer: Object Lifecycles: Modeling the World in States
Mellor and Shlaer: Object-Oriented Systems Analysis: Modeling the World in Data
Mosley: The Handbook of MIS Application Software Testing
Page-Jones: Practical Guide to Structured Systems Design, 2/E
Pinson: Designing Screen Interfaces in C
Putnam and Myers: Measures for Excellence: Reliable Software on Time, within Budget
Ripps: An Implementation Guide to Real-Time Programming
Rodgers: Oracle®: A Database Developer's Guide
Rodgers: UNIX®: Database Management Systems
Serbanati: Integrating Tools for Software Development
Shiller: Software Excellence
Toigo: Disaster Recovery Planning: Managing Risk and Catastrophe in Information Systems
Vesely: Strategic Data Management: The Key to Corporate Competitiveness
Ward: System Development without Pain
Ward and Mellor: Structured Development for Real-Time Systems
Yourdon: Decline and Fall of the American Programmer
Yourdon: Managing Structured Techniques, 4/E
Yourdon: Managing the System Life Cycle, 2E
Yourdon: Modern Structured Analysis
Yourdon: Structured Walkthroughs, 4/E
Yourdon: Techniques of Program Structure and Design

INFORMATION TECHNOLOGY IN ACTION
TRENDS AND PERSPECTIVES

Edited by

Richard Y. Wang

Sloan School of Management
Massachusetts Institute of Technology

With contributions by

Tim Andrews, William Bulkeley, Peter Chen,
Peter DiGiammarino, David Friend,
Paul Gillin, Jerrold Grochow, Henry Kon,
Stuart Madnick, Ed Oates,
David Rabinowitz, Adam Rin,
Charles Rossotti, Kenneth Rudin,
George Schussel, Stacey Schussel-Griffin,
Rick Sherlund, and Michael Zucchini

PTR Prentice Hall
Englewood Cliffs, New Jersey 07632

Library of Congress Cataloging-in-Publication Data

Information technology in action: tends and perspectives/edited by
  Richard Wang
  p. cm. — (Yourdon Press computing series)
  Includes bibliographical references and index.
  ISBN 0132210290
  1. Information technology. I. Wang, Richard Y. II. Series
  T58.5.I54 1993
  658.4'038'011—dc20   92-38651   CIP

Acquisitions editor: Paul Becker

Cover design: Wanda Lubelska

Copyeditor: H. Simón Bryce

Manufacturing buyer: Mary E. McCartney

Editorial assistant: Noreen Regina

Cover design director: Eloise Starkweather

Art production mnager: Gail Cocker-Bogusz

Illustrations by Vantage Art

Production team: Sophie Papanikolaou, Jane Bonnell, Janice McClam,
    John Morgan, Ann Sullivan, Camille Trentacoste, Brendan Stewart,
    Lisa Iarkowski, Mary Rottino, Harriet Tellem, and Phyllis Eve Bregman.

Proofreaders: Jane Byrne Smith,Kerry Reardon, Marielle Reiter, and Pat Guerrieri

Indexer: Barbara Palumbo

The book   was set in Microsoft Word and pages were made up using FrameMaker.

Published by PTR Prentice Hall
A Simon & Schuster Company
Englewood Cliffs, New Jersey 07632

T
58
.5
I54
1993

The publisher offers discounts on this book when ordered in bulk quantities. For more information, write: Special Sales/Professional Marketing, Prentice Hall, Professional Technical Reference Division, Englewood Cliffs, NJ 07632.

Printed in the United States of America
10 9 8 7 6 5 4 3 2 1

ISBN   0-13-221029-0

Prentice-Hall International (UK) Limited, *London*
Prentice-Hall of Australia Pty. Limited, *Sydney*
Prentice-Hall Canada Inc., *Toronto*
Prentice-Hall Hispanoamericana, S.A., *Mexico*
Prentice-Hall of India Private Limited, *New Delhi*
Prentice-Hall of Japan, Inc., *Tokyo*
Simon & Schuster Asia Pte. Ltd., *Singapore*
Editora Prentice-Hall do Brasil, Ltda., *Rio de Janeiro*

The following products are trademarks and/or registered trademarks of their respective manufacturers.

- Amdahl: UTS, Huron
- American Airline Reservation Systems: Sabre
- Andersen Consulting: Foundation
- Apple: Macintosh
- Ashton-Tate: Dbase
- ASK/Ingres: Ingres-Star
- Assymetric: Toolbook

- AT&T: UNIX, 3B2
- Borland: Object Vision, Paradox, Quattro Pro
- Chen & Associates: ER Modeler, Normalizer, Schema Generator
- Cincom: Advantage
- Cognos: Powerplay
- Computer Corporation of America: Model 204
- DEC: CDD+, Rdb, VAX 9000
- Fleet: Fleet One
- Fox: Fox Software, FoxBase
- Hewlett Packard: HP9000
- IBI: Focus
- IBM: AD/Cycle, DB2, DisplayWrite, DXT, ES/9000, IMS, MVS/XA, OS/2, OS/2EE, PI/I, Presentation Manager, Repository Manager, RM/MVA, System 390, VM/370, VMS, 3090
- Information Builders: Focus
- Informix: Informix
- Intel: IPSC, iWarp, 8086, 80286, 80386, 80486
- Intersolv: Excelerator
- KnowledegeWare: ADW, Information Engineering Workbench
- Lockheed: DIALOG
- Lotus: Lotus 1-2-3
- MCI: MCIMail
- Microsoft: DOS/MS-Windows, Excel, LAN Manager for Windows NT, MS-DOS, MS Multiplan, Visual Basic, Windows 3.x for DOS, Windows 4GL
- MIPS: R4000
- Motorola: 68000
- NCR: 3600
- nCUBE: nCUBE-1, 2 MPP Computer System
- Novell: Netware
- Oracle: Designer and Generator, Generator, Oracle DBMS, Oracle Server, Oracle 7
- Pilot Software: Lightship, Trend Spotter
- Seer Technology: HPS
- Software AG: Predict
- Software Publishing: Pro Flie

- Spinnaker: First Publisher
- Storage Technology: Iceberg
- Sun: SPARC
- Sybase: Sybase APT
- Symantec: Norton, Zortec, Q & A
- Teradata: DBC/1012, YNET
- Thinking Machines: CM2, CM5

The following names are registered trademarks or trademarks of their respective owners:

APT Workbench, Asset, Central Point, Cohesion, Concurrent, Corel, CP/IP LAN, Daisys, Data Based Advisor, DATACOM, DataEase, Deft, Empire, Enable, Enfin, Gpf, JYACC's JAM, Lansa, LU6.2, Maestro II, Mantis, Meiko, Micro Focus, Micro Rim, Motif, Netron, NeXT, OA Supercalc, Open Look, Pacbase, Paclan, Pacreverse, PL/SQL, Powerhouse, Predict CASE, PROMOD, Proteon, Pyramid, Quantum, Q & A,RPG III, S-Cubed, Sapiens, Seagate, Silicon Graphics, Simula, Slate, Small Talk, Smartstar, Softlab, SPX/IPX, SQL DS, SQL Forms, SQL Win, SQL Windows, SQL/400, Synon, System Engineer, Tandem, Thorn EMI, TECS, Tops, TRW, Uniface, VINECS, WordStar, Work Group, X3/H4, XDB Systems, XENIX.

Contents

Preface   xix

Contributors   xxiii

C H A P T E R   1   The Information Technology (IT) Industry   1

America's IT Industry   2

Participants in the IT Industry   4

Media   4

Investors   6

Firms in the IT Value Chain   6

Market Segments of Products and Services   7

Finding Information   8

Ask Experts   9

Bark up the Right Tree: Finding the Right Information   9

Get Your Hands Dirty   10

Get Ready for Prime Time   10

C H A P T E R   2   The Entity-Relationship Approach   13

Basic Concepts   14

Entities and Entity Types   14

Relationships and Relationship Types   15

Attributes and Values   17

Other Diagrammatic Notations   18

Advanced Concepts   19

    Weak Entities   19

    ISA Relationship   19

    Component-of Relationship   20

    Aggregated Entities   21

    The Gerund Entity Type   22

Pragmatic Skills in Developing
    an Enterprise Model   23

Market Segments of ER-Related Software
    Tools   24

    ER-Related CASE Tools   24

    ER-Related Repository Systems   27

    ER-Related DBMS's   28

Directions of the ER Approach   28

    Time Dimension Extensions   29

    Entity Lattice   29

    *Entity-Relationship vs. Object-Orientation
    30*

    Quality/Contextual ER Model   32

Concluding Remarks and Further Readings   33

Bibliography   34

    Conference Proceedings   35

CHAPTER 3   **Distributed and Client/Server DBMS:
Underpinning for Downsizing   37**

Introduction   38

Background on Distributed Database
    Computing   40

Background on Client/Server Database
    Computing   41

    The History Behind the Client/Server   42

    The Client   43

    The Network   44

    The Server   44

    The Benefits of Using SQL   45

More Details on Distributed DBMS's   46

    Basic Requirements for a Distributed DBMS   47

    IBM's Four Ways to Distribute Data   48

    Software Optimizers   50

    Two-Phase Commit Protocol   51

More Advanced Capabilities for Distributed (or Client/Server) DBMS's   52

More on Client/Servers   56

    Performance from a Client/Server Environment   58

Conclusion - A Reality Check   61

CHAPTER 4   Object Databases in Action: Technology and Application   63

Background   64

Persistent Language Environments   65

    Maintaining Object Identity   66

    Efficient Transfer of Objects   68

Databases of Objects   70

Component Object Databases   71

Approaches in Use Today   75

    Component Integration   76

    Adding Persistence: Inheritance and Registration   77

    The Storage Interface: Single-Level Stores and Seamlessness   79

Summary   81

References   81

C H A P T E R   5   **CASE and Application Development**
                      Technologies   **83**

CASE in State of Transition: A Brief Case
    History   84

> *What Problems Does CASE Address?*   *84*
>
> *CASE vs. System Development Methodologies*
> *85*
>
> *A Brief History of CASE*   *86*
>
> *Benefits and Pitfalls of CASE*   *88*

Technology and Industry Forces
    Affecting Applications Development
    Strategies and CASE   90

> *Client/Server Technology and Graphical*
> *User Interfaces*   *90*
>
> *Object-Oriented Technology*   *92*
>
> *Multiple Platforms in a World of Fragmented*
> *Standards*   *94*
>
> *Next Generation CASE and Application*
> *Development Environments*   *95*
>
> *A New Breed of Application Types*   *96*
>
> *The Need for CASE to Support*
> *Iterative Life Cycle (Process) Models*   *98*

Assessment of Alternative CASE and
    Applications Development Strategies and
    Vendor Classes   100

> *The Prototype-and-Build Approach*   *100*
>
> *Model-Prototype-Build, with Multiple*
> *Vendors' Tools*   *103*
>
> *Model-Prototype-Build, with a Single-*
> *Vendor's ADE and Tools*   *104*
>
> *Model-Prototype-Build with Multiple*
> *Vendors' Tools,*
> *But a Single Vendor's ADE*
> *Framework*   *110*
>
> *Combinations: Bottom-Up Revolution; Top-*
> *Down Evolution*   *111*

Which Way Should IS Organizations Go?   112

CHAPTER 6   **Database Computers**   **117**

Background and Motivation   118

*The Recognition of Relational Database
    Architecture   118*

*RDBM —Prodigious Consumers of Resources
    119*

The Micro-Processor Revolution   120

*The Need to Share Data Across
    Heterogeneous Platforms   121*

Connectivity Options for a Centralized Data
    Repository   121

Characteristics That a Database Computer
    Should Offer   122

Architecture of a Teradata DBC/1012   124

Keeping Up with Change   129

Scalability and Linearity   129

FALLBACK and Availability   130

The Future—NCR 3600 and 3700
    Implications   130

Conclusion   131

CHAPTER 7   **Massively Parallel Processing**   **133**

What is it?   134

Why Now?   134

Roadblocks to High Performance   136

Massively Parallel Architecture   138

Database Applicability   140

The Marketplace for Ultra-High Performance
    Applications   144

Case Study: Oracle for nCUBE   146

The Future: The New Mainframes?   152

CHAPTER 8   **Developing Strategic Business Systems**
             Using Object Technology 153

Introduction   154

Strategic Business Systems and Object
    Technology   155

Software Engineering for Object
    Technology   157

Life Cycle   157

Methods and Techniques   158

Tools and Languages   159

Design Repository   160

Estimating Methods   161

Training and Education   161

Ready for Prime Time?   162

Acknowledgments   163

References   163

CHAPTER 9   **Visual Information Access Systems   165**

Introduction   166

What is Visual Information Access?   167

The Problem with Paper   168

The Three Pillars of VIA   169

The Need for Middleware   170

Front-end GUI's   172

Back-End Database Servers   175

Conclusion   177

CHAPTER 1 0 **Toward Total Data Quality Management**
               (TDQM)   **179**

Social and Managerial Impacts
of Data Quality   180

Social Impacts: Privacy and Security   181

*Managerial Impacts: Customer Service,
Managerial Support, Productivity   181*

From Product Manufacturing to Data
Manufacturing   183

The Data Systems Life Cycle   184

The Data Product Value Chain   185

A Framework for Total Data Quality
Management   186

*Continuous Measurement, Analysis, and
Improvement   187*

*Economic, Technical, and Organizational
Perspectives   189*

Managing Data Quality   190

*Clearly Articulate a Data Quality Vision
191*

*Establish Central Responsibility for Data
Quality Within IS   191*

Educate Project and Systems Managers   193

*Teach New Data Quality Skills to the Entire
IS Organization   194*

*Institutionalize Continuous Data Quality
Improvement   195*

*Operationalizing Data Quality Management
195*

Concluding Remarks   197

CHAPTER 1 1 **The Media's Perspective: *Computerworld*   *201***

Introduction   202

The Understanding Gap   203

Understanding the Computer Press   207

How One Computer Publication Covers IT   208

    Audience   209

    Beats   210

    Staff   211

    What's News   211

    News Reporting   213

Caveat Emptor   214

CHAPTER 1 2 **The Media's Perspective:
The Wall Street Journal**   **217**

Effective Use of *The Wall Street Journal*   *218*

CHAPTER 1 3 **The Investor's Perspective:
Analyzing the IT Industry**   **221**

The Role of the Analyst and Efficient Markets
    222

Investment Considerations   223

Implications of Industry Trends   226

    New Generation of PC Software   226

Emergence of Client/Server Computing   228

CHAPTER 1 4 **The Consultant's Perspective**   **241**

Target Market   242

    General Market   243

    Market Segments   247

Service Framework   251

CHAPTER 1 5 **The CIO's Perspective:
Delivering IT Productivity**   **255**

Introduction   256

Why IT Has Assumed a Strategic Role in
    American Banking   257

What Can Consolidation Achieve?   260

The Re-Engineering of the Bank's Technology
  Infrastructures Is the Key to a Successful
  Consolidation   261

Consolidating and Re-Engineering the
  Infrastructure:
  Selected Cases   265

>   *The Consolidation of Data Centers   267*

>   *Commonality in IT Resources Means
>   Increased Consistency
>   and Quality   268*

>   *Check Processing: The Exception Case in
>   Consolidation   269*

Human Resource Management Is a Core
  Responsibility of the CIO in the Era of
  Technology-Inspired Reductions in Force   270

The Barriers to Successful Consolidation   272

A New Role for the CIO   274

>   *IT and the CIO Can Make Vital Contributions
>   to American Business in the 1990's   275*

Selected Readings   276

>   *Bank Mergers, Consolidations, and Related
>   Topics   276*

>   *Re-engineering and the IT Infrastructure
>   277*

>   *The Outsourcing Phenomenon   277*

>   *The Implications of Downsizing for Human
>   Resource Management   278*

>   *Information as a Strategic Corporate
>   Resource   278*

C H A P T E R   1 6 **Putting IT All Together Before It Falls Apart**

                                                                    279

The Double Threats: Business and IT Challenges
  280

Key Business Forces   281

Key IT Opportunities   282

Convergence of Business and IT Trends:
    Increased Connectivity   283

New IT Requirements   286

Conclusions: IT Is in Your Hands   286

Bibliography   287

Glossary   **289**

Index   **299**

Preface

If you would not be forgotten,
As soon as you are dead and rotten,
Either write things worthy reading,
Or do things worth the writing.

—Benjamin Franklin

The purpose of this book is to present information technology (IT) from the perspective of major players affecting the dynamics of the IT industry. These players include IT users, vendors, consultants, investors, and journalists.

This book is written for two types of readers:
- T professionals who wish to gain a broad understanding of the dynamics of the IT industry, and
- students who are interested in the IT industry.

A key message that we want to share with our readers is that in order to understand the dynamics of the IT industry, one must:
- have a general understanding of IT,
- have a good sense of emerging trends in IT, and
- have a broad understanding of the driving forces shaping the IT industry.

To get this message across, there is no better way than asking leading practitioners how they put IT into action. As such, Chapter 1 introduces the IT industry. The rest of the book presents trends and perspectives of different components of the IT industry, all written by leading practitioners in their fields.

This message, however, was not conceived spontaneously. It was an outgrowth of several semesters of teaching a graduate-level course, 15.565, offered as an IT concentration course for MBA students at the MIT Sloan School of Management. Historically, 15.565 was taught as a traditional database course. It first gave an overview of management information systems and the stages of information systems development. It then presented features and frameworks of database management systems (DBMS), followed by the three conventional database models (hierarchical, network, and relational). Next, it presented DBMS implementation strategies and compared commercially available DBMS's. Next, telecommunications and transaction management were presented. Finally, computer performance evaluation, capacity planning, and directions in database machines were presented to conclude this one-semester course.

Although well received, rapid changes in the IT industry necessitated us to cover trends and perspectives of the IT industry in addition to the fundamentals of information technologies. With the cooperation of Dr. Robert P. Goldberg, a co-founder and director of BGS, who was visiting MIT Sloan School, we started to experiment with a new approach for 15.565. Many Sloan MBA graduates also contributed greatly in numerous brainstorming sessions. As a result of this team effort, we identified major industry participants affecting the dynamics of the IT industry. We recognized that the best way to understand the IT industry is to listen to experts who put IT into action!

With 15.565 as a platform, we started to bring in industry participants to discuss their views and activities. All the contributors of this book participated in this course. Other practitioners have also helped shaping this course, such as

- Drew Brosseau (Vice President and Partner, Cowen),
- Maryann Burke (Senior Executive Vice President and CIO, Liberty Mutual),
- Gerry Cohen (Chairman and CEO, Information Builders),
- Robert Curtice (Vice President, Arthur D. Little),
- Mark Hansen (Principal, QDB Solution),
- Jesse Jacobson (President and CEO, Actuarial Solutions),
- Bill Jarosz (Director Connectivity Services, Fidelity Investments),
- Philippe Kahn (Chairman, President, and CEO, Borland International),
- John Landry (Chief Technology Officer, Lotus),
- Dick MacKinnon (Director, IBM Cambridge Scientific Center),
- Paul Newton (CEO, Bool and Babbage),
- Alan Sarasohn (VP of Customer Service, Bachman Information Systems),
- Mike Siemens (CIO, Bank of Boston),
- Dick Stuart (CEO, Computer Corporation of America),
- Michelle Swansen (Marketing Director, Charles Schwab),

- David Waltz (Director of Advanced IS, Thinking Machines), and
- Richard Winter (Chief Technology Officer, CCA).

In this process, we also came to articulate the message. This book is an attempt to convey this message to the reader and help the reader get started. There is no question in my mind that the contents of this book are timely and valuable. I hope that practitioners who are part of the IT industry will find this book insightful. And I hope that students will find this book not only interesting, but also a key to the IT industry.

Acknowledgments

There are many individuals to whom I want to express my gratitude for making this book project feasible.

First to Stu Madnick: without his continuous inspiration, encouragement and feedback, this project would have been short-lived. I also want to thank Gabe Bitran, head of the Management Science Area at MIT Sloan School of Management, for his full support of my academic activities in general and my course, 15.565, in particular. Bob Goldberg contributed not only ideas and industrial experience but also valuable time in helping to invite speakers and coordinating student projects in 15.565 over the past two years.

It is a privilege to express my appreciation to all the contributors of this book. All of them, when asked for help, simply said, "Yes, this is an interesting idea, I'll commit to write a chapter."

Thanks are also due to Deans Lester Thurow, Steve Graves, Bob McKersie, and Jeff Barks at Sloan School for creating an excellent environment for me to focus on my work, to all the guest lecturers who came to Sloan in the midst of their busy schedule, and to Sam Levine, Eileen Glovsky, Robert Young, and Marc Jedel who worked creatively as 15.565 teaching assistants.

Paul Becker, our publisher, not only has extensive publishing experience but also a great vision in supporting this book project. Gretchen Fisher, my book manager, is quite talented in coordinating people.

Last but not least, my wife, Yang, and my daughter, Forea, have been key sources of support, peace and joy during my work on this book project, as well as my intellectual pursuit at MIT.

To my father, I dedicate this book.

Richard Y. Wang
December 1992

Contributors

Chapter	Contributor	Affiliation	Job Title
1	Richard Wang	MIT Sloan School of Management	Assistant Professor of IT
2	Peter Chen	Chen & Associates	Founder and CEO
3	George Schussel	Digital Consulting, Inc.	President and Founder
4	Tim Andrews	Ontos, Inc.	Chief Technical Officer
5	Adam Rin	Gartner Group, Inc.	VP and Service Director
6	David Rabinowitz	Teradata/NCR	Senior Systems Engineer
7	Ed Oates	Oracle Corp.	Co-Founder, Oracle, and VP, Advanced Products Division
	Kennneth Rudin	Oracle Corp.	Senior Product and Marketing Manager
8	Jerrold Grochow	AMS, Inc.	Vice President and Chief Technology Officer

Chapter	Contributor	Affiliation	Job Title
9	David Friend	Pilot Software	Chairman
10	Richard Wang	MIT Sloan School of Management	Assistant Professor of IT
	Henry Kon	MIT Sloan School of Management	Ph.D. Candidate of IT
11	Paul Gillin	*Computerworld*	Executive Editor
12	William Bulkeley	*The Wall Street Journal*	Staff reporter and *The Information Age* columnist
13	Rick Sherlund	Goldman, Sachs & Co.	VP and Senior Analyst in the Investment Research Dept.
14	Peter DiGiammarino	AMS, Inc.	Senior Vice President
	Charles Rossotti	AMS, Inc.	Chairman, President, and Chief Executive
15	Michael Zucchini	Fleet Financial Group	Executive Vice President and Chief Information Officer
16	Stuart Madnick	MIT Sloan School of Management	John Norris Maguire Professor of IT
Glossary	Stacey Schussel-Griffin	Digital Consulting, Inc.	Managing Editor of Schussel's *Downsizing Journal*

P A R T 1

Introduction

C H A P T E R 1

The Information Technology (IT) Industry

Richard Y. Wang, Assistant Professor of Information Technologies, MIT Sloan School of Management and editor of this book, received his Ph.D. degree with a concentration in Information Technologies from MIT's Sloan School of Management. He has published extensively in the fields of database management systems, connectivity among information systems, and data quality management.

Professor Wang teaches a number of IT-related courses at the graduate level, including one that provides a broad coverage of trends and perspectives in the computer industry. He is a principal investigator of several information technology-related research projects. Most recently, he initiated a research program in Total Data Quality Management (TDQM). TDQM research investigates issues involved in data quality from both the technical and managerial perspectives.

Professor Wang is very active in professional services. He serves as a review for many research journals, conferences, and grant proposals. Most recently, he organized the annual workshop on Information Technologies and Systems (WITS), which brings IT researchers and practitioners together to exchange ideas and results.

A s I stated in the preface, this book is written for IT professionals who would like to gain a broad understanding of the dynamics of the IT industry and for students who are interested in the IT industry. A key message of this book is that in order to understand this industry, one must have a general understanding of IT, a good sense of the emerging trends in IT, and a broad understanding of the driving forces shaping IT.

People pursuing careers related to the IT industry are subject to a bombardment of information and pressure from all over. This industry is highly dynamic and exciting, but being part of it requires coping with many pressures. Vendors have their own agendas, users, another set of concerns, and the media and investment communities others still. The IT professional will hear from all these communities directly or indirectly because they all want to know what's on his/her mind. So understanding where these communities are coming from will make him/her that much better a professional.

This book is unique because it presents trends and perspectives that other IT texts do not and cannot accomplish—trends that come from participants shaping this industry and perspectives that many have overlooked. For example, each semester that I offer 15.565, a graduate-level M.B.A. course that covers trends and perspectives in the IT industry, some students ask why journalists, investors, and consultants should speak in the class. (The attendance of chief executive officers, CEO's, and chief information officers, CIO's, they understand because they want to become one someday.) And always after these guest lectures, those who wondered wanted to go to lunch with the guest speakers! Why? Because they enjoyed these lectures and wanted to know more. They realized the importance of understanding these communities. Enough for philosophy. Let's get started.

This chapter first reports the grade received by America's IT industry, then introduces the participants, the products and services, and information sources of this industry. The rest of the book presents key trends in the industry and perspectives from different communities. Enjoy IT.

1–1 America's IT Industry

This is an exciting time to be in the IT industry. In less than three decades, this industry has witnessed four generations of computing, rapidly changing from mainframe to minicomputer, to desktop systems, to distributed platforms. Just as historical-technological developments put their stamps on different eras, the revolution in information has brought the dawn of the information age. Today, IT is becoming a larger and larger part of the underlying infrastructure of our economy, culture, and daily lives. It is also one of the key technologies in which the U.S. still leads the rest of the world: "When examining the U.S. technological position, the American Council on Competitiveness gave America a B minus grade. Strong performances in some areas were offset by weak performances in others (Table 1-1)."[1]

Table 1–1 America's Technology Report Card[a]

A	Database systems, biotechnology, jet propulsion, magnetic-information storage, pollution reduction, software, voice recognition and vision in computers, computers
B+	Design and engineering tools, portable telecommunications equipment
B	Automotive power train, gallium arsenide, information networks, joining technologies, superconductors
B-	Electronic controls, materials processing, microelectronics
C+	Advanced materials, manufacturing process
C	Precision machining, printing and copying equipment, opto-electronic components
D	Chip-making equipment and robotics, electronic ceramic materials, electronic packaging, flat-panel displays, optical storage

a. Source: Thomas A. Stewart, "Where We Stand," in The New American Century, *Fortune,* Special Issue, 1991, p. 17.

America's IT industry, working hard and smart, received an A on database systems, magnetic information storage, software, and computers. This grade is well-deserved when one recognizes that U.S. corporations lead the rest of the world in all of these market segments. In 1991, for example:

1. Lester Thurow, "Head to Head: The Coming Economic Battle Among Japan, Europe, and America," William Morrow and Company, Inc., New York, 1992, p. 158.

- Borland dominated the low-end PC database market with more than 60% of the worldwide market share;
- Oracle and Sybase were the two key players in database applications in mid-range computers;
- IBM's DB2 dominated the mainframe database market;
- Teradata was the sole vendor in the database machine market, while Oracle, Kendall Square Research, and IBM were all poised to market database systems based on massively parallel processors.

U.S. firms also lead the rest of the world in many other emerging information technologies, particularly in the software area such as:

- spreadsheets, word processors, presentation graphics, and groupware,
- object-oriented database management systems (OODBMS),
- computer-aided software engineering (CASE) and application tools,
- graphic user interfaces (GUI), and
- system integration tools.

To understand the dynamics of the IT industry and how U.S. corporations succeed in it, one must first know who the key participants in this industry are, what kinds of products and services they produce and consume, and where to find the right information about the IT industry. These are discussed in the next three sections.

1–2 Participants in the IT Industry

There are many participants in the IT industry. They can be grouped into three classes: media, investors, and firms in the IT value chain, including vendors, intermediaries, and users (Figure 1-1).

Media and investors are two key participants in the IT industry that are often neglected. It is important to recognize that they are two major driving forces affecting the dynamics of the IT industry.

Media

For IT practitioners, there are two basic information sources:

- The IT media such as *Computerworld, PC Week, Byte*, and *Release 1.0*;
- The business media such as *The Wall Street Journal, Barron's*, and *Fortune*.

Major regional newspapers such as *The New York Times, The Boston Globe,* and *The Los Angeles Times* also carry a business section on IT news, particularly for firms in their region.

Media reports are based on press releases issued by firms and on research conducted by reporters. Stories are selected based on the journal's criteria and its target audience. In writing stories reporters may interview managers in IT firms, security analysts in investment firms, and experts in the IT industry. Given its discretion as to what stories to print and what constitutes "breaking news," the media has a significant influence in shaping the IT industry. The reader, however, has the responsibility to assess the credibility and accuracy in reported stories when utilizing these reports as input in making decisions— you certainly don't want to buy a product from a vendor if a credible source suggests that the vendor may go bankrupt.

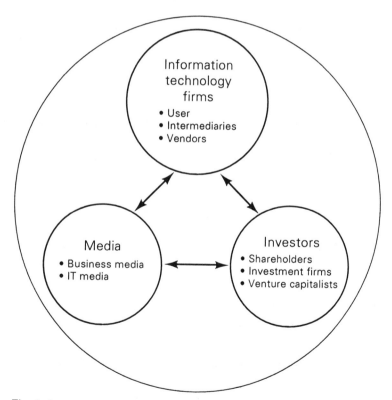

Fig. 1-1
Dynamics of the IT Industry

Investors

Investors also play an important role in the dynamics of the IT industry. Venture capital firms choose and fund corporations that are developing state-of-the-art technologies, with the expectation that the internal rate of return would be maximized over a period of, say, seven to ten years. For example, Picturetel, Bachman Information Systems, and Sybase were all heavily funded by venture capitalists. Investment firms assess the market value of a firm and convey judgment to their clients. Journalists also talk to security analysts in major investment firms and quote their opinions in the news. The news, in turn, is read by institutional investors and small investors alike. By understanding a vendor's financial strength and the perspective of the investment community, you will be in a better position to assess the vendor and its products for their technical merits and likelihood of sustained usefulness.

Firms in the IT Value Chain

Firms in the IT value chain consist of IT vendors, IT intermediaries, and IT users. IT vendors manufacture computer hardware and software. Firms in this category include IBM and Microsoft. Although IT vendors may distribute goods, offer consultancy, and provide after-sale services directly, these functions are also performed by IT intermediaries. Examples of IT intermediaries include Computerland, an IT distribution channel, and Arthur Anderson, an IT consulting firm.

Virtually all firms in business today are IT users. They use IT either for competitive advantage or out of competitive necessity. Examples of IT users include chain stores such as Wal-Mart and brokerage houses such as Charles Schwab. Each firm has an information systems unit (even if it is outsourced) which is responsible for the successful use of IT. Major corporations typically have a **chief information officer** (CIO) who interfaces with the CEO and line managers to make key IT decisions. The CIO is normally supported by technically oriented information systems (IS) managers. Together, members of the IS unit make recommendations about which IT platform to adopt and which products to make or buy.

Many firms in the IT value chain assume more than one role. American Airlines, for example, is an IT vendor providing airline reservation and information services through its Sabre airline reservation system. In addition it is an IT user in regular airline business.

By knowing where you are in the IT value chain, you will gain a better understanding of the driving forces shaping your career and impacting your daily work.

1–3 Market Segments of Products and Services

Many IT products and services are commercially available in the marketplace. They can be divided into the following categories:

- Software and DP services
- Large systems
- PC/workstations
- Communication and network services
- Peripheral and subsystems, and
- Other services.

The Software and DP services category can be further divided into many market niches. For example, in the CASE market, the key players include Intersolv, TI, KnowledgeWare, and Bachman Information Systems. Key players in the database market include Oracle, Sybase, Borland, Computer Associates, IBM, Information Builders, and Informix. In other market niches, AI Corp. markets knowledge-based DBMS's, Easel is in the GUI market, Slate is in the pen-based computing market, and BMC markets IBM's DB2 utility software.

In the large systems category, Cray Computer and Cray Research market supercomputers; Amdahl, CDC, DEC, IBM, and Unisys are in the mainframe market; while Sequent, Sequoia, and Tandem are in the "non-stop" computer market.

Sun Microsystems holds an industry-leading market share in workstations, but other companies have been working hard to close the gap. Hewlett-Packard, the number two player in the workstation market, has moved aggressively with a broad line of Unix-based workstations. HP offers faster machines than Suns at the high end and is competitively priced at the low end. IBM, Silicon Graphics, and DEC are also boosting product lines and marketing efforts in this sector.

The PC area has become a commodity market. As a result, shipments by direct-mail marketers have been steadily growing. By 1995, says WorkGroup President John Dunkle,[2] 30% of all PC's sold in the

2. *Business Week*, May 11, 1992, pp. 93-96.

U.S.— or about 9 million out of 30 million— will be via direct mail. The leader of the direct-marketing movement, Dell Computer, racked up a 63% sales gain, to $890 million for its fiscal year ended February 2, 1992.

Communications and network services are another huge category in its own right. In the wide-area network market, AT&T, GTE and MCI are major players. Novell is the leader in the local-area networks, Picturetel in the video-conferencing niche, and Cisco, Wellfleet, and Proteon in the bridge and router niche.

Peripherals and subsystems constitute another category of products which has a significant impact on the IT industry. For example, decreased costs of disk arrays helped the introduction of the Iceberg mass storage system by Storage Technology. The advancement of the high-density 3.5-inch disk drives also helped the evolution of personal computers. In the 3.5- and 2.5-inch disk drive niche, Seagate and Quantum are two key players for IBM PC-compatible and Macintosh computers.

There are many other services that the IT industry provides. For example, AMS offers many technology-based solutions such as credit management systems, Egghead Discount Software distributes software packages, and EDS is a key systems integration house offering outsourcing services.

Understanding the products and services available in the marketplace will enable an IS manager to make a more informed decision.

1–4 Finding Information

Information overload has become one of the biggest challenges facing IT professionals. *Computerworld's* readership studies, for example have consistently ranked lack of time and information overload as top concerns of IS managers. If you visit an IS manager at a major company, chances are you will find a table in his office stacked two feet high with publications. Similarly, if you visit a professor in the IS field, chances are you will find a bookshelf in his office stuffed with the latest journal transactions and conference proceedings. For students preparing to enter the IT industry, add text and reference books to the reading list. Unfortunately, there is no magic formula to solve the information overload problem; but fortunately the reward for meeting the challenge is high. We offer some tips:

- Ask experts whenever possible,
- Find the right information sources, and
- Get your hands dirty.

These are described in the following sections.

Ask Experts

Whenever possible, ask experts. They put you on top of the agenda right away. Many practitioners are experts in their own subfield, and interviewing them can often give you a very good sense of a particular topic. Experts are busy, but it pays to be patient. We have found that most leading practitioners love to discuss issues that they care about.

There are also many trade conferences where leading figures present their perspectives. Digital Consulting, Inc. routinely hosts conferences such as Client/Server World and Database World. Major vendors also participate in industry events such as Comdex, Networld, and DEC World.

Bark up the Right Tree: Finding the Right Information

If you don't have opportunities to interview experts, try a literature search. In general, IT literature falls into the following categories:

- Daily or weekly newspapers report company or product news. They tend to be application-oriented and most relevant today and in the near term. If you are interested in understanding what's happening today in the IT industry, you should thumb through trade publications such as *The Wall Street Journal's* technology section, *Computerworld, PC Week,* and *InfoWeek.*
- Monthly (or bi-monthly) magazines such as *Byte, Datamation, Software,* and *Corporate Computing* frequently feature a special issue about a specific technology, but normally do not offer market- or trend-oriented analysis such as changes in the market, size and growth rate of the market, and the outlook of a particular market or technology.
- High-end industry reports, such as the Gartner Group's reports and Goldman Sachs' reports, summarize and analyze IT firms and products in various market segments. Predictions of market size and growth rate are also available in these reports. But they are expensive to purchase and in many cases available only to their clients.

- Textbooks typically present fundamental background knowledge, but generally will not contain current news or trends.
- Academic journals and conference proceedings typically report research results that may become marketable from as few as five years to as long as decades from the time of publication, depending on how applied the journals or conferences are.

Get Your Hands Dirty

One of the best ways to appreciate the dynamics in the IT industry is to track its developments over time. It gives you first-hand experience of the driving forces. As a simple example, the day Microsoft announced the agreement to purchase Fox, Borland's stock price tumbled $7 from $60 to $53. If you had been tracking developments in the PC database market, you would have reasoned that Fox was in the same market as Borland and that the acquisition signaled that Microsoft was in a position to challenge Borlands number one position in the PC database area. Therefore, Borland's stock price tumbled.

In short, interviewing experts, attending conferences, reading publications, and tracking developments in the IT industry are different strategies for accumulating knowledge about the IT industry.

1–5 Get Ready for Prime Time

We are very fortunate to be in the IT industry today. It is exciting, challenging, and rewarding to be a participant in this industry. Those participants who meet the challenge have been rewarded with both excitement and wealth. For example, the personal wealth of Microsoft's founder and chairman, Bill Gates, soared $652 million, to $7.3 billion in late April, 1992, folloiwng a climb of almost $12 per share in Microsoft stock. The skill set needed to meet the challenge, however, ranges from marketing, to investing, to attaining technology. The question is how to attain such a skill set.

Throughout this book, we present trends in the IT industry, examine critical issues underlying these trends, and provide the perspectives from leading participants who contribute to the dynamics of the industry. Enjoy IT.

P A R T 2

Trends in the IT

Industry

In this part of the book we present trends in the IT industry. The entity-relationship (ER) approach, fundamental to information systems design, is first presented in Chapter 2 by Peter Chen, father of the ER model. Plain language is used here to describe concepts essential to ER modeling and trends in the ER approach.

In Chapter 3, George Schussel presents his perspective on distributed and client/server DBMS. George is in a unique position to present this subject due to his extensive experience in the database industry and his role as the founder of Downsizing Expo, a large industry trade show focusing on client/server databases, networking, and distributed computing.

In Chapter 4, Tim Andrews presents the technology and applications of object databases. As Chief Technical Officer at ONTOS, Tim writes this chapter with the aim of providing a perspective on the key characteristics of the object database.

The state of CASE and related application development technologies is presented in Chapter 5 by Adam Rin. Prior to joining the Gartner Group to oversee the CASE market, Adam served as a vice president at Bachman Information Systems, where he led product management and product marketing for the first commercially available database design and reverse engineering product.

As a senior systems engineer at Teradata, David Rabinowitz is very familiar with the DBC/1012. In Chapter 6, he examines DBC/1012 in detail as a successful implementation of database computers.

In Chapter 7, Ed Oates and Ken Rudin explore the evolution of massively parallel processing architectures, discuss the types of applications best suited to implementation on ultra-high performance hardware, examine the cost effectiveness of such machines for commercial applications, and analyze the implementation of Oracle's Relational Database Manager on a particular massively parallel computer, nCUBE, that they developed.

Issues involved in using object technology for industrial strength applications are discussed in Jerry Grochow's Chapter 8. As Chief Technology Officer at AMS, Jerry has extensive experience in supervising the introduction of new technologies into AMS business practice.

Putting data in the hands of the user in a friendly manner is the focus of David Friend's Chapter 9. Here David compares the fundamental differences between paper-based report writers and computer-based visual information access systems. For instance, paper-based reports are canned images of data, as opposed to live numbers that can be provided through friendly query tools. If users are the customers of the IT professional, then the IT professional must bear in mind that it is data that users really need; and data must come to users in a friendly manner.

Imagine that thousands of huge databases brimming with live numbers are easily accessible to you through friendly query tools! This is a great future to foresee; but what if the data quality is poor? In the past, personal familiarity with data may have been sufficient as a means of identifying, working around, or correcting bad data. This may not be the case in the future. As we rely more heavily on external sources of data and more frequently combine data from multiple sources, localized use of data becomes less effective as a policing aid for maintaining a good fit between what the user wants and what the information system provides. In Chapter 10, which concludes trends in the IT industry, Henry Kon and I discuss the impacts of data quality, an analogy between product manufacturing and data manufacturing, a framework for total data quality management, and an approach to data quality management in an organizational setting.

Enjoy IT.

The Entity-Relationship Approach

Peter P. S. Chen, the Foster Distinguished Chair Professor of Computer Science at Louisiana State University, Baton Rouge, Louisiana, is internationally known for his contributions to the original development of the Entity-Relationship (ER) model. Dr. Chen received his Ph.D. degree from Harvard University in 1973. In his thesis work, he discovered an interesting and unexpected rule to optimize system's throughput. That finding was called "Chen's rule" in a *Computerworld* article in the mid-70's and was incorporated into some commercial performance-optimization products.

He joined Honeywell (Waltham, Massachusetts) in 1973 and participated in the design of a new-generation distributed computer system. The need to handle multiple heterogeneous file and database management systems in a distributed environment motivated him to think about the fundamental concepts of information management—entity and relationship. In 1974, he spent the summer in DEC designing and developing a computer systems performance model for the DEC System-10. In September 1974, he joined the MIT Sloan School faculty, where he published the landmark paper on the "Entity-Relationship Model," which revolutionized the industry. In 1978, Dr. Chen moved to UCLA, where he taught one of the first courses in office automation in any university. In 1983, he accepted his current position at LSU. From 1986 to 1992, he held visiting professor appointments several times at MIT and Harvard.

Dr. Chen is very active in professional organizations. He was the founding chairman of the Technical Committee on Office Automation for the I.E.E.E. Computer Society. He was the program chairman, conference chairman, or steering committee chairman for over 15 international conferences. Dr. Chen was instrumental in starting the recent CASE revolution by serving as the keynote speaker in the first CASE symposium in the industry in 1986. He was an associate editor of *I.E.E.E. Computer, Information Sciences,* and *5th Generation Computing.* He is the editor-in-chief for *Data & Knowledge Engineering* and associate editor for other journals.

Dr. Chen received several awards including the Data Resource Management Award given by Data Administration Management Association (New York) in 1989.

He is an I.E.E.E. Fellow and is listed in *Who's Who in America* and *Who's Who in the World.* Dr. Chen is the founder of Chen & Associates (Baton Rouge, Louisiana), a firm providing tools, consulting, and training in data modeling and faster application development. The tools provided by the firm are aimed at a general audience and, therefore, accelerate the spread of the ER methodology to a wider audience.

T he entity-relationship (ER) approach, first proposed by Dr. Peter Chen, is extensively used in many database and information system design methodologies and has become a de facto standard of most manual and computerized design tools. It is the foundation for the understanding of CASE tools.

This chapter is unique in the sense that Dr. Chen distills his academic and industrial experiences and summarizes for the reader:

- Some of the subtle concepts often overlooked by ER modelers,
- Some pragmatic skills for developing an enterprise model,
- The market for ER related CASE tools and repository systems, and
- Research directions of the ER approach.

Enjoy IT.

2–1 Basic Concepts

Entities and Entity Types

An *entity* is a concrete object (such as a "person" or a "car") or an abstract concept (such as "project," "organization"). Entities are classified into different types such as PERSON type, DOG type, COMPANY type, etc. The concept of entity is the most fundamental concept in the ER theory and is the foundation for other concepts. Usually, the nouns in an English sentence are possible candidates for entities.

An **entity-relationship (ER) diagram** is a graphical notation to express entities, relationships, and other relevant concepts. In an ER diagram, an entity type is depicted as a rectangular box. Figure 2-1. shows entity type PERSON and entity type STOCK.

```
+-----------+        +-----------+
|  PERSON   |        |   STOCK   |
+-----------+        +-----------+
```

Fig. 2–1
Entity Types: PERSON and STOCK

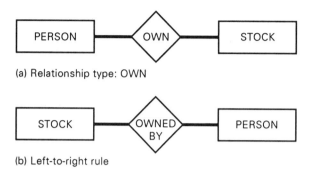

(a) Relationship type: OWN

(b) Left-to-right rule

Fig. 2-2
In ER diagrams, relationship types are depicted as diamond-
shaped boxes, as in (a). A left-to-right and top-down convention
is used for larger diagrams, as in (b).

Relationships and Relationship Types

Entities can be associated with other entities. A **relationship** is
the interaction of two or more entities. Usually, the verbs in an English
sentence are possible candidates for relationships. For example, when
we say, "Person X works for Project Y," the fact that "X works for Y" can
be viewed as a relationship between a PERSON entity, X, and a
PROJECT entity, Y. Relationships are also classified into types called
relationship types. For example, the relationship instances, "X works
for Y" and "W work for Z" can be viewed as belonging to the same relationship type called "WORK-FOR."

In ER diagrams, relationship types are depicted as diamond-
shaped boxes. For example, Figure 2-2(a) illustrates the relationship
type OWN between two entity types, PERSON and STOCK. Please note
that there is no direction expressed to show whether the relationship is
determined from a particular entity type to another. So, the relationship
type, in general, is non-directional. To make a large ER diagram read-
able, a left-to-right and top-down convention has been adopted. For
example, Figure 2-2(b) uses a semantic equivalent (in this case, passive
voice) verb phrase OWNED-BY to express the same relationship type as
OWN in Figure 2-2(a) because the relative positions of the two entity
types PERSON and STOCK are switched.

Most of the time, a passive-voice verb phrase (such as OWNED-
BY) would be sufficient, and there is no need to use different verbs for
each direction of the relationship.

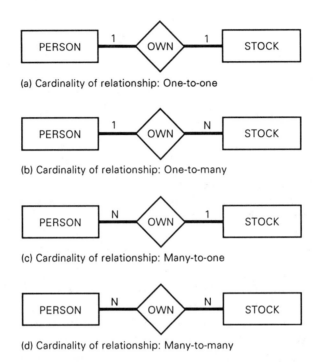

(a) Cardinality of relationship: One-to-one

(b) Cardinality of relationship: One-to-many

(c) Cardinality of relationship: Many-to-one

(d) Cardinality of relationship: Many-to-many

Fig. 2-3
Examples of Cardinality for a Binary Relationship.

When we model a relationship type, we should also characterize its **cardinality**, that is, the number of entities (of a particular type) which can participate in an instance of such a relationship. For example, a binary relationship type can be divided into four major categories based on the cardinality. Figure 2-3(a-d) depicts four such categories for the OWN relationship type: one-to-one, one-to-many, many-to-one, and many-to-many.

Note that the symbol "1" and "N" on the lines connecting entity types and relationship types is shorthand for "one" and "many." When we say the cardinality of the OWN relationship in Figure 2-3(d) is many-to-many, it means that "given a particular person, it is possible that this person can own many stocks" and that "given a particular stock, it may be owned by many persons."

So far, the cardinality information we are concerned with is the maximum number of entities of a certain type that can participate in a relationship. In certain modeling environments, we are not only interested in the maximum number, but also the minimum number of entities of a certain type that can participate in a relationship. In the current practice in the industry, the minimum values of interest are: 0 or 1. If the minimum value of the cardinality of a relationship is "0," it indicates that an entity of that entity type does not necessarily have to participate in that relationship; this type of relationship is called an **optional relationship**, to imply the relationship is optional. If the minimum value is "1," it indicates that an entity of that entity type must participate in that kind of relationship; this type of relationship is called a **mandatory relationship**. Figure 2-4 adds the minimum values of the cardinality information onto the ER diagram in Figure 2-3(d).

The "1:N" on top of the line between the PERSON entity type and the OWN relationship type indicates the minimum value is "1" and the maximum value is "N" for entities of PERSON type to participate in the OWN relationship. The minimum and maximum values of the cardinality information in Figure 2-4 can be interpreted as, "a person can own many stocks, but does not need to own any, and a stock can be owned by many persons, but must be owned by at least one person."

Fig. 2–4
Minimum Values of Cardinality

Attributes and Values

Entities and relationships have properties, which are expressed in terms of attributes and values. A **value** is a numeric value or a text string (or other forms) that is self-explanatory and is not an subject of our modeling effort. For example, "4" and "blue" may be considered as values. Values are classified into **value types.** For example, "3" and "4" belong to the value type INTEGER, and "blue" and "green" belong to the value type COLOR.

An **attribute** gives the meaning to a particular value associated with a particular entity or relationship. For example, the "age" of person

"X" is "34." In this case, "age" is the attribute to associate the value "24" with the person entity "X." The attribute/value pair is a mechanism to express the properties of entities and relationships.

In a **detailed ER diagram** or **attributed ER diagram**, the attribute types and value types are depicted as arrows and circles. Fig ure 2-5 shows the attributes and value types for entities in PERSON entity types.

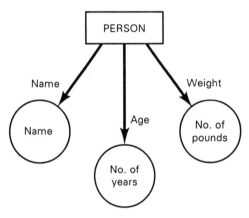

Fig. 2–5
Attributes and Value Types

Other Diagrammatic Notations

There are many variations of the ER diagrammatic notations. Figure 2-6(a)-(c) illustrates three variants of the ER diagrams.

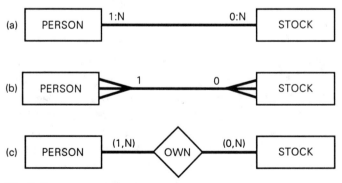

Fig. 2–6
Variants of ER Diagrams

2–2 Advanced Concepts

The basic concepts discussed in the above sections are the fundamental building blocks in developing an enterprise model. However, if we try to model the complex world more closely, we need more advanced concepts such as weak entity, ISA relationship, component-of relationship, and aggregated entity. In the following, we will describe each one in more detail.

Weak Entities

There are certain entities whose existence depends on the existence of other entities. One example occurs if the company policy states: "After an employee leaves the company, all his/her dependent information should be deleted." Figure 2-7 illustrates a **weak entity** type, DEPENDENT, and the arrow of the relationship indicates that the regular entity type, EMPLOYEE, determines the existence of the DEPENDENT.

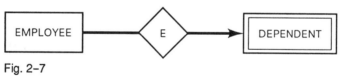

Fig. 2–7

Weak Entity DEPENDENT

ISA Relationship

In the modeling of the real world, one of the most frequently encountered relationship types is the **ISA relationship**, which describes the subtype relationship between two entity types. The term "ISA" is the concatenation of two English words, "is a(n)," which is used to describe the subtype relationship as demonstrated in the following sentence: "A female person is a person." Figure 2-8 shows several ISA relationship types in an **entity hierarchy**, which is a hierarchy of entity supertypes and subtypes. Note that the ISA relationship types use arrowheads to indicate the supertypes.

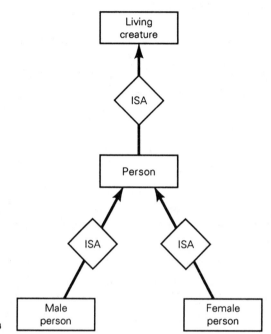

Fig. 2–8
An Entity Hierarchy
with ISA Relationships

Component-of Relationship

Another useful relationship type is the **component-of relation-ship** type, which describes the fact that the entities in one entity type are the components of one (or more) entities in another entity type. For example, a steering wheel is a component of an automobile. Figure 2-9 illustrates a component-of relationship type. Note that an arrowhead is used to point to the entity type containing the other entities.

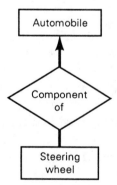

Fig. 2–9
A Component-of
Relationship

Fig. 2–10
An ER Diagram

Aggregated Entities

An ER diagram can be abstracted as a high-level entity type called aggregated entity type. For example, Figure 2-10 depicts an ER diagram with two entity types, PRODUCT and CUSTOMER, linked by a relationship type SHIPPED-TO. This diagram describes which products were shipped to which customers. This ER diagram can be conceptualized as a high-level entity type called SHIPPING, which can be linked to other entity types via relationship types.

Figure 2-11(a) shows that the SHIPPING entity type is linked to SHIPPING CLERK entity type via PERFORMED-BY relationship type. This ER diagram describes which shipping tasks were performed by which shipping clerks. These high-level entity types, which were abstracted from a lower-level ER diagram, are called aggregated entity types. This concept can be used to hide the low-level details. For example, Figure 2-11(b) shows only the SHIPPING entity type without the detailed information on how it was constructed or where it came from.

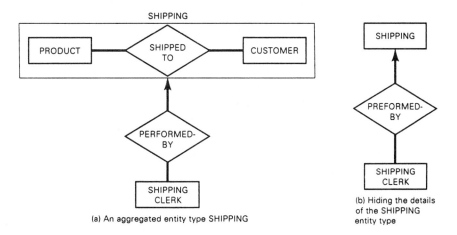

(a) An aggregated entity type SHIPPING

(b) Hiding the details of the SHIPPING entity type

Fig. 2–11
Aggregated Entity Types

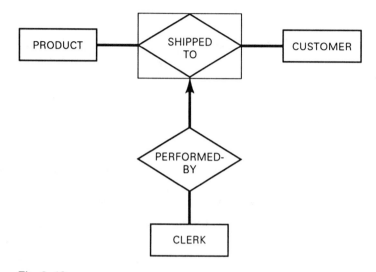

Fig. 2-12

The Gerund Entity Type SHIPPING

The Gerund Entity Type

In some situations, there is a need to model the "relationship of relationships." Remember that relationship types are defined by entity types. If so, how can one model the relationship of relationships? In order to do so, we need to convert a relationship type into an entity type so that it can be used as the foundation to build another relationship type. The construct in the ER diagrammatic technique useful in this situation is the **gerund entity type**, which is an entity type converted from a relationship type. Figure 2-12 illustrates the gerund entity type SHIPPING, which was a relationship type SHIPPED-TO in Figure 2-10 and is now an entity type together with entity type CLERK to build the relationship type PERFORMED-BY. The name "gerund" is derived from the concept in English grammar in which a noun was converted from a verb but still maintains some of the properties of the verb with respect to its old subjects. In the ER diagrammatic technique, a gerund entity type such as SHIPPING in Figure 2-12 is an entity type with respect to the relationship type PERFORMED-BY, but still maintains certain relationship properties with respect to the entity types PRODUCT and CUSTOMER.

2–3 Pragmatic Skills in Developing an Enterprise Model

There are two major ways of developing an enterprise model: the top-down approach and the bottom-up approach. The top-down approach uses the principle of multi-level refinement; it starts from a few high-level entity-relationship types, which are then refined, recursively, into lower and lower levels of entity-relationship types. The bottom-up approach uses the principle of multi-level abstraction: starting with low-level entity-relationship types, which are then abstracted, recursively, into higher and higher levels of entity-relationship types.

The concept of aggregated entity type is central in both the top-down and the bottom-up approaches. When we do a top-level ER diagram for a large corporation, we may have ten to thirty high-level entity types at the corporate levels, and some of them can be refined into low-level ER diagrams, in which some of the entity-relationship types could be refined further into even lower-level ER diagrams, and so on. This is compatible with the current practice of business systems analysis: Starting with company missions and objectives, use them to derive company policies and detailed action plans for divisions and departments.

On the other hand, the bottom-up approach starts with several low-level ER diagrams; some of them can be grouped into aggregated entity types, which become a part of a higher-level ER diagram. This abstraction process can be done several times to build a multi-level ER diagram.

Which approach is better, the top-down or the bottom-up? In theory, there is no difference— because if you can build a multi-level ER diagram top-down, you can also build it bottom-up, or vice versa. However, there are some differences in their conceptual appeals and pragmatic usages. Conceptually, the top-down approach is more appealing since it is compatible with the business systems analysis approach and compatible with how the human mind works: It starts from simple things and then gets into more details. However, in practice, building a top-level corporate ER diagram needs the involvement of most, if not all, senior executives of the company. This is usually not feasible because most senior executives are very busy, and some of them may not recognize the benefits of developing such a top-level ER diagram. So, in practice, the bottom-up approach occurs more often.

2-4 Market Segments of ER-Related Software Tools

Many new software tools on the market are based on the ER model or its extensions. Most of them are CASE tools, and the rest are Repository Systems or DBMS's.

ER-Related CASE Tools

CASE tools can be divided into two categories: those emphasizing-process and those emphasizing data.

Most CASE tools belong to the first category because most people today still practice the older process-based methodologies. More than 80% of these tools support ER diagramming. The following is a small subset of such CASE tools.

CASE Tool Name	Vendor Information
Excelerator	Intersolv Rockville, Maryland
PROMOD	McDonald Douglas St. Louis, Missouri
PACBASE	CGI Systems Poughkeepsie, New York

The second category of CASE tools emphasizes data-oriented methodologies. Most CASE tools in this area are based on ER diagrams (even though the diagram notations supported may be slightly different).

Some such CASE tools are listed below and followed by analysis of the market segments they try to address.

CASE Tool Name	Vendor Information
IEF (Information Engineering Facility)	Texas Instruments Dallas, Texas
IEW/ADW (Information Engineering Workbench/Advanced Development Workbench)	KnowledgeWare Atlanta, Georgia
Bachman Workbench	Bachman Info. Systems Burlington, Massachusetts
Chen ER-Modeler	Chen & Associates, Inc. Baton Rouge, Louisiana

The IEF by TI is, primarily, a mainframe-based tool while the other three are PC-based tools. The IEF is basically a large application system running on top of IBM's DB2 DBMS. It is priced at $200,000 and more. It starts with ER diagrams and action diagrams and generates SQL codes for DB2 and a few other DBMS's.

The IEW/ADW by KnowledgeWare and the Bachman Workbench by Bachman Information Systems are priced around $7,000 to $50,000 (for each workstation). They also concentrate on DB2 and a few other DBMS's. Since IEF is a mainframe-based tool, it is claimed to be more integrated, while IEW and Bachman Workbench are PC-based tools and are claimed to be more flexible, supporting more diagrammatic techniques and less expensive to start with.

Among all CASE tools, the Chen ER-Modeler Workbench by Chen & Associates probably supports the most comprehensive versions of the ER model. It supports not only the ISA relationship, but also the gerund relationship and multi-level ER diagrams. Figure 2-13 (next page) shows an architecture diagram of the basic modules in the Chen ER-Modeler package. The user starts with ER-Designer, then can use the Normalizer module to normalize it to third Normal Form or BCNF relations. Then the user can use the Schema Generator to generate optimally-designed, syntactically-correct database schemas for any one of more than thirty DBMS's. To specify processes, the user can employ the DFD-Designer to draw data flow diagrams and then link to a 4GL/SQL/COBOL code generator. The DDS-Link module is used to upload the analysis and design data from Chen's PC-based data dictionary into a mainframe or mini-based data dictionary system or vice-versa. The CASE-Link module offers users the capability to link their existing CASE tools (such as Excelerator, IEF) via Chen Workbench to the DBMS/Data Dictionary systems (such as Sybase) not supported by that CASE tool. The reverse-engineering module can reverse existing file/DB descriptions from COBOL Copybook and many commercial database systems. That is, you may recapture the data design in existing application systems into ER diagrams and use it to redesign the system as a blueprint for migration to a new file system or DBMS.

Depending on the number of modules you need, Chen ER-Modeler Workbench is priced from $1,000 to $10,000 per station. Its strength lies in the advanced ER diagram capability, a very sophisticated Normalizer module (probably the most advanced on the market today), and the support of over 30 DBMS's, seven data dictionary systems, and five other

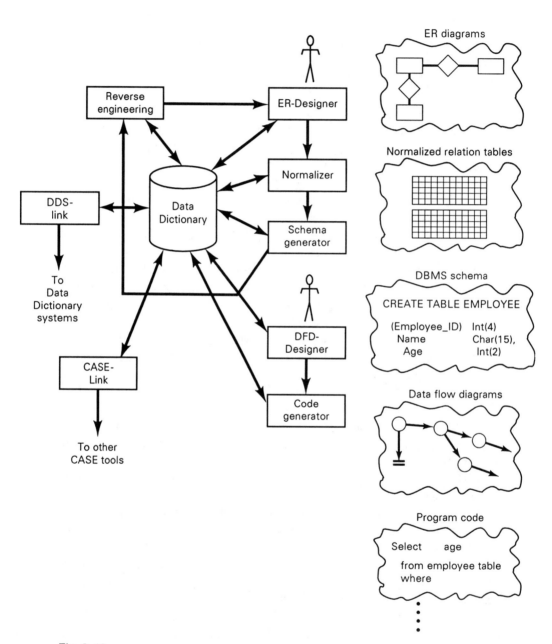

Fig. 2–13
An Architectural Diagram for the ER-Modeler Package

vendors' CASE tools. Although its schema generator on certain DBMS's such as Sybase, Informix, Ingres, and Unisys DBMS's is very sophisticated, its DB2 schema generator is not as comprehensive as Bachman's. However, the cost is only a fraction of that of a Bachman Workbench.

Another important difference is that IEF/ADW/Bachman concentrates on the OS/2 market while Chen concentrates on the DOS/MS-Windows market. Furthermore, Chen Workbench supports the client/server architecture and runs on LAN environments.

Note that it is almost impossible to have the complete CASE solution from only one vendor. It is often necessary and, perhaps, desirable to have several CASE tools with the best CASE tool in its class for your shop. For example, it may be feasible to run Bachman on your OS/2 server and run Chen on the Windows clients, or, IEF on your mainframe and Excelerator/Chen/ADW on your PC's. So, try different configurations to find the most cost-effective solutions to fit your company's requirements.

ER-Related Repository Systems

So far, we have the use of the ER model in systems analysis and design, and the software tools (CASE tools) to support this process. Now, we focus our attention to software systems which are the direct implementation of the ER model. In this respect, the repository system is qualified to be called a major direct implementation of the ER model. A **repository system** is a special kind of database management system in which the data is not the operational data of the organization, but rather the data about the information resources in the organization. It is an extended concept of the so-called data dictionary system, which primarily keeps track of the data about existing files, databases, and programs, and not data about other information resources such as data from each stage in the software development projects or about hardware resources.

The ER model was adopted by **American National Standards Institute (ANSI)** in 1989 as the meta-model for Information Resource Dictionary System (IRDS), which is another term for repository system. This is the result of a multi-year study by ANSI's X3/H4 committee on the architecture of IRDS. In 1990, the National Institute of Science and Technology of the U.S. government also issued a FIPS (Federal Information Processing Standards) on IRDS specifying the ER model as the meta-model for the repository systems to be acquired by federal agencies.

On the commercial side, the ER model was adopted by several major vendors as the meta-model for their repository systems. For example, IBM's Repository Manager, RM/MVS, uses the ER model as the meta-model. However, the version of the ER model used in RM/MVS is slightly different from the version of the ER model used in the ANSI/IRDS. This is no surprise to industry observers since IBM has not always followed completely the ANSI directions in the past thirty years. However, the differences in these two versions of the ER model are relatively minor so that it is possible that IBM can build patches to make RM/MVS compliant with ANSI/IRDS standards. There are other vendors' repository systems, such as DEC's CDD+ and Software AG's Predict, that use the ER model as the meta-model of their systems.

ER-Related DBMS's

Another possible direction for implementation of the ER model is ER database management systems (DBMS's). The key question is, why do we need to do things in two steps, first modeling it using the ER model and then converting the ER specifications into the constructs supported by conventional DBMS's, which are based on the hierarchical, network, or relational data models? This is the current practice in the industry, no matter if it is done manually or with the assistance of a CASE tool. As a result, a lot of important semantic information (such as business rules of the organization) are lost during this translation process. A natural question that comes into mind is, is it possible to execute the ER specifications directly without translating them to something else? In order to do so, an ER DBMS is needed.

There are several research prototypes of ER DBMS in research laboratories. For example, Bellcore in New Jersey has implemented, using C++, an ER DBMS which is used internally to handle a large amount of data. As another example, IBM researchers [Malh 89] have designed and implemented an ER language prototype on top of IBM's SQL/DS.

2–5 Directions of the ER Approach

Since the first paper published on the ER approach in 1976 [Chen 76], there have been numerous papers written on the extensions of the ER model. In the following, we will discuss some of the most important extensions and applications of the ER approach in the next decade.

Time Dimension Extensions

One of the active research topics is how to introduce the time dimension into the ER model. Is "time" an entity or an attribute? Or something else? In the past, the ER model was primarily used for modeling the real world at one specific time instance. In essence, we are taking a snapshot of the real world. For many applications, whether the data is very up-to-date or whether the data has been changed several times in the past five years (and the exact dates the data were changed) is not crucial. However, in certain applications (such as those in the legal field), it is important to keep track of the events and dates. In those applications, time becomes an important dimension in the ER model. Currently, researchers are still debating the best mathematical structures and the most appealing diagrammatic notions to represent the time concept in the ER model. Interested readers may refer to [Theo 91].

Entity Lattice

The entity hierarchy described in Section 2-2 has its limitations. A broader concept is an entity lattice [Chen 87] which allows multiple parents (entity supertypes) for a given entity type while an entity hierarchy allows at most one parent (entity supertype) for any given entity type. Each entity lattice has one universal supertype, which is the supertype of all entity types in the lattice. Each line in the vertical direction indicates the supertype/subtype relationship, with the one on the top being the supertype. Figure 2-14 illustrates an entity lattice of EMPLOYEE. In this entity lattice, the EMPLOYEE entity type is the universal supertype. Note that MALE PROFESSIONAL EMPLOYEE has two parent supertypes: MALE EMPLOYEE and PROFESSIONAL EMPLOYEE. This demonstrates that the world cannot be modeled as simple hierarchical structures.

The lattice concept is very useful in modeling more precisely the real world as well as in developing efficient storage and retrieval structures for DBMS's. For example, most database queries can be viewed as selecting one or more subtypes in entity lattices. A query like, "select employees who are male and are in the professional ranks," is aimed at the MALE PROFESSIONAL EMPLOYEE subtype. So, research on the lattice structures can provide us better modeling techniques and faster DBMS's in the future.

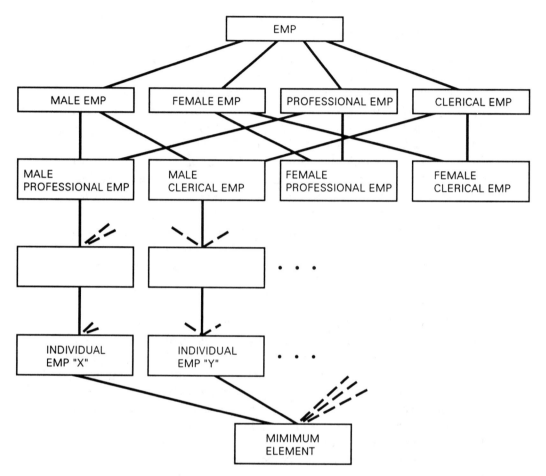

Fig. 2–14
An Entity Lattice of EMPLOYEE

Entity-Relationship vs. Object-Orientation

What is OO? Object-Orientation is a new paradigm of program-ming. While many people talk about OO, most of them talk only about what the (potential) benefits of OO are. Very few of them give a global perspective—at the level of the whole computer industry - concerning where this OO idea came from and the reasons why the OO idea attracts so much attention. In addition, very few compare OO with ER and dis-cuss their roles in the system's development life cycle. Here we will give you such a perspective.

The concept of OO starts with the field of computer languages. In some sense, OO is a way to get away from low-level programming techniques involving pushing bits and bytes. The programming language people realized that they could not stay in such a low level forever and that they need to move to a higher conceptual plateau. What conceptual level is higher than bits and bytes? The answer is the "real world," or more precisely, the "representation of the real world." What do we see in the real world? Objects (or entities)! So, OO is motivated by the need to program in a higher level of abstraction than what we have today.

Many ideas in OO are very similar to those in ER. In general, ER is richer than OO in terms of structuring capabilities while OO is stronger in the specification of the processes of the system.

The field of OO is very confusing because almost everybody has a different definition. We will accept a definition of OO if it satisfies three criteria: (1) **inheritance**, (2) **encapsulation**, and (3) **polymorphism**. Each object is a collection of data and all the methods (procedures) which can operate on the data. Inheritance means that the objects in the object hierarchy can inherit both the data and methods from their parent objects in the object hierarchy. Encapsulation means that the methods of an object are hidden from some other objects. Polymorphism means that the same method name can be applied to objects with different names.

Let us look at each concept in more detail. The object hierarchy is very similar to the entity hierarchy we discussed in Section 2-2. However, the world is not just a hierarchy or a collection of hierarchies.

It is interesting to note that the evolution of programming paradigms mirrors the evolution of data models in the past twenty years. Initially, database management systems used the hierarchical model (such as IMS database system). Then, the database people found out the world is not just a collection of hierarchies; so, it evolved into a more complex data model— the network model (a typical DBMS using this model is the Computer Associates' IDMS database management system). Later, the data model evolved into the relational model (such as IBM's DB2) and the ER model. In some sense, the programming people followed the same path as the database people. The first natural structured relationship detected in the real world was the hierarchical structure. Now, the programming language people are realizing that the hierarchical model is not sufficient to model the complexity of the world; that is the reason that the concept of the so-called multiple inheritance was developed to handle the case of an object having multiple parents. In some sense, multiple inheritance is similar to the network model. However, there are many other types of relationships in the world which still cannot be handled by the network model, or by multiple inheritance. So, a more general mechanism of relationship such as those available in the ER model is the natural next step. Please keep in mind that we do not intend to say that the programming language field is ten years behind the database field. To the contrary, the programming language field has many advanced concepts which should be learned by the database people. What we try to convey here is that, on this particular aspect of adopting structured relationships, the evolution of programming paradigms is similar to that of data models.

Let us look at another concept—encapsulation. "To group all methods with the data they operate on" is a completely different paradigm than the previous paradigm of grouping data with an operation. In our view, this new paradigm opens up solutions to new sets of problems. But we should keep in mind that, as with the current programming practice which uses a procedure-oriented view, the new paradigm will not be able to solve all kinds of problems. A more balanced view would be: a complete application, dynamically binding data to procedures, or vice versa. The shifting of the paradigm is just like the swinging of a pendulum, from one side to the other, and, we think, it will eventually settle down in the middle.

In the future, we are going to see both ER and OO learn from each other. For example, more dynamic constructs will be added to the ER model, and more structured relationship types will be added to the OO programming paradigm. So, we will see the merging of OO with ER to become some kind of "OOER" model, and finally, a fully active ER model. Figure 2-15 illustrates the convergence of the ER and OO concepts which will provide a basis for almost all the fields in the computer software area.

Quality/Contextual ER Model

Another research direction is to define the criteria for a quality data model. Data quality has become an important issue in the past years. Most data modules (including the ER model) assume that all data given is correct. We need a scientific way to assess the quality of the data in (or to be put into) the database. We also need to incorporate such quality measures into the ER model as well as to develop algebra- or calculus-based operations to manipulate such data quality descriptions.

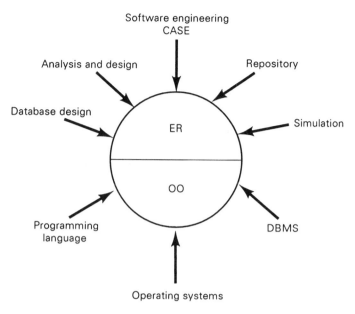

Fig. 2-15
Merging of ER and OO in the Future

Similar to data quality, the context of the data to be modeled is also an important issue. For example, an ERD for an automobile manufacturing company is expected to be quite different from the ERD for a supermarket chain since some entity types are very important in one industry, but can be ignored in another industry. Each industry has its own assumptions and domain knowledge, and an ERD built for a specific industry will implicitly assume that the readers of the ERD will be familiar with the basic assumptions and domain knowledge. In the past, this kind of contextual information (i.e., the basic assumptions and knowledge for a specific domain) was not documented. Thus, some people are confused by the vast differences in ERD's for different industries. Therefore, we think it is important to define a "contextual ER model," which can be used as the foundation for modeling contextual information explicitly.

2-6 Concluding Remarks and Further Readings

In the past 15 years, the ER model has emerged as the most widely used model for enterprise modeling and has served as the basis for many CASE tools, repository systems, and the future generation of DBMSs. It has become the "must-know" knowledge for students and professionals in the fields of MIS, database, software engineering, and systems analysis.

For further readings, there are several books specifically on the ER model [Teor 90, Nava 92]. There are also books on the general subject of databases [Ullm 86, Korth 88, Elma 89], which start with a chapter on the ER model and then discuss other conventional data models and how to translate the ER model into them. There are also books on database [Gold 85, Kroe 88, McFa 88], which have discussed the ER model and its applications. In terms of database design, a very comprehensive work can be found in [Hawr 89] and two simple, easy-to-understand monographs are [Howe 83, Chen 91]. For those interested in application of the ER model to systems analysis, they can read [Mode 90]. Also, refer to [Fide 87] for applications to information retrievals.

Each year, there is an international conference on the entity-relationship approach, which is held in North America and the rest of the world, alternately. Each volume of the conference proceedings contains approximately 25-50 articles on new research results or practical applications. Besides the conference proceedings, the reader may find ER-related papers in several journals such as [ACM, IEEE, DKE].

2-7 Bibliography

[ACM] Transactions on Database Systems (TODS), Communications of the ACM (CACM), Association for Computing Machinery (ACM), NYC.

[Chen 76] Chen, P. P. "The Entity-Relationship Model— Toward a Unified View of Data," *ACM Trans. on Database Systems, Vol. I, No.1.* March 1976.

[Chen 83] Chen, P. P. "English Sentence Structure and Entity-Relationship Diagrams," *Information Science 29*. May 1983, pp. 127-149.

[Chen 87] Chen, P. P. and Li, L. "The Lattice Concept in Entity Set," *Entity-Relationship Approach*. ed. S. Spaccapietra. North-Holland, 1987.

[Chen 91] Chen, P. P. Entity-Relationship Approach to Database Design, Q.E.D. Information, 161 Linden Street, Wellesley, Massachusetts, 1991.

[DKE] Data & Knowledge Engineering, North-Holland/Elsevier Publishing Co., Amsterdam/New York City.

[Elma 89] Elmasri, R. and Navathe, S.B., *Fundamentals of Database Systems*. Benjamin/Cummings Pub. Co., 1989.

[Fied 87] Fiedel, R., *Database Design for Information Retrieval,* John Wiley & Sons, 1987.

[Gold 85] Goldstein, R. C. *Database: Technology and Management,* John Wiley & Sons, 1985.

[Hawr 88] Hawryskywz, I. T. *Database Analysis and Design.* Science Research Associates, 2nd Ed., 1989.

[Howe 83] Howe, D. R. *Data Analysis for Database Design* Edward Arnold, 1983.

[IEEE] "Transactions on Knowledge and Data Engineering," *IEEE Software Magazine.* IEEE Computer Society, Washington, D.C.

[Korth 88] Korth, H. and Sibershaltz, A. *Database Systems Concepts.* New York City: McGraw-Hill, 1988.

[Kroe 88] Kroenke, D. *Database Processing: Fundamentals, Design, and Implementation.* Science Research Associates, 1988.

[Malh 89] Malholtra, A., Markowitz, H., Tsalalikhin, Y., Pazel, D. P. and Burns, L.M., "An Entity-Relationship Programming Language," *IEEE Transactions on Software Engineering,* August 1989.

[McFa 88] McFadden, F. R. and Hoffer, J. A. *Database Management.* Benjamin/ Cummings Pub. Co., 1988.

[Mode 90] Model, M. *Practiced Systems Analysis.* New York City: McGraw-Hill, 1990.

[Nava 92] Navathe, Batini, and Ceri, *Entity-Relationship Approach.* New York: Wiley and Sons, 1992.

[Teor 90] Teorey, T. J. *Database Modeling and Design: The Entity-Relationship Approach.* San Mateo, CA: Morgan Kaufmann Publishers, 1990.

[Theo 91] Theodoulis, C., Loucopoulos, P. and Wangler, B. "The Entity-Relationship Time Model and the Conceptual Rule Language," *Proc. 10th International Conference on Entity-Relationship Approach.* ER Insititute, 1991.

[Ullm 86] Ullman, *Principles of Database Systems,* Computer Science Press, 1986.

Conference Proceedings

Chen, P.P. (ed.) *First ER Conference Proceedings: Entity-Relationship Approach to Systems Anaysis and Design.,* 663 pages, Amsterdam/New York: North-Holland/Elsevier Science Publishing Co., 1980, (hardcover).

Chen, P.P. (ed.) *Second ER Conference Proceedings: Entity-Relationship Approach to Information Modeling and Analysis.* 664 pages, Amsterdam/New York: North-Holland/Elsevier Science Publishing Co.,

Davis C., Jajodia S., Ng P., Yeh R. (eds.) *Third ER Conference Proceedings: Entity-Relationship Approach to Software Engineering.* 867 pages, Amsterdam/New York: North-Holland/Elsevier Science Publishing Co., 1983, (hardcover).

Proceedings of the 4th International Conference on Entity-Relationship Approach. 323 pages, October, 1985. ISBN 0-8186-0645-2, IEEE Catalog # 85-CH2226-9, IEEE Computer Society order # 645.

Spaccapietra, Stefano, (ed.) *Proceedings of the 5th International Conference on Entity-Relationship Approach.* Amsterdam/New York: North-Holland/ Elsevier Science Publishing Co., 1987. ISBN 0-444-70255-5.

March, Salvatore, T., (ed.) *Proceedings of the 6th International Conference on Entity-Relationship Approach.* Amsterdam/New York: North-Holland/Elsevier Science Publishing Co., 1988, ISBN 0-444-7-440-X.

Lochovsky, F. (ed.) *Entity-Relationship Approach to Database Design and Querying (Proc. of the 8th International Conference on Entity-Relationship Approach).* Amsterdam/New York: North-Holland/Elsevier Publishing Co., 1990, ISBN 0-444-88716--4.

Distributed and Client/Server DBMS: Underpinning for Downsizing

Dr. George Schussel is the president and founder of Digital Consulting, Inc., the largest American information systems seminar and conference company. An expert on database, downsizing, and information management issues, his lectures are held all over the world typically before audiences that number in the hundreds. Schussel writes extensively on the database and downsizing subjects and has published over 100 articles in leading computer industry journals such as *Computerworld*, *Datamation*, and *Data Based Advisor*. He is also the editor of *Schussel's Downsizing Journal* (SDJ), a monthly publication. He serves as Chairman of Database World, a conference/trade show held twice a year and drawing over 10,000 attendees per year. He is also the creator of the Downsizing Expo, a large industry trade show focusing on client/server databases, networking, and distributed computing.

Schussel undertakes a wide variety of consulting and education assignments in private industry and government. Prior to founding Digital Consulting, Inc., Dr. Schussel was vice president at the American Mutual Group of insurance companies in Wakefield, Massachusetts. He was the senior manager responsible for administration of a multi-million dollar computer budget and 200 full-time personnel handling all data processing for the American Mutual Group.

Schussel is a fellow of the American Association for the Advancement of Science, holds a CDP certification from the Data Processing Management Association, and has received an Outstanding Industrial Engineer of the Year award from the American Institute of Industrial Engineers.

Schussel's academic background includes a doctorate from the Harvard Business School (D.B.A., managerial economics & computer science); master's degree from Harvard University (M.S., applied mathematics & computer) and bachelor's degree from the University of California (B.A., physics & mathematics). He has lectured or held faculty appointments at the University of Southern California, Harvard University, MIT, and the University of Alabama.

$\mathbf{C}$lient/server computing is hot and is changing the IT industry. But what is it? Is it a concept, an architecture, or a product?

"Client/server computing is the poor man's Mercedes Benz of distributed DBMS," according to Dr. George Schussel. In this chapter, George presents his perspective on client/server database computing, its relationship to distributed DBMS, and why it is a fundamental enabling technology for downsizing. Enjoy IT.

3–1 Introduction

One of the key trends in modern computing is the **downsizing** and distributing of applications and data. This paradigm shift is occurring because companies want to take advantage of modern microprocessor technology which allows them to benefit from the new styles of software which employ graphical user interfaces (GUI). **Client/server** and **distributed database** technologies are two fundamental enabling technologies involved in downsizing.

The benefits of client/server computing are so compelling that most companies will find it impossible to ignore. Those benefits are

1 *Cost savings* By distributing processing over a number of microprocessor-based computers rather than a few larger machines, one can take advantage of computer instruction cycles selling for $100 per million (on PC's) versus cycles selling for $60,000 per million (discounted mainframe prices).

2 *Scalability* The modular nature of client/server approaches means that such networks can be easily expanded by adding more nodes or migrating to newer processors on existing nodes. This offers a developer or user the tremendous advantage of keeping application software constant as the size of the application moves from a small LAN all the way up to environments as large as supercomputers.

3 *Robustness* One of the disadvantages of downsized systems based on file/server approaches has been that the security and integrity functions of true DBMS-based systems were not available on file servers. Client/server approaches, on the other hand, are based on SQL relational DBMS servers and offer all of the robustness,

security, and data integrity of the traditional mainframe computing environment.

4 *Interoperability with the desktop*   As Windows evolves to become a standard on the desktop, facilities like the Windows' clipboard allow the tight coupling of typical desktop applications like word processing with data processing and client/server applications. For example, the results of an SQL-based query (a data table) can be cut and pasted directly into a Word document or Excel spreadsheet.

5 *GUI interfaces*   There is not much doubt that graphical interfaces like Motif, Presentation Manager, and Windows offer many learning, use, and productivity benefits for users. Although straight DOS environments can certainly be supported on the client, many client/ server users are building on these GUI bases for their client-side computing.

6 *Faster application development*   Development of client/server applications is now available with screen painting.

Client/server approaches usually are implemented with individual applications running over multiple computers. Usually the database(s) resides on server machines while applications run on client computers. While the type of computer used as a server varies widely (e.g., you could have a mainframe, minicomputer, or PC), most clients are PC's. **Local area networks** (LAN's) provide the connection and transport protocol used in linking clients and servers.

A **distributed DBMS (database management system)** offers the capabilities of client/server DBMS and then some. The most fundamental difference between the two architectures is that the distribution of data within a distributed database is both pervasive and invisible. In this style, a DBMS resides on each node of the network and allows transparent access to data anywhere on the network. This means that the user is not required to physically navigate to the data.

Note: In the remainder of this chapter the term "DBMS" is used to mean the systems software that controls data, while the term "database" is meant to be the actual data itself.

The distributed database setup is different from the client/server approach in which the application must be aware of knowing the physical location of data, at least to the extent of on which server it's located. With a distributed DBMS, once an SQL query or remote procedure call is directed to the appropriate server, its query optimizer for SQL will handle the internal database navigation. Many of the advanced functions described later in this chapter, such as stored procedures, triggers, and two-phase commits, are available in both client/server and distributed DBMS environments.

Client/server DBMS and distributed DBMS have much in common. Both are based on the SQL language invented in the 1970s by IBM and standardized by ANSI and ISO as the common data access language for relational databases. Both are appropriate for distributing applications.

3-2 Background on Distributed Database Computing

The market for modern distributed DBMS software started in 1987 with the announcement of INGRES-STAR, a distributed relational system from RTI (now the Ingres Division of ASK Computers) of Almaden, California. Most of the original research on distributed DBMS technology for relational systems took place at IBM's two principal California software laboratories, Almaden and Santa Theresa. The first widely discussed distributed relational experiment developed within IBM's laboratories was a project named R-Star. It is because of IBM's early use of the word *Star* in describing this technology that most distributed DBMS systems have *Star* incorporated into the name. Today, the market for distributed DBMS is almost entirely based on the SQL language and extensions. (The principal exception is Computer Associates, which inherited IDMS and DATACOM prior to relational systems and has implemented distributed versions both with and without SQL.)

Distributed DBMS products can be thought of as occupying the Mercedes Benz echelon of the marketplace. These products support a local DBMS at every node in the network along with local data dictionary capability. This requirement that a piece of the DBMS exists on each node is the essential difference between distributed DBMS's and client/server systems. In a client/server approach, the DBMS resides on one (or a few) nodes, rather than all of them, and is accessed from a requester piece of software residing on the client.

The market for distributed DBMS has grown slowly for two reasons: (1) users are not sure of how to use the products, and (2) vendors are taking the better part of a decade to deliver a full range of functionality. Another important and unanswered concern is that companies do not know what communication costs to expect for functions that historically have been run internally to single computers. Now, however, with the imminent widespread availability of 100-bps capability across LAN's (with fiber and/or copper), concerns about communication costs and availability with distributed databases are disappearing. The growth in usage of distributed DBMS software in the 1990's is likely to be significant.

3–3 Background on Client/Server Database Computing

If distributed DBMS products represent the top tier of the market, then client/server DBMS engines are the Fords and Chevrolets. By accepting a reduction in functionality from what a distributed DBMS provides, vendors have developed client/server DBMS's that run exceedingly well on modern PC's and networks. Important capabilities like two-phase commits and distributed JOIN's across multiple servers are becoming available in both distributed DBMS and client/server DBMS. It is very likely that both markets will merge over the mid-term future.

Much of the impetus for downsizing comes from the fact that many companies want to implement applications that were previously forced to reside on mainframes onto faster, cheaper PC's or workstations. But, before committing to downsizing such applications, assurances about the integrity of the data and applications are necessary. In addition, PC's, as well as LAN's, have had reputations for not offering a mainframe level of security. Client/server computing is a solution that combines the friendly interface of the PC with the integrity, security and robustness of the mainframe. Server databases located on PC LAN's use implementations of the SQL database access language — the standard database language used on mainframes. Once you have decided to build a client/server environment, you will be on your way to building an applications architecture that will be economical, flexible, and portable for a long time into the future (Figure 3-1).

The functionality delivered by today's client/server systems is not too different from that of a distributed DBMS. The key difference is that a client/server approach places the DBMS and DBMS dictionary at certain designated nodes where the data resides. The client program is required to navigate the system and find the correct server node for access to the necessary data.

Distributed database vs client servers

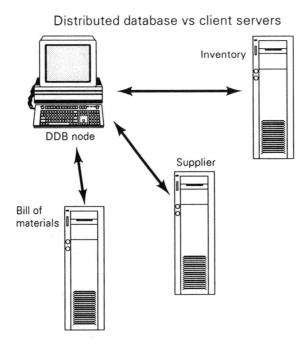

Fig. 3–1
One solution is to use a true distributed DBMS with a node in the client. This node does the join optimization using the system dictionary. This can also handle distributed transactions and can support a global schema view.

The History Behind the Client/Server

The idea for client/server computing grew out of database machine and relational approaches. One early visionary was Robert Epstein who, while working for Britton Lee, envisioned creating a database machine environment with a server that was a virtual machine rather than a physically unique piece of hardware. The systems software, then, was separated into a front end (client) which ran the program (written in a 4GL) and a back end (server) which handled the DBMS chores. The advantage of this idea was that the back end (the virtual database machine) could physically be moved out onto a different piece of hardware if desired. What made this different from Britton Lee's traditional approach was that Epstein planned for the server to be a generic VAX,

UNIX, or PC machine, rather than a unique, custom-built database machine. By moving the database machine onto a standard piece of hardware, this approach picked up the advantage of a vastly improved price performance for generic small systems. About the same time that Epstein was honing his ideas and starting Sybase to market them (mid-1980's), Informix Corp., a well-established relational DBMS vendor, embarked on a redevelopment path that would lead to a client/server architecture and distributed DBMS. Also at this time, Umang Gupta had pictured the same situation and left Oracle to form Gupta Technologies, a company which has emerged as a leader in PC-based, client/server DBMS and tools market. Bing Yao, the former University of Maryland professor who founded XDB Systems, was another early developer of client/server approaches to database computing.

By now, most SQL DBMS vendors have jumped into the client/server game. One exception is IBM; when IBM talks about client/server computing, what it is really referring to is distributed computing. IBM is in the process of building a fully functional, distributed architecture for all of its SQL products: DB2, SQL/DS, SQL/400, and OS/2EE. IBM is taking several years to develop this approach.

A client/server computing environment consists of three principal components: client, server, and network (Figure 3-2).

The Client

The client is where the application program runs. Normally, client hardware is a desktop computer such as an IBM PC, PC clone, or Apple Mac. The application program itself may have been written in a 4GL or third-generation language such as C or COBOL. There is an entirely new class of Windows 4GL's that allows the painting of applications under leading desktop, Windows-based operating systems.

Such Windows 4GL's support both Windows-oriented application development and execution. Leading examples now on the market include Powersoft's PowerBuilder, JYACC's JAM, Uniface, and Gupta's SQL Windows. Using any of these application-building approaches will result in a runtime configuration where the I/O and application controls come from the client, while the database and associated semantics run on the server. At the desktop level, most software will support the emerging Windows-based standards: Windows 3.x for DOS, Presentation Manager, Motif, and Open Look for UNIX and the Macintosh (Table 3-1).

Client - Server Functions

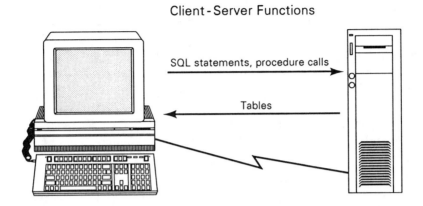

SQL statements, procedure calls

Tables

Client
Application program
Screen forms
Generation of SQL
Application control
Task switching

Network
Hardware/wire
Communications software
Multiple C and S

Server
Optimize and execute SQL
Manage transactions
Business rule enforcement
Stored procedures and triggers
• Security
• Concurrency management
• Logging and recovery
• Database creation and definition
• Data dictionary

Fig. 3–2
Client Server Functions

The Network

The network connects the clients and server(s). Normally, networks are based on either Ethernet or Token Ring topologies and have appropriate interface cards in both the client and server boxes. The communications software typically handles different types of transportation protocols such as SPX/IPX, LU6.2, and TCP/IP. Most network environments provide support for multiple clients and servers.

The Server

The server is responsible for executing SQL statements received from a client. Sometimes data requests are not communicated through SQL, but through a remote procedure call which triggers a series of precompiled, existing SQL statements.

The server is responsible for SQL optimization, determining the best path to the data, and managing transactions. Some server technologies support advanced software capabilities, such as stored procedures, event notifiers, and triggers. The server is also responsible for data security and requester validation.

The server will also handle additional database functions such as **concurrency management, deadlock** protection and resolution, **logging** and **recovering, database creation** and definition. The idea of managing data on a separate machine fits well with the management approach of treating data as a corporate resource. In addition to executing SQL statements, the server handles security and provides for concurrent access to the data by multiple users.

Table 3-1 Client/Windows 4GLs

End User	Occasional Programmer	Professional Programmer
Quest GUPTA TECHNOLOGIES	Dataease DATAEASE	Open Insight REVELATION TECHNOLOGIES
Personal Access INFORMIX	Forest & Trees CHANNEL COMPUTING	SQL Windows GUPTA TECHNOLOGIES
Objectvision BORLAND INTERNATIONAL	Infoalliance SOFTWARE PUBLISHING CORP	Informix 4GL INFORMIX
Notebook LOTUS	Focus INFORMATION BUILDERS	Paradox BORLAND INTERNATIONAL
Q + E PIONEER SOFTWARE	Visual Basic MICROSOFT	PowerBuilder POWERSOFT
Impromptu COGNOS	Windows 4GL ASK/INGRES	Uniface UNIFACE
Oracle Card ORACLE		Ellipse COOPERATIVE SOLUTIONS
		dBase Iv, Server Edition BORLAND INTERNATIONAL
		Oracle SQL Forms ORACLE

The Benefits of Using SQL

An important benefit that the set-oriented SQL language provides is network efficiency. When using traditional, file-serving, PC LAN approaches, the entire data file must be transmitted across a network to the client machine. Using SQL as a basis in the database management system on the server solves this problem since only the necessary query-response data (a subset of a table/tables) is transmitted to the client machine.

Having SQL on the server also allows the database implementation of advanced facilities such as triggers and automatic procedures. As relational DBMS evolve, they will confer the ability to build rules directly into the **database engine**. Systems that are built with this approach will be more robust than traditional application-based logic approaches.

Although client/server computing is being planned for environments which use minicomputers and mainframes as servers, the largest market likely to develop will have a mix of Windows 3.x, Windows NT, MS-DOS, OS/2, and Macintosh on the client, and either UNIX, Windows NT, NetWare, or OS/2 for the server. Server software will provide mainframe levels of security, recovery, and data integrity capability. Functions such as automatic locking and commit roll-back logic, along with deadlock detection and a full suite of data administration utilities, are available on the server side. Another way of looking at this, then, is that SQL client/server technology allows cheap PC's to be made into industrial strength computing engines.

3–4   More Details on Distributed DBMS's

Distributed DBMS's are where the most interesting action is happening in the large systems DBMS market (minicomputer to supercomputer). As SQL emerges as the standard DBMS language, the principal methods by which DBMS vendors are differentiating their products are by adding various functions including

- distributed or client/server computing,

- support for object approaches,

- database semantics, and

- more relational functionality (typically semantics).

Distributed DBMS software needs to provide all of the functionality of multi-user, mainframe database software, while allowing the database itself to reside on a number of different, physically-connected computers. The types of functionality distributed DBMS must supply include data integrity, maintenance through **automatically locking** records, and the ability to roll back transactions that have been only partially completed. The DBMS must attack deadlocks to automatically recover completed transactions in the event of system failure. There should be the capability to optimize data access for a wide variety of different application demands. Distributed DBMS should have specialized I/O handling and space management techniques to insure fast and stable transaction throughput. Naturally, these products must also have full database security and administration utilities.

The discussion below first focuses on the basic, and then the advanced functions for a distributed DBMS. However, it will not be helpful to use this section as a feature checklist since there is a great disparity between performing these functions at a minimum level and accomplishing them at an advanced level.

Basic Requirements for a Distributed DBMS

- *Location transparency*   Programs and queries may access a single logical view of the database; this logical view may be physically distributed over a number of different sites and nodes. Queries can access distributed objects for both reading and writing without knowing the location of those objects. A change in the physical location of objects without a change in the logical view requires no change of the application programs. There is support for a distributed JOIN. In order to meet this requirement, it is necessary for a full local DBMS and data dictionary to reside on each node.

- *Performance transparency*   It is essential to have a software optimizer create the navigation for the satisfaction of queries. This software optimizer should determine the best path to the data. Performance of the software optimizer should not depend upon the original source of the query. In other words, because the query originates from point A, it should not cost more to run than the same query originating from point B. This type of technology is rather primitive at this time and will be discussed later in this chapter.

- *Copy transparency*   The DBMS should optionally support the capability of having multiple physical copies of the same logical data. Advantages of this functionality include superior performance from local, rather than remote, access to data and non-stop operation in the event of a crash at one site. If a site is down, the software must be smart enough to reroute a query to another data source. The system should support fail over reconstruction: When the down site becomes live again, the software must automatically recon-struct and update the data at that site.

- *Transaction transparency* The system needs to support trans-actions that update data at multiple sites. Those transactions behave exactly the same as others that are local. This means that transactions will either all commit or abort. In order to have distrib-uted commit capabilities, a technical protocol known as a two-phase commit is required.

- *Fragmentation transparency* The distributed DBMS allows a user to cut relations into pieces, horizontally or vertically, and place those pieces at multiple physical sites. The software has a capabil-ity to recombine those tables into units when necessary to answer queries.

- *Schema change transparency* Changes to database object design need only be made once into the distributed data dictionary. The dictionary and DBMS automatically populate other physical catalogs.

- *Local DBMS transparency* The distributed DBMS services are provided regardless of the brand of the local DBMS. This means that support for remote data access and gateways into heteroge-neous DBMS products are necessary. (This is very much a future capability, as no vendor offers this feature today.) These require-ments are summarized in Table 3-2.

IBM's Four Ways to Distribute Data

Most vendors have been taking many years to develop software that offers distributed DBMS capability. As a way of bringing its distributed SQL products to market, IBM has proposed a phased implementation with four discrete steps to achieve distribution of data. These four princi-pal steps are defined as follows:

- *Extracts* provide the ability to extract data. This simply means that there exists a batch process which unloads and reformats opera-tional data into a relational view. For example, IBM's DXT allows for **batch unloading** of IMS and reformatting into DB2. This extraction is manually managed.

- *Snapshots* are becoming a popular technique among many vendors. A snapshot is an extract (as defined above), along with a date and time stamp. The advantage of a snapshot is that after it's defined to the system, it is automatically created and managed. Snapshots are read-only and provide an alternative method for decision support access to production data.

Table 3-2 Distributed DBMS - Requirements

Location Transparency	Queries can access distributed objects (distributed Join) for both read & write - without knowing the location of those objects. There is full local DBMS & DD.
Performance Transparency	A query optimizer must determine the best (Heuristic) path to the data. Performance must be the same regardless of the source node location.
Copy Transparency	Multiple copies of data may optionally exist. If a site is down, the query is automatically routed to another source. Fallover reconstruction is supported.
Transaction Transparency	Transactions that update data at multiple sites behave exactly as others that are local. They commit or abort. This requires a two-phase commit protocol.
Fragmentation Transparency	The distributed DDBMS allows a user to cut a relation into pieces, horizontally or vertically, and place them at multiple sites.
Schema Change Transparency	Changes to database object design need only to be made once into the distributed data dictionary. The DBMS populates other catalogs automatically.
Local DBMS Transparency	The distributed DDBMS services are provided regardless of the local DBMS brand. This means that RDA and Gateways into heterogeneous DBMS products are necessary

- *Distributed tables* can be thought of as the first level of real-time, read/write distributed DBMS functionality that meets the fragmentation requirement previously mentioned. Such a system, which can support distributed tables, will normally manage a single physical copy of data to support the system's logical views.

• *Replicates* are a more sophisticated version of the distributed DBMS capabilities classified under copy transparency. These can be thought of as support for a single logical view by up to n physical copies (of the same data). These data replicates must be updatable (not snapshots). At a minimum, updatability of physical data replicates will require a software optimizer (as discussed below) and a two-phase update commit protocol. Figure 3-3 summarizes IBM's approach to distributed database.

Software Optimizers

When a DBMS is spread over many different physical sites, the cost difference between the best and worst ways of accomplishing a function such as a JOIN can easily be a million to one. Because of this, a distributed DBMS absolutely must have a cost-based software optimizer. Without a cost-based optimizer, navigation to data is under programmer control, violating a basic precept of relational theory (this is what must be done with several earlier RDBMS's such as Oracle prior to 7.0). In the absence of such an optimizer, only known queries can be handled because the performance of an unanticipated query may be extremely poor.

A reasonable software optimizer has to be intelligent enough to ask tough questions and to develop a correct search strategy based upon the answers to those questions. Examples of the types of issues that should be dealt with are:

1   How busy are the various machines on the network?

2   What are the relative speeds of these machines?

3   What are the sizes of the tables that have to be accessed?

4   How are the tables organized?

5   What is the line speed between various nodes on the network?

6   How busy are the lines between the various nodes?

7   What are the access patterns in indexes?

8   Where should the software optimizer itself run?

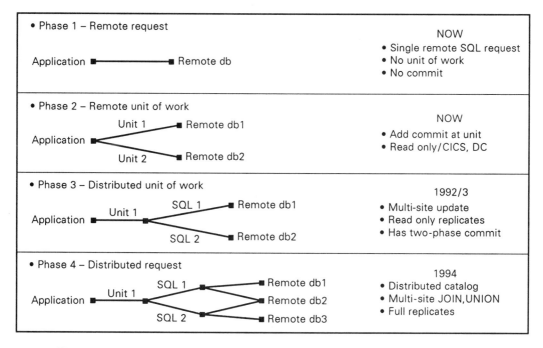

Fig. 3–3
IBM's Approach to Distributed Database

Two-Phase Commit Protocol

The goal of the two-phase commit protocol is to allow multiple nodes to be updated synchronously as result of a group of SQL statements which are either committed or rejected together.

The following is the general procedure for a two-phase commit.

1 One node is designated as a master. The master sends notice of an upcoming query out to all of the slaves.

2 The slaves respond with ready messages when all of the data necessary for the protocol is available.

3 The master sends out a *prepare* message to the slaves.

4 The slaves lock the necessary data and respond with a *prepared* message to the master.

5 The master sends a *commit* message to the slaves.

6 The slaves respond with a *done* message.

For the DBMS software vendor, developing two-phase commit protocol is one of the most challenging tasks. The additional complexity in this type of software comes from the fact that there are different types of failure nodes and the software needs to recover from any combination of failures over all of the supported environments. For the user, operation in an environment requiring a two-phase commit may be very costly. The extra cost is incurred since a two-phase commit requires an extra round-trip message above the normal amount of messages that occur in single computer systems.

There are no standards for implementing a two-phase commit. Various vendors have offered different, partial implementations. It is likely that we will see a future ISO standard dealing with two-phase commit protocol.

3–5 More Advanced Capabilities for Distributed (or Client/Server) DBMS's

- *Gateways* Many of the distributed DBMS and client/server DBMS products have optional gateways that allow access to data stored in other DBMS's. Lower levels of functionality provide for read-only access, while higher levels of function allow write access also. This higher level should be accompanied by two-phase commit capability across the different systems (general availability of this capability is still in the future).

  Distributed access is a technology that is closely related to distributed DBMS. Distributed access is about the building of gateways that allow one DBMS to access data stored in another. This can properly be thought of as a subset of the technologies being delivered by vendors selling distributed DBMS or client/server DBMS technologies. The demand for distributed access, of course, is greatest in popular mainframe file and database environments such as IBM's IMS, DB2, VSAM, and DEC's Rdb. This is because local DBMS capability is not a requirement for distributed access. Instead, most vendors provide a piece of software known as a requester to be run on the client side of the RDA environment. Some of the products in this market are not finished gateways, but tool kits so that users can build custom gateways.

- *Relational integrity* An important server function that supports increased productivity in application development is relational integrity. This can include features such as referential integrity, or the ability to state business rules directly into the database using stored procedures or program triggers.

* ***Triggers***   Triggers are small SQL programs, written in SQL-extended language, that are stored in the DBMS catalog. Each trigger is associated with a particular table and an SQL update function (e.g., update, delete, and insert). They are automatically executed whenever a transaction updates the table. You can write triggers to enforce any database validation rule, including referential integrity.

    Since triggers are stored in the catalog and automatically executed, they promote consistent integrity constraints across all transactions. Triggers are easy to maintain because they are stored in only one place. They result in rules that are enforced for any application that accesses the database, such as spreadsheet programs.

* ***Multi-threaded architecture***   For the best performance, distributed (or client/server) DBMS should implement a multi-threaded, single-server architecture. Multi-threaded servers perform most of their work and scheduling without interacting with the operating system. Instead of creating user processes, multi-threaded servers create a thread for each new user. Threads are more efficient than processes — they use less memory and CPU resources. A multi-threaded server DBMS can service ten to 40 users simultaneously on a machine as small as a 33-MHz 80386 PC with 10-MB of RAM.

* ***Symmetric multi-processing***   Another advantage of DBMS servers is direct support of multi-processor hardware architectures in a symmetric multi-processing (SMP) mode. Most operating systems either currently (UNIX, Windows NT, VMS) or soon (OS/2) will offer support for this functionality. Therefore, there needs to be effective integration between the DBMS and the operating system in order to take advantage of the potentially improved throughput.

    Direct support for SMP means the DBMS can take advantage of several parallel processors under the same skin (with an appropriate operating system). These processors can be either tightly or loosely coupled.

- **Cursors**   A cursor stores the results of an SQL query and allows a program to move forward through the data one record at a time. Sometimes, programmers are also able to move backward within a cursor. Without a cursor, it's harder to program transactions that browse through data.

- **Text, image, date, and other extended data types**   Support for different types of data can make any DBMS useful in a wider variety of applications. To store a picture, it would be useful to have something like IMAGE data types of binary data. Another useful item is TEXT data types, which are printable character strings.

- **Remote procedure calls (RPC's)**   RPC's allow an application on one server (or client) to execute a stored procedure on another server. Stored procedures enhance computing performance since all of the commands can be executed with one call from the application program.

- **Multi-platform implementations**   Another primary advantage of a robust DBMS is multi-platform portability and networking. If your software runs on many different vendors' hardware, then you have that much more flexibility. For example, Informix has been implemented on approximately 400 different hardware systems.

- **Disk mirroring**   For companies wanting the reliability of mainframe environments on the PC LAN, disk or server mirroring capability is necessary. Mirroring implies that dual operations are executed for each computing step with error reports whenever there is any difference between the results of the dual steps. Mirroring also allows the system to continue to operate at essentially full speed, even after one of the processors or disks has failed. Disk mirroring is supported through the process called shadowing. This is a very useful facility for applications that require extremely low amounts of down-time — if one disk fails, then the system will automatically divert and use the other disk without interrupting operations.

- **BLOB data types**   A BLOB data type (binary large object bin) has no size limit and can include unstructured, non-relational types of data such as text, images, graphics, and digitized voice. One way to handle BLOB's is as a single field in a record, like a name, date, or floating point number. It can then be governed by concurrency and transaction control.

The ability to create database macros which can be executed by the database engine should be supported within the DBMS. These macros would be implemented as centrally-stored, user-written procedures that tell the database system how to translate BLOB data to another format. Because they are stored in one place and managed by the database, BLOB macros are simpler to create and maintain than similar codes in an application.

- *Application specific functions* This capability allows a user to easily extend the range of database commands by adding new functions, coded in C, to the DBMS *kernel*. This facility is helpful in the manipulation of BLOB data.

- *Event alerters* An event alerter is a signal sent by the database to waiting programs that indicates that a database change has been committed. Event alerters work remotely and can span across multi-vendor networks. Although it would seem to be simple to add event alerters to a system that supported the concept of triggers, implementation of the technology is made difficult by the need to support an asynchronous, heterogeneous environment.

Event alerters offer many benefits.

  - The waiting programs consume neither network traffic nor CPU cycles.

  - Notification is effectively instantaneous, not dependent on some polling interval.

  - Event notification works remotely, even across differing platforms. The notification mechanism is managed by the DBMS.

  - Unlike a trigger, an event alerter can affect programs running outside of the database.

- *Multi-dimensional arrays* In scientific processing or time-series commercial types of applications, array support for the database is useful. Arrays are stored as a single field in a record so that retrieval is expedited. Arrays are widely used in scientific processing and are very expensive to normalize for a relational DBMS — normalization typically means creating redundant data to generate separate records for information that is really only different at the field level.

3–6 More on Client/Servers

Almost all of the advanced functions listed in the previous section on distributed DBMS (such as BLOB data types and RPC's) are also available from leading DBMS-server vendors. To repeat our previous definition, the primary difference between a server DBMS and a distributed DBMS is whether or not each node on the network has a full copy of the DBMS. Added functionalities are not a good way to tell the difference between these two cousin technologies.

Many companies are delivering client/server DBMS and associated tools at this time. The very large and active market of the 1970's and 1980's for mainframe DBMS and 4GL's that featured companies like Cullinet, IBM, Software AG, Cincom, and Applied Data Research, has been replaced by a new market. This new environment is built around the client/server or distributed DBMS model with open availability (connectivity) between GUI-oriented tools running principally on the client and server DBMS principally executing SQL. The reasons behind the current and impending growth of this market are many:

- Developers can use PC's instead of time-sharing terminals as primary development platforms.

- Security, integrity, and recovery capabilities comparable to mini-computers result even though the PC is used as the principal platform.

- The efficiency of SQL queries and transmissions greatly reduces the network communication load (from that of a PC LAN/file-server-based approach).

- Gateway technologies, which are an important component of client/server computing, will allow PC users to gain access to data located in mainframe and minicomputer DBMS products such as DB2, IMS, and Rdb.

- The client/server model isolates the data from the applications program in the design stage. This allows a greater amount of flexibility in managing and expanding the database and in adding new programs at the application level.

- The client/server model is very scalable because as requirements for more processing come up, more servers can be added to the network or servers can be traded up for the latest generation of microprocessors.

- A lot of flexibility comes from a computing environment based upon SQL since the language is standard. Commitment to an SQL-server engine will mean that most front-end, 4GL, spreadsheet, word-processing, and graphics tools will be able to interface to an SQL engine.

- Client/server computing provides the industrial strength security, integrity, and database capabilities of minicomputer or mainframe architectures, while allowing companies to build and run their applications on relatively inexpensive PC and minicomputer networks. The use of this hardware and software combination can cut 90% of hardware and software costs when building industrial= strength applications.

The client/server model offers users choices between many different hardware and software platforms. The hardware choices are too expansive to be listed here, but the principal choices for operating systems are multi-user, multi-tasking, protected products such as UNIX, OS/2, Windows NT, and NetWare. The microprocessor engine driving the hardware is typically a single or dual processor Intel x86 or RISC chips such as SPARC or the MIPS R4000.

UNIX today, and OS/2, NT, and NetWare in the future will support symmetric multiprocessing on the server, and this, importantly, will allow scalability of database applications well up into supercomputing performance categories. Today, Sequent Computer and its multiprocessing server product line is probably considered the leader in high-transaction-rate, database-oriented processing.

The client environment is typically a smaller, but powerful, PC that has enough power to run applications on top of multi-tasking, single-user operating systems such as Windows 3.1 or OS/2.

The concept of using a large mainframe such as a VAX 9000 or ES/9000 as a database server to networks is discussed by the mainframe vendors. For these machines to play a role in future networks, however, it is clear that they will have to adopt server functionality by acquiring and supporting emerging downsizing standards such as UNIX, NetWare, LAN Manager for Windows' NT, and LAN Server for OS/2. Players in the downsizing open systems server market are summarized in Table 3-3.

Performance from a Client/Server Environment

The reader might be skeptical of the claim that PC's running server software can perform as well as mainframes, but there is documented evidence to this effect. The most efficient PC-server operating system at this time is probably NetWare. Tests run in conformance with the **Transaction Processing Council**'s standards have shown that products like Informix and Gupta's SQLBase are capable of running about 50 transactions per second (TPS) on 486-based PC's.

I have visited and witnessed mid-sized banks with over 100,000 transactions per day running complete on-line teller systems against an SQL DBMS server running on a single processor 486 server (this was for a mixed DOS and NetWare environment with a DOS server running the database and a NetWare server handling file management and transport services).

Table 3-3 Players in the Downsizing Open-Systems Server Market

Corporation	Program
Gupta Technologies, Inc.	SQLBase
IBM	OS/2EE
Informix Software Inc.	Informix Online
ASK/INGRES Division	Intelligent Database
Microsoft/Sybase	SQL Server
Novell	Netware SQL
Oracle	Oracle Server
Sybase	SQL Server
XDB Systems Inc.	XDB-Server
Borland/Interbase	Interbase
Progress Software	Progress
Computer Associates	IDMS/R, Datacom
DEC	Rdb, ACMS

Hyatt Hotels implemented a UNIX-based client/server approach using AT&T minicomputers and Informix SQL-based software to completely replace its mainframe reservations system for 600 hotels worldwide. This is the kind and size of application that has historically been relegated to strictly mainframe, transaction-style processing. Although Hyatt has reported an overall 25% savings in running the client/server system, the most important benefit for them is the improved maintain-ability and functionality of the new application.

These kinds of systems and performance numbers definitively prove that SQL-style client/server systems can be implemented on generic hardware platforms and deliver performance that is the equivalent of an expensive mainframe running IBM's DB2. And, in fact, the banks I have seen being run on PC servers have used those machines to replace mid-sized mainframes.

The transaction capabilities of client/server software working with low-end PC servers or super-servers (minicomputer-style cabinets built with merchant microprocessors such as the 80486 or R4000) are quite astounding. PC hardware can support disks with 4-millisecond access time and 8-MB transfer rates. Such a machine can be configured with 600-MB of disk for under $5,000!

If you have had a chance to build PC-based database applications in the last few years, you may be suspicious of any claim that a PC hard-ware environment could be capable of performing on a level comparable with minicomputer technology. However, it is important to remember that the processing capability of a typical PC has increased by forty-fold between 1984 and 1992. A PC built around the Intel 80486 microproces-sor chip running at 33/66-MHz has at least 60 times the computing power of a PC/XT. This high level of service can provide on-line transac-tion processing capabilities at a cost under $2,000 per TPS (Table 3-4).

Table 3-4 Database Server Performance

Low End

- 486 PCs, low-end RISC, 12 ms ACCESS/4MB Transfer Rate
- 10-20 MIPS @ $6,000 to $18,000
- 8 - 15 TPC-B/SEC
- 90 workstations simultaneously on a single server
- 250 ATM's on a single server
- Ethernet - 100 TPS Across Network

High End

- Parallell CISC or RISC gives hundreds of MIPS
- SCSI and API Channels - comparable to 3090 channels

Result:

- OLTP at $1K - $4K per TPS

This cost is much less per TPS than existing minicomputer and mainframe systems can provide. Using proprietary minicomputers, you can expect to spend between $25,000 and $40,000 per TPS. IMS-based MVS mainframe environments typically yield a cost of $50,000-$75,000 per TPS. Alternatively, using the combination of MVS and DB2 as a transaction processing engine will typically cost over $100,000 per TPS. What all of this means is that, based upon full development, maintenance, hardware, software, and staff costs, SQL client/server computing is likely to result in finished systems that cost only a small fraction of what building transaction systems has cost in the past. Actual case studies confirm this type of important savings in finished, delivered systems.

Of course, there are many applications which are simply too large to contemplate running on (even fast) PC's. Client/server architectures allow you to design the application once and then, without change, port that application to whichever server has the database processing power you need to manage your database. This allows application development on PC-style servers, with the porting to the new generation of super servers, minicomputers built to run open operating systems powered by multiprocessing versions of merchant CPU chips. The approach is to take microprocessor-based technologies and combine them with high speed buses, channels, and parallel computing architectures to create platforms that can run with the fastest minicomputers. Vendors such as Compaq, Pyramid, and Sequent are building parallel processing machines using CISC or RISC microprocessor units capable of reaching a sustained processing capability of hundreds of MIPS. Do not be surprised, then, to see a combination of these new hardware systems with software from companies like Informix, Sybase, Gupta, Microsoft, and Oracle delivering computing technologies comparable to IBM's largest machines, but at a tiny fraction of the price.

As a first project, it is clearly more comfortable to use client/server computing for mostly-read or decision support environments. The very large, tough, performance-based applications, such as retail credit card verification or airline reservations, require reliable processing of hundreds of transactions per second and are still relegated to mainframes only. However, as mentioned earlier, there is no shortage of serious transaction processing applications that have already been successfully implemented on top of client/server SQL environments.

In the future, I expect multiprocessor-based client/server architectures to regularly take on mainframe types of applications. It is very reasonable to envision products like Informix, Oracle, and Sybase in combination with high-end super servers from companies such as Sequent, Pyramid, Concurrent, Compaq, IBM, or DEC. This high-end super-server hardware is typically built with parallel Intel 486, 586, and/ or RISC chips from MIPS, DEC, or Sun. By configuring a server with a multiprocessor design and an open operating system that supports it (e.g., UNIX, VINES, NT, OS/2, or LAN Manager), a vendor can build a machine with hundreds of MIPS processing power and 250-GB of disk data storage for well under $500,000. Combining this technology with high speed channels and a client/server DBMS, allows a configuration of new technology hardware and database server to be considered as a replacement for a $14 million IBM System 390 running DB2. With a potential savings of almost 95%, this would appear to be an offer well worth considering for many situations.

3–7 Conclusion - A Reality Check

The various advantages of distributed processing and distributed DBMS are both well-documented and considerable, especially for companies that wish to take advantage of new computing styles featuring graphical interfaces and distributed implementation. Migrating to these new technologies, however, requires serious investments in the training and building of expertise for the new systems. There do exist potential problems associated with taking advantage of the advanced capabilities of distributed DBMS's. Below is a quick summary of some of the problems associated with this technology.

1   Communication costs can be quite high, and using a two-phase commit protocol tends to generate a considerable amount of communications traffic.

2   There is the need for gateway technology to handle the SQL differences among different DBMS vendors.

3   The predictability of total costs for distributed queries is variable. In other words, it is difficult to predict how much it will cost to get a job done.

4   Supporting concurrency, in addition to deadlock protection, is very difficult.

5   Supporting full recovery with fail over reconstruction is very expensive.

6   Performing a JOIN across different physical nodes is very expensive using current technology and networks.

7   Some advanced relational functions, reasonable for single computers, are difficult and expensive across distributed networks (e.g., the enforcing of semantic integrity restraints).

8   The job of database administrators is more difficult because, above and beyond their current functions, they need to understand the integrity, optimizer, communication, and data-owner issues of the distributed world.

9   Data security issues are neither well-understood nor proven. It would appear that a distributed environment is more susceptible to security breaks than is a database which is contained in one box.

Please recognize this as a list of potential pitfalls that await (in most cases) the advanced user of this new technology. As is the case of most new technologies, the well-advised user would take small steps while mastering the approach before moving onto the more complex conversions/implementations. Many companies will find the client/server approach to be more simple to implement initially. Investments made in such an approach will likely migrate towards a distributed database if later desired.

At a rate of 50 TPC-B transactions per second, a (currently) large PC is capable of running an SQL DBMS and delivering services comparable to most of the IMS applications in existence today. The ability to create those applications with the ease associated with SQL databases and GUI screen painters is something that we only could have dreamed about in the mid-1980's. Prototyping approaches in building those applications means that significant time-savings will be realized in better looking and more flexible approaches of the 1990's. The era of PC LAN-based systems has arrived and will dominate the systems building paradigm for the foreseeable future.

Be sure to pay close attention to picking your software partner. The vendor who provides you with a DBMS and tools should be selected most carefully. In an era of open and replaceable hardware and operating systems, your development tools and DBMS vendor will be most important.

Object Databases in Action: Technology and Application

Mr. Tim Andrews has been Chief Technical Officer at ONTOS, Inc. since 1988. He is one of ONTOS's two primary designers and has a unique background in object technology, database implementation, and technical marketing.

Mr. Andrews joined ONTOS 1986 as a key member of the initial design team. During 1987 and 1988, he was Manager of Technical Programs; in this role he worked extensively with all critical customers and led seminars and workshops worldwide. Since his appointment to Chief Technical Officer in 1988, Mr. Andrews has helped shape the strategic direction of the ONTOS product architecture and has continued his work with critical customers, most notably IBM. He has appeared in numerous forums around the world, giving speeches and lecturing on object database technology.

I n the late 1980's, *The New York Times* commented that object-oriented technology had become the software industrys equivalent of oat bran, wondering if it was a fad. Today, object-oriented technology has become a major force in the IT industry. Object-oriented databases have also been widely cited as the most likely contender to succeed relational databases, much like the network data model was replaced by the relational.

In this chapter, Tim Andrews gives an in-depth analysis of object databases from both technology and market viewpoints. As opposed to other object-oriented articles, Tim approaches this chapter as an active practitioner participating in the object database market. Because of the need to explain to his customers what an object is, why it is here to stay, and what it can do for firms, Tim is in a unique position to shed light on this subject.

The object database represents a new database technology that is rapidly gaining acceptance in the marketplace. Object database technology is complex, and its associated products are relatively new. There is some confusion surrounding the impact of object database technology and the segmentation of the products available. A full discourse on object database technology is well beyond the scope of this chapter because, as Andrews explains, "it represents the convergence of two substantial technology streams: languages and databases." A complete understanding of object database technology requires in-depth knowledge of both object-oriented programming languages (OOPL's) and database management systems (DBMS's). In fact, one of the challenges of trying to explain object databases is that most technical people have a heavy bias in either the DBMS or OOPL direction and, as a result, are missing an important body of knowledge needed to properly interpret the technology.

This chapter is written for readers with a background in both OOPL's and DBMS's with the aim of providing a perspective on the key characteristics of the object database (ODB). It is hoped that readers will gain some insight into how the object database products are segmented and what the most important characteristics of object databases are from a technical perspective. The reader should begin to understand the various possible uses of an ODB and the utility of products in this category for a given application or suite of applications. Enjoy IT.

4–1 Background

The object database represents the convergence of two substantial technology streams: languages and databases. Objects were originally a language phenomenon, first appearing in the language Simula in 1967 and embodied today in C++, Smalltalk, and a host of other languages. Databases originated in the 1960's with the IMS system from IBM and have evolved into relational database products such as Oracle, Ingres, and Sybase and PC database products such as Paradox, Dbase, and Fox-Base.

Much research and development has been conducted in each of these technology streams, and a familiarity with both object languages and databases is needed to fully understand the object database technology stream. This chapter will assume the reader has a background in object languages and databases. There are many excellent references where such background information is available. The reader is referred to [DATE] and [WIED] for background reading on database technology. [MEYE, TAYL, WIRF] provide background on object language technology. Other ODB references are beginning to appear [ZDON, MART, KIM].

Products in the object database market fall into three categories: *persistent language environments (PLE's)*, databases of objects (DOB's), and *component object databases (CODB's)*. These categories are more or less functionally layered. In other words, databases of objects provide a superset of the functionality of persistent language environments, and component database objects add additional capabilities to databases of objects (Figure 4-1).

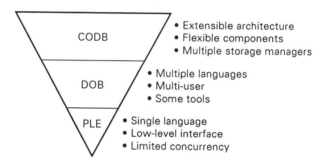

Fig. 4–1

4–2 Persistent Language Environments

Persistent language environments' (PLE's) primary function is to facilitate the storage and retrieval of objects from within a given language environment. This category is focused on developers who use a specific language with the products generally very closely bound to the language, usually C++ or Smalltalk. Because of the single language focus, these products are used more in single-user environments where a single developer creates an application, e.g., by converting an existing C++ application. CAD applications, in particular, are well-suited to this approach in the workstation marketplace.

One reason for the development of PLE's is the desire of programmers using an OOPL to store and retrieve objects from a secondary storage device such as a hard disk. Since the objects in an OOPL are created and managed by the language environment, support must be added if the programmer wants to save objects for use in a subsequent session. The programmer has a range of choices in this case: write code to save and recall objects from disk, use an existing DBMS, such as a relational database management system (RDB), or use an ODB.

In order to add persistence to the OOPL, a programmer is forced to write code that is not generally relevant to the task at hand. Furthermore, writing this code is not a trivial task. There are many significant subtasks which must be accomplished, the most important of which are the proper maintenance of *object identity* and an efficient mechanism for transfer of objects between the program and the storage device.

Maintaining Object Identity

Object identity is one of the key advantages of using objects in design and programming. Simply put, identity allows one to point at an object independent of any particular feature of that object. For example, identical twins may have the same hair color, eye color, height, and weight. In fact, they can be very hard to distinguish based on features alone. They are, however, two distinct people. In the case of twins, we identify them by giving them unique names. To identify objects in a program, we use unique names called references. These references are assigned and managed by the OOPL and are crucial in the performance of an OOPL.

OOPL's assume that objects of interest are created when the program starts and are destroyed when the program ends. Consequently, OOPL's manage references only during execution of a program. Maintenance of references beyond the scope of execution is a feature which must be added. There are two primary reasons to add support for object references beyond the execution of a program: 1) to allow access to objects in multiple executions of the same program; 2) to allow access to objects from different program executions, which may occur simultaneously.

PLE's are concerned primarily with the first reason. They add the ability to remember object references beyond a single program execution so that objects persist beyond the execution of the program in which the references were originally created. Thus the moniker persistent language environment.

Ultimately, proper maintenance of object references will involve translating values stored in the persistent memory (typically a hard disk) into pointers that an executing program can manipulate and vice versa (Figure 4-2)

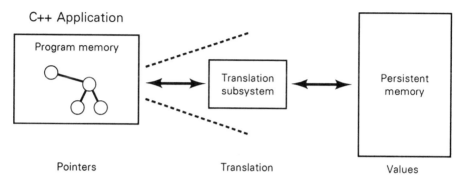

Fig. 4-2

This general concept is true for any program interacting with a persistent store, such as a file or a database. Pointers are the only mechanism by which programs can manipulate structures and are only valid during a single program execution. A C++ program using an RDB must read values from the database and translate these values into structures containing data and pointers as well as translate the data and pointers in the program structures to values when updating the database (Figure 4-3).

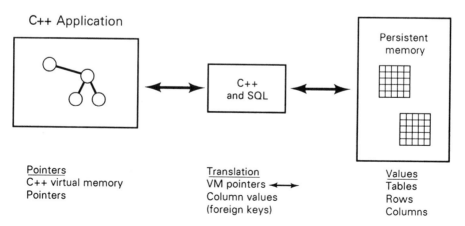

Fig. 4-3

The major difference introduced by a PLE is that the translation is managed automatically, thereby reducing the programmers time and effort (Figure 4-4).

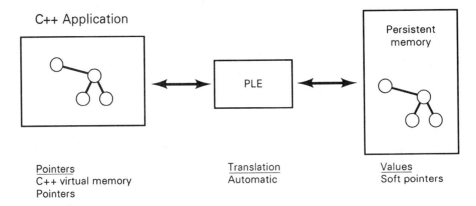

Fig. 4-4

This automatic translation is an example of Tesler's Law of Conservation of Complexity, an informal, but very elegant insight into software coined by Larry Tesler. The rule states, "complexity is never eliminated; its just moved around." In this case, the complexity of managing the translation of object references is moved out of the hands of the programmer and into the hands of the system. The complexity is not eliminated, but rather moved around so that the programmers efforts are focused on the application problem (Figure 4-5).

Efficient Transfer of Objects

OOPL's rely on pointers to implement object references. As a result, traversing an object reference means traversing a pointer (or perhaps many pointers - another famous informal law of software states that every difficult problem in software is solved by another level of indirection). However, introducing persistence into the equation means that traversing an object reference may involve accessing the persistent memory. Understanding the effect of adding persistence is critical because the difference in execution time between accessing program pointers and accessing persistent storage is at least three orders of magnitude. For example, consider a simple application which draws a geometric model of

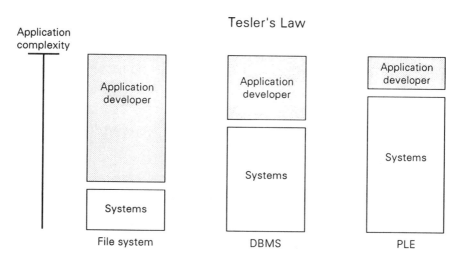

Fig. 4–5
Tesler's Law: For less application developer effort, the same application can be built.

a manufactured part on the screen. Assume that this part is represented graphically by one million point objects. An OOPL would traverse a minimum of 1,000,000 pointers to draw the part object. Assuming it takes a microsecond to traverse an in-memory pointer; this means it will take a minimum of one second to draw the part. However, if the objects are persistent, the same operation could take 1,000 seconds, or over 15 minutes. Consequently, PLE's use a variety of techniques to provide efficient transfer of objects so that the actual performance experienced by applications is far better than the example cited above.

The most important techniques used by PLE's are *caching and clustering*. Caching reduces the average access time into persistent memory by keeping objects in program memory after the first access. Thus, if the same object reference is traversed 1,000 times, the first access will be to persistent memory and the subsequent 999 accesses will be to program memory pointers. The average access time will be:

(millisecond + 999 microseconds)/1,000 accesses =
1.999 microseconds

In this case, the average access time experienced by the application is only twice the original rather than 1,000 times the original. This technique has proven to be very effective in practice because the trend of adding large amounts of program memory capacity to application machines is growing; this added memory allows large caches to be maintained by the PLE.

Clustering of objects refers to the ability to co-locate the physical representations of objects in the persistent memory. Clustering allows the system to transfer a large number of objects to/from persistent memory with one access. The amount of time required to access persistent memory is not affected significantly by the amount of data transferred. For example, many hard disk drives have average access times of 15 milliseconds. However, that 15 millisecond access can typically read 1,000 objects into program memory instead of just one. If all of those objects are needed by the program, then we have just reduced the per object access time to fifteen microseconds. Clustering provides the programmer with the ability to place objects close together so that each transfer of objects reads into program memory those objects most likely to be used by the application. This is a statistical phenomenon; applications may not access a consistent group of objects with each execution, so the results of clustering, while good, never reach the ideal.

Caching and clustering make the average access time to objects in persistent memory close to that of objects in program memory. The combination of this access time with the automatic maintenance of object identity makes PLE's a very attractive option to programmers. They can easily add persistence and benefit from it without a significant loss in average application performance.

4–3 Databases of Objects

Databases of objects (DOB's) are systems aiming at a more general market than PLE's by providing, in addition to the basic persistence of PLE's, storage and retrieval of objects from multiple languages along with more sophisticated database features such as concurrent access, 4GL's and higher-level tools for developing database applications. Currently, the languages supported are C++ and Smalltalk, with LISP and other languages garnering some support. These systems allow for the development of multi-user applications.

In the discussion of PLE's, the features normally associated with database systems such as multi-user access and reliable transactions, were not mentioned. PLE's approach the problem from the language perspective; if database features are present, they are generally secondary to language interface support. DOB's approach the problem from the traditional database perspective and concentrate on adding objects to the typical database mechanisms. These systems can be viewed as an evolution of the current RDB, with classes and objects replacing tables and rows. DOB's use OOPL's as data definition and data manipulation languages and provide the PLE functionality which integrates the data definition and data manipulation languages with the OOPL.

However, in contrast to PLE's, DOB's place more emphasis on multi-user transaction capabilities than language integration. DOB's offer more flexible locking protocols and are designed to be used in multi-user environments. For example, PLE's often offer no locking at all or page-level locking. DOB's provide locking at the object level. This feature makes the DOB a more complex system, but offers the flexibility needed to support concurrent use effectively.

Another distinction between DOB's and PLE's is that DOB's emphasize support for multiple languages and tools to ease application development. Where PLE's are targeted for low-level system programming in a particular language, DOB's are targeted at higher-level programming for a broader class of developers. DOB's trade off the very tight coupling with a single language with the ability to support more than one language. Vendors of DOB's also apply their resources to developing higher-level graphical tools rather than debuggers and low-level language support.

4–4 Component Object Databases

Finally, there are component object databases (CODB's) using an entirely new architecture based on object technology. This architecture adds unique extensibility and flexibility to the capabilities of PLE's and DOB's. For example, the object-oriented architecture of CODB's allows for undisruptive integration into existing environments, enabling the user to take advantage of the advanced capabilities of the CODB while leaving the data where it is. An insurance company can integrate existing systems, such as CICS applications, with new policy objects using a CODB, such as ONTOS DB.

Another unique advantage is that the extensibility of CODB's enables new technology to be integrated without changing systems. This category of product aims at the largest market: commercial corporate environments seeking to move computing into distributed environments without abandoning the significant investment in existing systems.

Component object databases (CODB's) build on top of both PLE functionality and DOB functionality by using objects to change the implementation architecture of the database. PLE's and DOB's are implemented as large, closed systems similar to the previous generation of RDBs (Figure 4-6).

CODB's, in contrast, are implemented in modular component class libraries. These component class libraries can be accessed and extended independently which makes CODB's flexible, accessible, and extensible at all layers of the system (Figure 4-7).

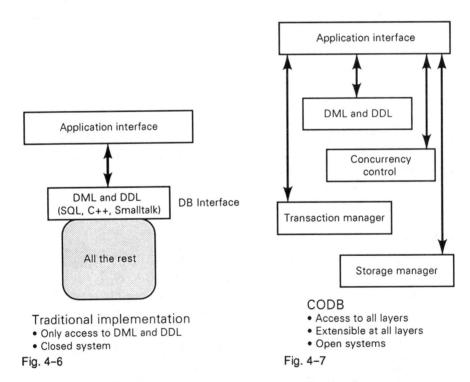

Traditional implementation
• Only access to DML and DDL
• Closed system

Fig. 4-6

CODB
• Access to all layers
• Extensible at all layers
• Open systems

Fig. 4-7

An example of the difference in this approach is the storage management component. The *storage manager (SM)* handles the physical representation of an object including its layout in program memory, its transfer to and from persistent memory, and its layout in persistent memory. Capturing this functionality into an extensible component enables the CODB to provide alternatives for storage independent of the logical model. As an extensible component, the SM also enables both vendor and customer to add more alternatives over time (Figure 4-8).

Performance tuning and integration of existing systems are two of the most important ways that SM's benefit the developer. Performance is dramatically affected by the physical representation of the objects used by an application; SM's enable the programmer to change physical representations without changing the application code. This capability is radically different from traditional implementations which provide only one vendor-supplied SM. The only performance tuning options available are more vendor-supplied mechanisms such as indices, caching, and clustering. CODB's also provide these standard mechanisms, but, rather than limiting them to a single vendor-supplied approach, CODB's *encapsulate* each approach into an SM.

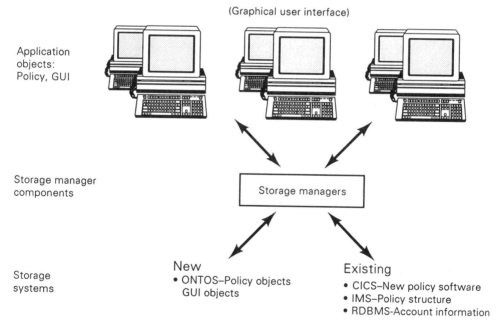

Fig. 4–8

By using a class component approach, multiple SM's can be supplied by the vendor and by third parties. Developers can then choose from a variety of SM's and can mix and match multiple SM's within a single CODB. This choice enables the developer to match the physical representation to the actual application needs with a far more significant impact on application performance than secondary mechanisms such as indices and clustering.

The ability to add new SM's enables the CODB's to address evolving requirements. This capability is especially important when programming with objects because of the number of different kinds of data that can be defined and managed with any ODB. RDB's, for instance, only store and retrieve tables, and the result is that the variation in structure between databases is not noticeable. However, since new object classes can be defined by the programmer, ODB's exhibit significant variations in the kinds of structures managed within a single database. SM's enable the development of new physical representations to provide effective implementations of this wide variety of logical object classes. Furthermore, these SM's are modular components and can be reused, which leverages the investment in developing a new SM. For example, a mapping system may store point objects representing a coordinate system for a map as well as satellite images from which the map is derived. Point objects are very small, typically just a few bytes, and are generally accessed in large numbers. Satellite images are very large and are usually accessed one at a time. SM's allow the use of different physical layouts for these two different data types, resulting in much better performance since each representation can be more precisely matched to the data it represents.

This concept can be effectively applied when integrating different systems. Data available in an existing RDB or a mainframe DBMS or an application with a custom file system can be left where it is and encapsulated in an SM.

Once in an SM, it can be used transparently from any application object in the CODB, enabling the programmer to develop new applications. Advantages of the features of the CODB are gained while using the existing information assets of the organization. For example, an insurance company develops a workstation application with a graphical interface to track the movement of a policy from initial proposal to actual issue. Typically, the movement of the policy object through the organization will cause information to be captured by a variety of databases and applications.

SM's allow the application to be developed using policy objects which add new information in the CODB. SM's can then be developed to

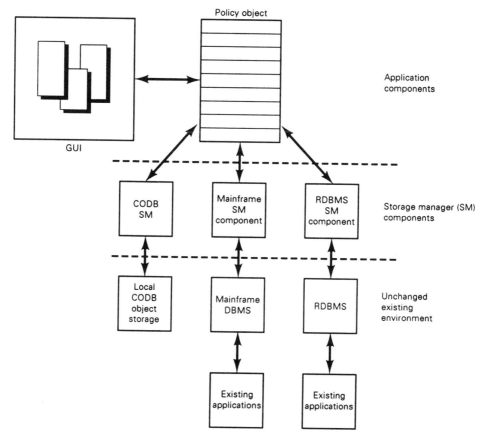

Fig. 4-9

interface with each of the existing systems. The result is the new application built as desired while all of the existing data assets remain in place. Furthermore, these SM's are now reusable components which can be used in other applications. This approach is only possible with a CODB (Figure 4-9).

4-5 Approaches in Use Today

Another perspective on object database technology is taken from the developer's viewpoint on the use of an object database. This section examines issues that are routine across PLE's, DOB's, and CODB's with a focus on the commonly evaluated aspects of system interface.

Component Integration

Developers evaluating ODB's today are concerned with how easily the ODB will work with other tools that the developer's organization has chosen. Languages, design tools, and other software components must be integrated with the ODB to leverage the investment in each piece of software purchased. The most effective mechanism that an ODB can provide to facilitate integration with other software components is an *active data dictionary*. An active data dictionary for an ODB consists of two components. First, there is a set of classes and objects which describes the type of information in the ODB. For each class defined in the ODB, there is a set of objects describing that class which constitutes the data dictionary of the ODB.

The second component of the active data dictionary is a runtime support system which makes the data dictionary objects available from a program while applications are running with the database. Programs interact with the data dictionary of the ODB without shutting down the system; this feature makes the data dictionary active. An active data dictionary can also be modified at any given time, allowing new components to be integrated into a running system.

An active data dictionary also provides a common base for describing the type system of any software component, thereby facilitating the integration of arbitrary software components (Figure 4-10).

Connecting components

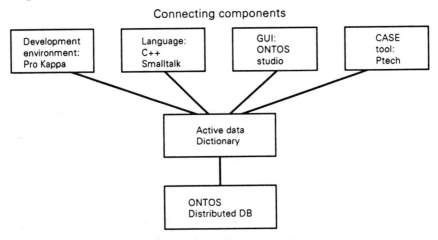

Fig. 4-10

Integrating different software components requires that the description of each component's interface, called its external type system, be integrated. Storing each component's external type system in an active data dictionary enables an application to dynamically integrate the external type systems of a set of components. An application can then pass information between components, thus providing effective integration of the components. As part of an ODB, an active data dictionary maintains this information which can be updated over time to add new components or to adjust the information on existing components.

The use of objects as the description mechanism for the active data dictionary also extends the kind of information that can be maintained and thus, the kinds of software components that can be integrated. GUI components, for instance, have an external type system describing the screen objects and events involved in a GUI. This information can be very naturally described using objects. In contrast, this information would be very difficult to describe using tables in an RDB. The active data dictionary of an ODB provides greater benefit because it can be used to manage a wider variety of software components within an organization.

Adding Persistence: Inheritance and Registration

There are two approaches in use today to add persistence to objects within an OOPL: *inheritance and registration.* Among the commercially available ODB's, ONTOS DB uses the inheritance approach. Class definitions are altered to inherit from an ONTOS DB base class which introduces the necessary messages to make objects of those classes capable of persistence. The inheritance model is conceptually simpler; the programmer knows immediately if objects of a given class can be made persistent. The inheritance model does not force every object of a given class to be persistent. It adds a message that causes objects to become persistent. Thus, if an object never receives this message, it does not become persistent. Adding persistence to objects can be handled on an object-by-object basis.

The inheritance model also allows the developer to use object programming techniques to customize the logic involved in storage and retrieval of objects. One major advantage of object programming is its ability to encapsulate complex operations. For example, the ONTOS DB system uses a base class with a putObject message to store objects. Every persistent class inherits the putObject message and uses it to store objects into the database. Any class can then override its own putObject message to perform specialized functions and be assured that every object of that class and any subclasses of that class will have those functions performed. This capability makes it much easier to enforce integrity constraints and, generally, simplify the programming task for the user of the class. For example, a company is creating a class library to describe its payroll. The first step is to create a Payroll class. When a payroll object is modified, certain related actions must be performed. For instance, appropriate taxes must be withheld and the appropriate tax accounts updated. The implementation must be written carefully to ensure that the payroll objects work. In a system using inheritance to add persistence, the developer can add this code to perform all the necessary actions within the putObject message for the Payroll class:

```
    Payroll::putObject(...) // the putObject
message for the Payroll class
    {
    calculate new withholding rates

    update tax account objects
    }
```

The company can now be confident that every payroll update will cause the proper related information to be entered into the appropriate systems.

Moreover, subclasses of Payroll such as Hourly and Exempt can be created, and the company knows that all these objects will go through the appropriate code. Finally, this code can be added or updated even after the class library has been created, with classes guaranteed to perform the new actions. The use of inheritance to add persistence is a very powerful technique.

The registration model takes a different approach: Class library definitions are not altered. Instead, messages are added or altered to provide the information necessary for persistence. The major advantage of the registration model is that existing class definitions do not have to be altered to inherit from a base class. However, class implementations usually will need to be altered, because the implementations almost always involve some form of composite behavior. Composite behavior is the use of a composite object to encapsulate the behavior of other related objects. For example, a square object is composed of four line objects. The code to create a square will create four lines, the code to draw a square will draw the four lines created earlier, and so on.

The definitions of the square and line classes do not need to be altered in a registration-based system. However, the code that implements squares will need to be altered because the code which creates and manipulates line objects must be altered to add the registrahe registration model information in order to add persistence. Furthermore, the use of inheritance to encapsulate shared code as described above is more difficult to implement.

The Storage Interface: Single-Level Stores and Seamlessness

The most obvious distinction between ODB's and RDB's is that the language interfaces of ODB's are much more integrated with the database. Rather than use a single database language, such as SQL, and then interface SQL to each programming language, ODB's use the extensibility of OOPL's to create a tailored interface within each OOPL. Extensibility is a simpler and more natural method for the programmer, and it overcomes the "impedance mismatch" regularly cited as a difficulty of using the declarative SQL language with an imperative programming language. In the extreme, the ODB integrates so tightly into the OOPL that it provides a completely seamless interface; persistent objects and transient objects become virtually indistinguishable. This interface is also known as a single-level store because the second level, the database, is transparent, so that the programmer only sees one "level" of objects.

The seamless interface is the easiest interface for the developer to use. Typically, the developer does not have to write any special code to save objects to the database or retrieve objects from the database. The number of lines of code that the developer must write and the complexity of the programming model are significantly reduced when compared with an RDB. The programmer cannot forget to save an object or traverse a reference to an object that is not yet in program memory. However, there are two problems with a seamless interface: the lack of access to the database storage interface and the conflict between the memory model and the transaction model.

In a truly seamless environment, the programmer has no direct access to the storage interface where objects are saved to and retrieved from the database. This can be problematic for two reasons. First, it eliminates the possibility of using messages to encapsulate integrity constraints and complex functions, one of the major advantages of using the OOPL. Second, it prevents the programmer from tuning the way objects are moved between disk and memory. While this may seem like an advantage, it must be remembered that single-level stores are an illusion to simplify the interface for the developer. In reality, access to the database is 1,000 times slower than access to memory, and thus the ability to have control over the interface between the program memory and the database is crucial. One unnecessary access to the database is as bad as 1,000 unnecessary accesses to the program memory.

The seamless environment creates the illusion that there is only one level of memory. The programmer cannot distinguish between objects in program memory and objects in persistent memory (Figure 4-2(a)). In reality, there is a difference between program memory and persistent memory. For example, if the programmer wants to save objects, then those objects must be transferred from program memory to persistent memory. In a seamless environment, the programmer has no direct control over this transfer because it is handled automatically.

A transaction is used to group logical units of work into an atomic action against the database. In order to be saved into the ODB, any objects in program memory that were modified during a transaction must be transferred from program memory to persistent memory by the end of the transaction, and program memory must be cleared so that a new transaction can begin. The programmer has no direct control over both the transfer of objects and the clearing of memory in a seamless environment. The programmer can only exert indirect control over memory by ending a transaction. However, this uses the transaction model to control the memory model.

Specifically, in a seamless environment there is no way to remove an object from program memory without also removing the object from persistent memory. An application reading a large number of objects from the database will be unable to manage the program memory used by those objects. In the extreme, the program memory is exhausted and the application fails. In a seamless environment, the only option available to the programmer is to break up the application into smaller transactions so that the end of the transaction will clear program memory. Breaking up transactions could interfere with computations in the application.

In summary, a seamless programming interface to an ODB, when it is the *only* interface to the ODB, has significant drawbacks. However, ODB's do provide a much easier-to-use programming interface than RDB's by integrating the language and the database models using objects. The ODB interface provides greater application development productivity and alleviates the impedance mismatch between languages and RDB's.

4–6 Summary

The object database represents a new database technology that is rapidly gaining acceptance in the marketplace. In order to understand the acceptance of this technology, the object database products have been placed in three distinct categories: PLE's, DOB's, and CODB's. A technical perspective on PLE's, DOB's, and CODB's has been provided along with examples of features and functions of each of these products. PLE's are targeted at low-level system programming in a particular language. DOB's are targeted at higher-level programming for a broader class of developers. CODB's allow integration with existing environments without disruption of data.

Each product category offers significant benefits which result ultimately in investment returns for organizations that implement object database technology. To understand how object database technology can benefit an organization, each product category must be carefully reviewed from a technical perspective. Only after a complete evaluation of each of these categories can the inherent benefits of object database technology be appreciated.

4–7 References

[ATKI] Atkinson, M., F. Bancilhon, D. J. Dewitt, K. R. Dittrich, D. Maier, and S. Zdonik. The Object-Oriented Database System Manifesto, *Proc. of the DOOD Conf.*, Kyoto, Japan, (December, 1989), 40-57.

[CARD] Cardenas, Alfonso F. and Dennis McLeod, ed. *Research Foundations in Object-Oriented and Semantic Database Systems.* Englewood Cliffs, New Jersey: Prentice Hall, 1990.

[DATE] Date, C.J. *An Introduction to Database Systems,* 4th ed., Reading, Massachusetts: Addison Wesley, 1986.

[FISH] Fishman, D. H., D. Beech, H. P. Cate *et al.* Iris: An Object-Oriented Database Management System, *ACM Trans on Office Information Systems,* vol. 5, no. 1, (January, 1987), 48-69.

[HAMM] Hammer, M. and D. McLeod. Database Description with SDM: a
    Semantic Database Model, *ACM Trans. on Database Systems*, vol. 6, no. 3,
    (September, 1981), 351-386.
[KIM] Kim, W. and F. Lochovsky, ed. *Object-Oriented Concepts, Databases, and
    Applictions*. Reading, Massachusetts: Addison Wesley, 1989.
[MART] Martin, James and James J. ODell. *Object-Oriented Analysis and
    Design*. Englewood Cliffs, New Jersey: Prentice Hall, 1992.
[MEYE] Meyer, Bertrand. *Object-Oriented Software Construction*. London:
    Prentice Hall International (UK) Ltd., 1988.
[TAYL] Taylor, David A. *Object-Oriented Technology: A Managers Guide*.
    Alameda, California: Servio Corporation, 1990.
[WIED] Wiederhold, Gio. *Database Design*. New York: McGraw-Hill Book Com-
    pany, 1983.
[WIRF] Wirfs-Brock, R., B. Bilkerson, and L. Weiner. *Designing Object-oriented
    Software*. Englewood Cliffs, New Jersey: Prentice Hall, 1990.
[ZDON] Zdonik, S. B. and David M., ed. *Readings in Object-oriented Database
    Systems*. San Mateo, California: Morgan Kaufmann Publishers, Inc., 1990.

CASE and Application Development Technologies

Adam Rin is Vice President and Service Director for the Applications Development and Management Strategies service at Gartner Group, Inc., a service that analyzes strategies, technologies, methods, products, industry trends, and vendors that aid in the development of applications systems. Gartner Group is by far the leading analysis firm for the computer industry. Dr. Rin's areas of expertise are in computer-aided software engineering (CASE), client/server computing, and application development strategies and tools.

He joined Gartner Group in the fall of 1988 after an extensive career in the independent software products industry. After a brief academic career, he conceived, proposed, and led the development of IDEAL, a highly productive and commercially successful fourth-generation language (4GL) at ADR, Applied Data Research, Inc. (now part of Computer Associates). He later served as Vice President of Product Planning at ADR. Following that assignment, he served as a vice president for product development at Computer Corporation of America on the Model 204 product line, the high-performance mainframe DBMS. Prior to joining Gartner Group, he was a vice president at Bachman Information Systems, where he led product management and product marketing for the first commercially available database design and reverse engineering product.

Adam Rin earned a Ph.D. in computer and information science in 1976 and a B.A. in mathematics in 1971, both from the University of Pennsylvania.

Is CASE dead? Absolutely not; it is evolving. IS organizations are discovering that CASE requires an investment that pays off in years, not months. Similarly, a new generation of applications development tools, including client/server, 4GL's, GUI builders, and object-oriented programming environments, are coming to challenge more traditional CASE approaches. Moreover, new industry forcesincluding downsizing, client/server architectures, open systems, and heterogeneity—are reshaping development technologies and IS strategies.

In this chapter, Adam Rin analyzes the changing face of CASE and applications development, and provides an assessment of alternative strategies as we enter the next era of applications development. Enjoy IT.

5–1 CASE in State of Transition: A Brief Case History

What Problems Does CASE Address?

Applications development over the last 20 years has been plagued by numerous problems:

1 Islands of automation;

2 Piecemeal evolution of systems;

3 Lack of integration in systems (redundant data, inconsistent/incomplete data, and inconsistent user interfaces);

4 Informal and imprecise specifications and designs; and

5 The program code as the only documentation (and so the organization is not aware of what information exists and/or how to get it).

Unfortunately, it has not been uncommon for specifications to be non-existent or for them to be far too informal and imprecise. Battles over the system functionality are fought between analysts and end-users much too late in the development cycle. The end-user's perception of the functionality often evolves during development. Traditional specifications in text form often become obsolete before the system is developed. Frozen specifications often fail due to their constant "defrosting" or because of a premature "freeze." Also unfortunately, even when the original system was well-specified, its maintenance and evolution over subsequent   months   and   years   goes   undocumented   and   grows unsystematically. It is a common phenomenon that the only representation of the system is the code itself, which is often obscure. New functionality is hindered due to a lack of information about the system or a lack of awareness of the side-effects of changes.

This implies additional problems:

6 User requirements not fully met;

7 Difficulty in maintenance, quality, and reliability;

8 Loss of productivity;

9 Lost business opportunities; and

10 Technological lock-in to specific platforms, devices, or proprietary DBMS's.

The fallout from the accumulation of the foregoing problems has been the inability of getting the right system built or modified in a timely fashion. Productivity is but one problem. Lack of responsiveness to change—be it from new business needs, regulatory requirements, or technology changes—and lost business opportunities can result.

CASE vs. System Development Methodologies

CASE, *computer-aided software engineering*, has been aimed at addressing some of these problems. To understand what CASE really attempts to address, we must first define a system development methodology. A *systems development methodology* (Figure 5-1) is a framework for building systems, which consisting of a work breakdown structure with phases, subphases, and tasks. Each type of task should result in a set of deliverables and uses specific formal techniques to produce and

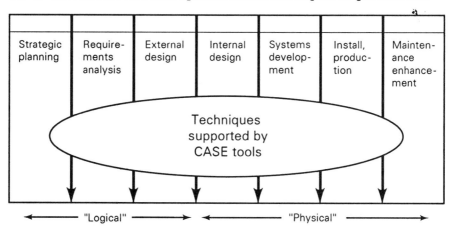

Fig. 5-1

Systems Development Methodology vs. CASE

represent those deliverables. A technique is a formal representation of some aspect of the system under planning, design, or development and can be presented in the form of a diagram, chart, structured text, matrix, or table. Many of the structured (or formal) techniques (sometimes called methods) have been around since the mid-1970's, but did not become adopted widely until the mid-1980's with the advent of commercial robust CASE tools. CASE tools automate the representation of these formal models, particularly the diagramatic ones, and help ensure their consistency and completeness. Some of the techniques automated by CASE are oriented toward the organization, some toward the data modeling, and others toward the processes or functions of the enterprise.

A Brief History of CASE

CASE is simply a set of technologies that provides automated support for the usage of techniques across the system's life cycle. A brief history of commercial CASE can begin in the 1970's when formal diagrams for specifying system processes emerged under various names. However, these were variants of structured analysis and design techniques, offered as precise ways to specify requirements and design specifications. Diagrams included dataflow diagrams, structure charts, and later, functional decomposition charts. Similarly, there emerged complementary data modeling techniques (for conceptual designs of databases) called entity-relationship diagrams. Although useful and employed by many progressive organizations, these diagrams on the whole fell into disuse until the mid-1980's due to lack of automation. It was impossible to manually maintain these diagrams as changes occurred and tough to validate them for completeness and consistency beyond simple applications.

In the early-to-mid 1980's CASE tools emerged to automate the drawing and mechanical validation of structured analysis/design techniques. These tools were retrospectively called upper CASE to distinguish them from more programming-oriented tools. Nastec, of Southfield, Michigan, now defunct, offered one of the early upper CASE commercial tools called CASE 2000, but by the mid-1980's it was outgunned by Index Technology's Excelerator. These first-generation CASE products were later overtaken by KnowledgeWare's IEW and ADW products and Texas Instrument's Information Engineering Facility. In the technical (embedded systems, engineering, and aerospace) sector, Cadre Technologies' Teamwork (still going strong) emerged as a leader.

Also in the early 1980's, various tools to aid programming emerged, including screen painters, report generators, code generators (from macro-technology) and fourth-generation languages (4GL's), which provided increased programming productivity over native 3GL programming. These tools also often hid the details of invoking database and data communication systems. In 1987, these tools were retrospectively called lower CASE to distinguish them from the upper CASE analysis and design tools (and by some to exploit the then-rising popularity of the CASE term). By the late 1980's interfaces between upper tools and lower CASE tools emerged; but these tended to be partial and awkward interfaces, as the products had overlaps and gaps between them.

In the late 1980's, so-called integrated CASE tools from a single vendor emerged from KnowledgeWare (IEW and, later, ADW) and from Texas Instruments (Information Engineering Facility or IEF). These tools were introduced to support a successor set of formalisms under the generic umbrella of "information engineering," an integrated set of data and process modeling techniques tied to business modeling, and by the late 1980's to code-generation from higher-level program specifications, thus spanning much of the life cycle. IEF remains the most integrated tool set on the market today.

One of the contributions of CASE is enabling separation of the logical system requirements from the physical design and development; i.e., it enables concentration on enterprise business requirements to be automated independently of the target hardware, system software, display devices, user interface and presentation details, target DBMS, or any other physical aspect of the target system (Figure 5-2). An example of a CASE tool set that cleanly separates between the logical enterprise models and the physical design and programming tools is offered by Bachman Information Systems.

CASE techniques fall into numerous categories, two of the most important of which are data-oriented techniques and process-oriented techniques. A data-oriented technique at the logical level is called **data modeling**, a formal representation of the basic entities (persons, places, organizations, things that are central to an enterprise) and their interrelationships. Earlier CASE tools stored the actual diagrams (e.g., data flow, function decomposition, or entity-relationship diagrams) or their representation in proprietary files. In order to use a combination of tools, interfaces had to be written.

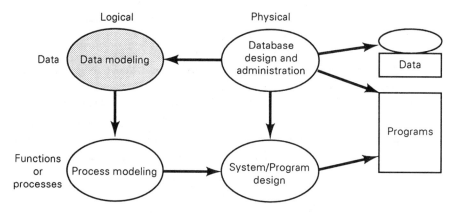

Fig. 5-2
CASE Concepts

A **repository** is an integrated DBMS for CASE and other application development tools to represent, store, and manage the deliverables of each phase of the system development life cycle. It contains a definition of all the objects that are produced by or input to each of the tools/techniques of its intended CASE products and other types of tools. Many independent integrated CASE tools have had a repository or its precursor for the past several years (e.g., Texas Instruments, Oracle, CGI). IBM and DEC have each released preliminary versions of their repositories (Repository Manager/MVS and CDD Plus, respectively) as part of their CASE strategy (AD/Cycle and Cohesion, respectively) although these still have a way to go to maturity.

Benefits and Pitfalls of CASE

CASE has had its benefits and its pitfalls. The benefits of CASE are the rigor and discipline it introduces through a set of successive deliverables in a life cycle; that is, the structured techniques, with validation and easier modification, support an orderly system development methodology. The results of properly implemented CASE are better quality and precision in systems. CASE is less about delivering systems faster (although much hype and exaggeration about productivity led to disappointments and setbacks with CASE) and more about delivering the right systems. When implemented well, it can save money in several respects: 1) it is less expensive to fix defects earlier in the life cycle than later in the life cycle; 2) flexibility of platforms, maintenance, and support is improved due to the separation of logical from physical design; and 3) in the long term, after a lengthy learning curve and with integrated code generators that cross platform boundaries, productivity is improved somewhat.

However, CASE has had pitfalls that have hurt its reputation. It requires an investment in methodology, techniques, hardware, tools, and training. Its return-on-investment is lengthy, often several years. Many of the techniques automated by CASE are aging and are only slowly being modernized (for example, to incorporate object-oriented analysis and design techniques). Code generators added to integrated CASE tools have been, until recently, aimed at mainframe applications, and only recently, vendors have been scrambling to append client/server generators and graphical user interfaces (GUI's) in the target application (while stand-alone client/server development tools, although just programming tools, catch the market's eye). CASE has also been hurt by lack of standards and inter-operability of tools and by exaggerations and unfulfilled promises of vendors. For example, IBM's 1989 AD/Cycle announcement of an application development environment (an ADE) that would unify diverse CASE tools into a cohesive framework has not substantially materialized even three years later and still does not appear particularly promising.

CASE technology is far from perfect, but in the cases of failure it was usually the organizational, cultural, or implementational efforts that failed, not the tools. Organizations that have been successful with CASE have tended to invest in methodology, education, testing, technology transfer, and ongoing support. They also carefully match the culture and organizational profile to the type of tool set and methodology selected, and furthermore, they have set realistic expectations and instituted a phased implementation plan.

On average, application development productivity will increase between 4% and 10% annually during the next five years. Organizations at the upper range will pay attention to the following critical success factors (especially if they wish to be successful with CASE and related development technologies): methodology, matching tools to culture, setting appropriate expectations, setting up a technology transfer program, commitment to education, training, and a phased implementation plan.

At present, CASE is at a juncture and is continuing through its evolution. Section 5-2 explores some key technological and industrial forces that will affect CASE and development strategies during the next five years. Section 5-3 assesses alternative strategies in selecting and implementing CASE and client/server development technologies, and Section 5-4 outlines some considerations for organizations deciding on which way to proceed.

5–2 Technology and Industry Forces Affecting Applications Development Strategies and Case

Despite CASE and other development tools, application development organizations remain under increasing pressure from diverse sources (Figure 5-3). Corporate business process re-engineering (BPR) activities are demonstrating that many of the information systems in place today are in support of largely outdated and inefficient business processes that can and should be streamlined. User demands for new functionality and easier-to-use systems that exploit client/server architectures and workstations are on the rise. As demand for increased productivity and quality (P and Q in Figure 5-3) in developing systems rises, external options to central applications development organizations, including outsourcing and systems integrators (SI), challenge traditional internal development organizations.

Enabling a new generation of applications, however, are a number of maturing technologies that can meet the challenges of the next five years (see the shaded areas of Figure 5-3):

1   Client/server architectures and graphical user interfaces (GUI);

2   Object-oriented (OO) technologies;

3   Tools to support multiple platforms in a world of fragmented standards; and

4   Increasingly more sophisticated CASE and **application development environments (ADE's)**.

These technologies will enable a new generation of applications, but will also require new skill sets and methodologies and application development strategies, CASE strategies, and development tool sets (the subject of Section 5-3).

Client/Server Technology and Graphical User Interfaces

Client/server is an architecture or model of computing that is rapidly gaining momentum and is affecting the methodology, CASE tools,

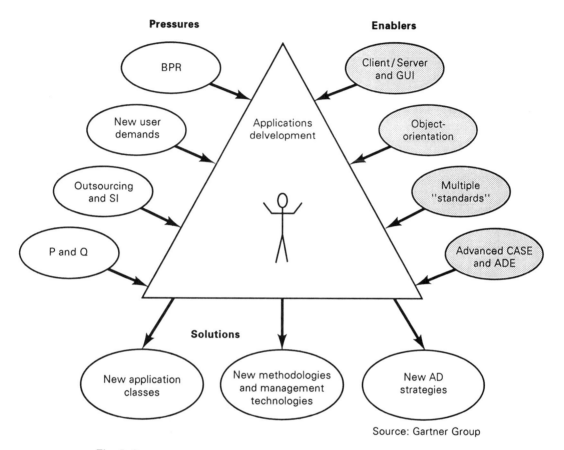

Pressures **Enablers**

BPR

Client/Server and GUI

New user demands

Applications delvelopment

Object-orientation

Outsourcing and SI

Multiple "standards"

P and Q

Advanced CASE and ADE

Solutions

New application classes

New methodologies and management technologies

New AD strategies

Source: Gartner Group

Fig. 5-3
Pressures, Enablers and Solutions for the Next Generation of Application (Source: Gartner Group).

other development tools by which the next generation of applications will be built.

Client/server computing is actually a special case of cooperative processing, which is two or more complementary programs interacting and executing concurrently on two or more machines (often different tiers) as part of an overall business function, whereby each component exploits the operating characteristics of its respective platform. Client/ server, although used in loose conversation interchangeably with cooperative processing, is an architecture of cooperative processing with predefined roles for two types of components, clients and servers. The client is the driving or initiating component, typically on a workstation, delegating predefined types of tasks to a responding component satisfying the request, the server, usually for which it awaits a response. The server acts on behalf of a client for a predefined class of functions, e.g., database requests.

Client/server computing is being driven by demands for easier-to-use interfaces on desktops, improved price/performance of desktop and server platforms, more access to decision data, and LAN SQL DBMS technology and high-productivity tools for client/server application development. The percentage of new, multi-user online applications that employ a client/server architecture will grow to 75% by 1996 and 90% by the year 2000.

Since a client/server application splits an application between workstations and servers, it requires first separating the application into logical layers, such as presentation services, core business logic, and database services.   The advantages of client/server include improved ease of use, productivity, and quality for the end-user via GUI presentation, more efficient use of computer resources (which will lower overall costs), improved functionality with GUI, multimedia, data integration, easier access to shared data, and technology leverage for competitive advantage.

Client/server will be deployed to exploit each platform for benefits such as exploiting the IWS for presentation services, optimizing processing load, accessing shared data, and making resource locations transparent to users and developers. Implementations of client/server applications, however, will remain slow through 1995 due to a shortage of methodology and tools for designing the client/server topology, immature tools, lack of uniform tools across platforms, lack of bridges from CASE technology to client/server design and code generation, lack of expertise and methods in development organizations, and the initial investment needed in hardware, system software, tools, training and support. The challenge for CASE is to extend its technology from conceptual enterprise models and aid in generating monolithic applications to the design, configuration, and code generation of client/server applications.

Object-Oriented Technology

Another evolving technology that will affect development and CASE tools is the maturation of *object-oriented (OO)* technology. Simply stated, OO technologies are a major paradigm shift in the way application components are organized and maintained, embracing several concepts of encapsulation, message passing, inheritance, and dynamic binding (Figure 5-4).

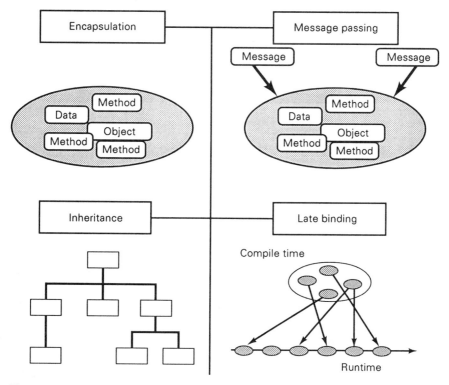

Fig. 5–4
Object-Oriented Concepts

These notions of organizing and manipulating the objects of an application system translate into benefits of reusability, easier real-world modeling, and eventually, productivity. Analogous to the shift to structured approaches in the 1970's and 1980's, OO technologies are first affecting programming, then design, and then analysis techniques; but we expect the OO evolution to occur more rapidly than did the structured evolution of the past.

CASE technology is a threat and an opportunity for CASE. Many of today's CASE tools automate structured techniques and information engineering techniques developed in the late 1970's and early 1980's. Leading CASE vendors will evolve their tools to incorporate OO analysis and design techniques between 1993 and 1996. Similarly, OO technology will penetrate mainstream commercial developers through OO CASE-driven generators, OO languages such as Smalltalk for GUI and proto-typing, C++ in C-trained organizations, and eventually OO-like extensions to COBOL.

Still, barriers to OO adoption exist, most notably culture changes, reeducation requirements, immature tools, and lack of integration with other technologies, such as CASE, change control, methodologies, and project management; these barriers are all the more reason a gradual evolution and a new generation of CASE technology will be likely.

Multiple Platforms in a World of Fragmented Standards

An important requirement for the next generation of applications is the desire for portability and inter-operability of applications across hardware, operating systems, windowing systems, communication systems, and database environments. One approach toward this goal is building applications based on standards in an open systems environment. The much-abused term "open" can mean some degree of support for any one or more of the following: software that uses protocols established by a neutral body and available from multiple suppliers, a development environment that can support multiple tools and available on multiple platforms, an execution environment that runs on multiple platforms, and/or an environment with published interfaces accessible to any party.

Standards are a prerequisite for open development environments and building open systems. As important as the quest for open systems is, multiple standards will proliferate. Such standards will emanate from standards bodies, from consortia and de facto standards that are simply popular, but proprietary offerings at some level of enabling software (e.g., Windows or Macintosh user interface environments). For the next five years, proprietary application development tools and CASE-driven generators that can target multiple client and server platforms will provide a more robust, practical, and cost-effective solution to portability and inter-operability than will waiting for the stabilization, consolidation and/or maturation of standards.

Next Generation CASE and Application Development Environments

The next generation of CASE is on the horizon. The ideal CASE environment is likely to be characterized by an advanced repository-based application development environment (ADE) founded in OO modeling techniques, iterative development, support for multiple client and server platforms and databases, and integrated work-flow and project management tools. Such environments will emerge in 1993 and mature by 1997.

By 1997, the next generation CASE and ADE will consist of the following layers (Figure 5-5).

- *Consistent user interface* for all tools: with on-line expert assistance and tutorials.
- *Management technologies:* on-line methodology and work-flow management, with methodological enforcement; project management tools to plan, estimate, schedule and monitor all development activities against goals; a decision-support system to forecast alternatives; work-group support; software change management; software distribution facility; and measurement tools for forecasting and capturing productivity and quality metrics.
- *Development-support tools:* interpretive technologies to animate models, simulate designs and debug programs; intelligent browsers to navigate, query and report against the repository; change impact analysis tools; tools to test and verify incrementally growing designs and systems.
- *Development tools:* increasingly OO tools will span planning, analysis, prototyping, design and code generation. The tools will assist in design decisions, particularly with the complexity of client/server design and heterogeneous networks. Code will be generated from models for common client and server platforms and runtime environments. Prototypes will be kept in synchronization with formal models. And CASE environments will be more capable of inter-operating with other categories of tools, such as personal productivity tools (e.g., word processors, spreadsheets, calendars, reporting tools).
- *Repository:* all design and development data and project-progress data will be integrated in a unified, readily accessible and shareable

environment; catalogued and indexed reusable objects will be the basis for future productivity and quality; versatile browsing, impact analysis, configuration management and reporting capabilities will leverage repository system information.

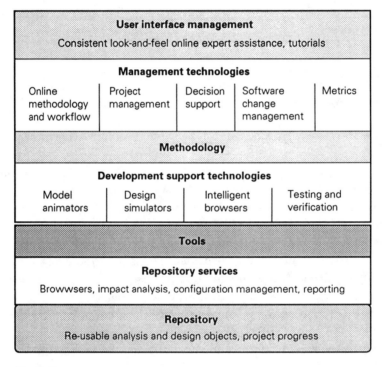

Fig. 5–5
An Ideal CASE and ADE in 1997 (Source: Gartner Group)

A New Breed of Application Types

The combination of these maturing application development and execution technologies, when used in the redesigning of the fundamental business processes in corporations, will enable new classes of applications during the next five years (Figure 5-6).

Applications of the past were largely for survival, e.g., automating routine operations such as batch processing and then on-line transaction processing (OLTP). Decision-support systems (DSS) emerged to provide managers operational decision-enabling information. Applications in the coming years, such as business process automation (BPA) applications

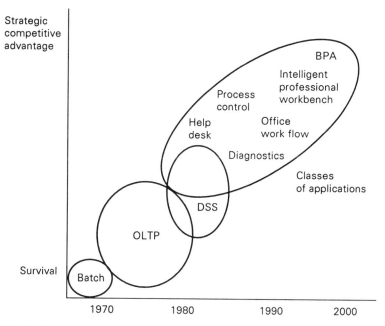

Fig. 5-6
New Classes of Applications (Source: Gartner Group)

will increasingly be critical components for re-engineered business processes at the heart of the enterprise's mission. BPA is the automation of core processes that add value to an overall business function. Most likely, the next generation of applications will uniquely exploit various combinations of advanced technologies, including client/server architectures, graphical user interfaces, knowledge-based systems, and object-oriented technologies. These new classes of applications will have to be addressed by the next generation of CASE, ADE's, and development tools.

The applications to be built during the next five years will require a mix of new technologies and their appropriate usage. These technologies will also need a shift in skill sets and in the life cycle methodology for building applications.   Firstly, the new classes of applications will require the assimilation and coordinated use of a number of complementary technologies (Figure 5-7), only slowly to be integrated into next-generation CASE suites. These technologies will require new skill sets and will create new classes of business and technology specialists in organizations (e.g., business analysts, JAD facilitators, OO class-library administrators, client/server topology architects, GUI designers, database designers, multi-media specialists, etc.). By 1997, 85% of new applications will require a mixture of skill sets not prevalent in today's typical IS organization.

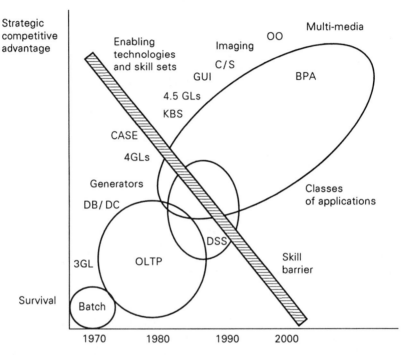

Fig. 5-7
Technologies and Skill Sets for Evolving Application Types (Source: Gartner Group)

The Need for CASE to Support
Iterative Life Cycle (Process) Models

New life cycle methodologies (also known as process models) will have to be supported by next-generation CASE tools and the organization. The traditional waterfall model (refer back to Figure 5-1) whereby a linear progression of phases, each with frozen specifications or deliverables feeding the next phase, has been a vast improvement over no or informal methodologies that in many organizations had reduced to a "code and repair" mode of operation. In recent years, even the waterfall model has shown its limitations: It relies on the difficult challenge of intense, formal requirements analysis and concurrence among end-users and analysts, before proceeding to subsequent design and coding stages with tangible deliverables. In addition, it relies on CASE models without visualizing partial systems or prototypes like those now easily possible with GUI client/server technology.

Inspired by the spiral development model espoused by Barry Boehm of TRW[1], progressive organizations have instituted various adaptations of this approach. Our version of an iterative process model (Figure 5-8) focuses not just on the iteration of life cycle deliverables to ensure accuracy and, therefore, quality, but also focuses on the necessity to regularly review the project's status, refine estimates, and allocate resources throughout the life cycle. This is a powerful model for not only ensuring the accuracy of the application systems in meeting user needs, but also ensuring that projects that are not appropriate, either in scope, or financial, or technical feasibility, do not proceed. This process model,

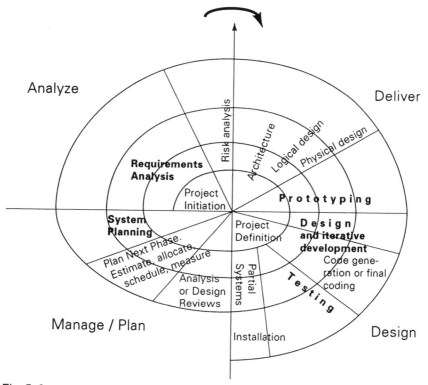

Fig. 5–8
An Iterative Process Model (Source: Gartner Group's Modification and Extension based on Barry Boehm's Spiral Model)

1. "A Spiral Model of Software Development and Enhancement," *Computer Magazine*, May, 1988.

from the inside out, relies on iterations of formal modeling and prototyping, with the latter as a means to verify the formal models or elicit additional requirements. Commercial methodologies are slowly evolving toward including an iterative process model, and emerging CASE tools will support such methodologies. Iterative and cyclical development methodologies exploiting CASE, client/server, prototyping, and/or OO techniques and tools will be used by 50% of new systems development by 1997.

5–3 Assessment of Alternative CASE and Applications Development Strategies and Vendor Classes

In an era of client/server architectures, emerging OO technologies, contemporary methodologies, and evolving CASE technology, it is important to revisit and analyze strategies for applications development. We see five classes of application development and tools approaches that are viable. These approaches are just beginning to unify CASE and client/server issues:

1   Prototype-and-build

2   Model-prototype-build, with multiple vendors' tools

3   Model-prototype-build, with a single-vendor's ADE and tools

4   Model-prototype-build, with multiple vendors' tools, but a single vendor's ADE

5   Combinations: bottom-up revolution, top-down evolution.

The pros and cons of each of these are explored below.

The prototype-and-build strategy is one of giving up on classical upper CASE, focusing rather on either traditional, monolithic lower CASE 4GL's or generators or on their modern client/server counterparts that concentrate on the construction (including prototyping) phases of the life cycle (Figure 5-9).

The Prototype-and-Build Approach

There are numerous products already on the market that concentrate on the construction phases of the life cycle. These products, useful for physical design of the user interface, prototyping, and high-level coding phases of the life cycle, fall into one of five subcategories that we used to call lower CASE. The categories and sample products are depicted in Figure 5-10.

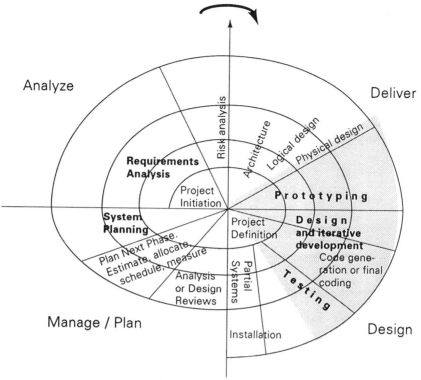

Fig. 5-9
The Prototype-and-Build
Approach (Source: Gartner Group)

Client/server categories of tools have had counterparts in main-frame and mid-range platforms. Some products have analogous development and execution technologies, and strengths and pitfalls (albeit different user interface environments) across selected mainframe, mid-range, and client/server platforms. Although the environment and details differ significantly, the business tradeoffs among these categories are uniform across the platforms.

In general, using any of these development tools for client/server or traditional application has its advantages and disadvantages. Prototype-and-build tools will significantly increase productivity compared to 3GL and native-API programming. As tools focusing on programming, they tend to have a shorter learning curve than formal upper CASE tools, and hence, a shorter time to attain their return-on-investment. These tools produce highly visible results (unlike models produced by upper CASE). They have strengths in prototyping and iterative development and are available now for client/server applications.

Their disadvantages, as a whole, are that as tools to aid detailed design, prototyping, and construction, they yield only tactical benefits. They entail little reuse or enterprise leverage, as they are project-focused, not enterprise-oriented, and islands of automation may result. This approach of constant change of a system can also allow developers to fall into the "moving target" trap and yield inflexible architectures. This approach uses no formal requirements analysis approach of upper CASE, and no durable model of the enterprise results from its use.

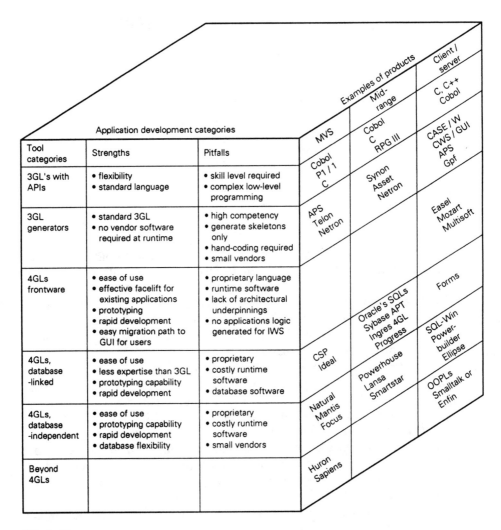

Fig. 5-10
Categories and Examples of Prototyping and Building Tools (Source: Gartner Group)

Model-Prototype-Build, with Multiple Vendors' Tools

This approach attempts to take advantage of the strengths of formal modeling of upper CASE technology, combined with modern development tools for construction. The strategy entails implementing tools that work reasonably well together, including traditional 4GL's or generators or their modern client/server tool counterparts, as a complement to upper CASE to attain the benefits of both. Optionally, it uses a dictionary as a focal point for enterprise model management, reusability, and data/database administration. This approach covers a wide span of the life cycle as illustrated in Figure 5-11.

This approach also uses prototyping as a means to verify the formal models or to elicit further requirements that get reformalized into the upper CASE models.

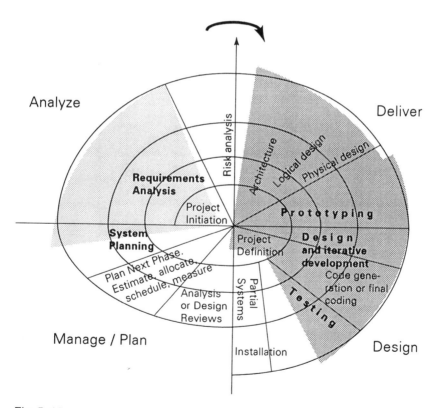

Fig. 5-11
Model-Prototype-Build Approach with Multiple Vendors' Tools (Source: Gartner Group)

The advantage of this approach compared to the prototype-and-build approach alone is that it preserves the long-term advantages of CASE (leverageable, reusable, formal models of the enterprise—independent of physical implementation considerations), while exploiting state-of-the-art client/server development tools today. Compared with the single-vendor approach (discussed next), it entails using the best of each breed of technology or at least the best combination of technologies that have interfaces.

The disadvantages of this approach include a greater initial cost than the prototype-and-build approach alone. Upper CASE technology requires adoption of a methodology and entails a significant investment not returned in the first year. This approach requires a manual methodology to fill the gap between the analysis tools and the construction tools. Design of client/server architectures, topologies, and platform and database selection are not assisted by either upper or lower CASE tools yet. This approach is one of suboptimizing the tasks addressed by each tool. As a result of using multiple tools from multiple vendors, there is a less integrated solution than going with a life cycle, single-vendor approach. Often the tools have redundancies in the information they maintain, and interfaces, even when they exist, are often awkward.

Complementary prototype-and-build tools with upper CASE modeling tools are currently not integrated, leaving a gap in the design phase, particularly for client/server applications, and requiring an investment in a CASE-driven technology and methodology. However, this approach will improve long-term quality and productivity compared with prototype-and-build tools used alone.

Model-Prototype-Build, with a Single-Vendor's ADE and Tools

An alternative is to acquire a tool set from a single vendor that provides a relatively integrated ADE spanning the life cycle of building applications. This strategy embraces a so-called integrated CASE or *I-CASE* vendor of choice, where the client/server design and generation capabilities are one factor. Although the degree of integration of the user interface, meta-data, process, and control of these suites of tools varies significantly among the products on the market, there have emerged a number of successful suites of products that span all the phases of the application life cycle (although with some of these vendors the focus until recently has been entirely the generation of traditional, monolithic, terminal-based applications).

Many of the I-CASE vendors and products (e.g., Texas Instruments' Information Engineering Facility, KnowledgeWare's ADW, Oracle's CASE*Designer and Generator, Andersen Consultings Foundation, or Seer Technology's HPS) have already (or will soon) introduce versions of client/server application generators as back-ends to their upper CASE capabilities. Those committed to an I-CASE vendor supporting traditional monolithic applications or those considering I-CASE vendors and willing to implement client/server applications at the rate that the I-CASE vendor is providing support for their target platforms and environments may find this the best long-term solution. Figure 5-12 illustrates the life cycle coverage that these tool sets partially support.

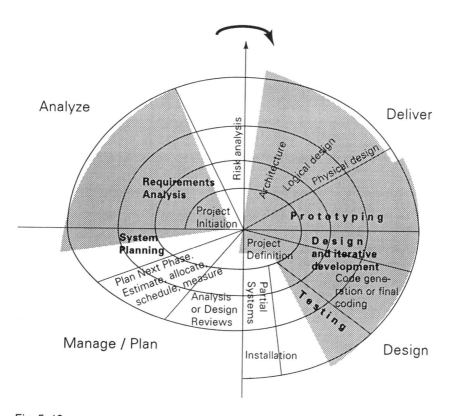

Fig. 5-12

I-CASE Will Span the Life Cycle of Applications Development (Source: Gartner Group)

The advantages of implementing a single-vendor solution are that it has a single point of support, it can be more integrated than mix-and-match solutions (although this depends on the product), and it ties client/server as well as monolithic applications to business models. The disadvantages of this approach include the fact that typically I-CASE implementation entails a high, up-front investment and provides a good return-on-investment, though only in the long-term. These environments are typically closed in that it is difficult to exploit the benefits of other tools. This type of solution is not a best-of-breed approach, and in particular, the products are in the very early stages of supporting the design and generation of client/server applications. Finally, as a group, such products are still weak in prototyping and iterative development.

Partially integrated model-prototype-build solutions targeting popular client and server platforms are emerging from leading I-CASE vendors in 1992-93, but will not mature or target sufficient platforms until 1995.

Evaluating Specific CASE Toolsets

The evaluation and selection process for I-CASE tools or even upper CASE tools that complement development tools is complex and beyond the scope of this chapter. Given that no CASE strategy or environment is ideal for all purposes, development organizations will be more likely to be successful with CASE if they prioritize selection criteria in accordance with their goals and profile. A critical success factor for the selection and implementation of a CASE strategy will be its fit with the profile of the organization, application types to be built, methodology, and practices.

Following that assessment, an evaluation of numerous capabilities is necessary. Criteria for evaluation can be grouped into the following eleven categories: (1) the development environment; (2) the life cycle coverage of the tool set; (3) the degree of integration of the constituent tools; (4) the methodology and techniques supported by the tools; (5) the ease of use; (6) the repository technology that the tool set uses; (7) any management technologies supported by the product (such as project management, version control, configuration management and metrics); (8) the breadth (batch, online transaction processing, decision support, client/server, etc.) and technology (3GL, 4GL, etc.) of the target application; (9) the degree of support of design and generation of client/server applications and their target platforms; (10) the degree of reverse engineering of components of legacy systems; (11) the usual business issues in evaluating a vendor, such as its vision, credibility, financial strength, market share, marketing, momentum, support quality, and technology base.

The following is a short survey of some representative CASE vendors (with product names in parentheses) on the market today with a brief highlight of their positions, strengths, and challenges:

Amdahl (Huron) Not really a CASE tool, but an advanced, rules-driven mainframe (MVS) language, moving next to Unix. It is not as object-driven as its rival Sapiens, but it has a lower initial learning curve. Client/server modeling tools are under development. Its major challenges are market penetration and improvement of its perception as a real player.

Andersen Consulting (Foundation) This was the first of major CASE vendors to deliver a client/server generator. While its upper CASE tools are not particularly integrated with its generator, its methodology and professional services are effective. It needs to establish a distinct product identity to offset its perception as a Big 6 firm selling systems integration or services.

Bachman (Analyst, Designer, and DBA) It has excellent data and process modeling for enterprise analysis and unique DB2 database (re)design tools. Its major challenge is the current lack of a comprehensive application generation strategy, as its CSP and Telon bridges are of limited value. Its longer-term direction, however, is to provide design products for client/server applications driven from enterprise models and an architecture to interface to leading client/server development tools.

Cadre (Teamwork) This is a long-time leader in the technical market (embedded systems, process control, aerospace, engineering), but is repositioning toward commercial sectors (exemplified by interfaces and marketing agreements with commercial players and the introduction of database design tools). It has integrated, multi-platform tools for analysis/design and skeletal code generation for C/C++ and some re-engineering. Its challenges in the commercial sector include competition and marketing.

CGI (Pacbase, Paclan, PacReverse) Traditional life cycle application generation for the mainframe world, it has strengthened its products with LAN-based repository and reverse engineering. It also acquired technology from Transform. CGI has strong European presence, but its major challenges are an aging mainframe-targeted product, late-ness in addressing client/server (it is developing a next-generation application builder for client/server due in 1993), and North American presence and marketing.

Cincom (Advantage and Mantis) It has a versatile 4GL targeting traditional monolithic applications, with import bridges from KnowledgeWare and Intersolv models. It has also introduced complementary text and project management tools. Its major challenges include lack of a complete solution, an aging 4GL, and late to get to client/server.

Intersolv (Excelerator II and APS) This vendor reentered the CASE market with Excelerator II, a tool set with classical diagramming for analysis, good multi-user repository, and extensibility, but nothing revolutionary. However, APS is an excellent generator, soon to have client/server generation capability. The firm also markets PVCS, a software change manager. Its major challenge is to unify the products, largely still unintegrated, and to regain momentum in the market.

KnowledgeWare (ADW) Widely used, this modular, life cycle set of tools supports multiple methodologies. It is beginning to support client/server, GUI, and is re-engineering via acquisitions, but with somewhat fragmented modules. Its major challenges are to regain momentum, to fill product gaps, to integrate the product line, and to address next-generation applications.

LBMS (System Engineer) This versatile Windows-based upper CASE tool, has a newly released code generator for mainframe applications and also a project manager (Project Engineer). Its major challenges are North American expansion and getting to client/server computing more quickly.

Oracle (CASE*Designer, CASE*Generator, SQL*Forms) Oracle provides a strong and elegant I-CASE environment for multi-platform applications. With improved quality, it is enjoying the growing loyalty of its user base with improved quality, but needs to continue overcoming its past reputation for poor quality. Its challenges are unbundling from its Oracle DBMS and expanding the CASE product line with such capabilities as process modeling and generation of more generalized topologies of client/server applications.

S-Cubed (Daisys) This is a small company with a unique approach to CASE and client/server application generation through forms-driven analysis; diagrams are automatically generated and client/server applications are sophisticated. However, this vendor lacks presence, capital, marketing, and distribution muscle.

Sapiens This vendor, with a product by the same name, is not a classical CASE environment, but rather an advanced, object-based, and rule-driven mainframe language and self-contained development environment. It has had European success and, more recently, has established a North American presence with an IBM partnership. Its object diagrammer has been introduced, yielding a form of I-CASE. Its challenges include getting beyond its current primitive client/server support, increasing its marketing, and overcoming a hard-sell when its product requires a cultural shift to a new paradigm.

Seer (HPS) This IBM-backed spin-off from First Boston builds and markets CASE tools, designware, packages, and services focused on the financial industry. HPS, however, is a general purpose I-CASE suite of tools for IBM distributed environments. It is a well-integrated set of tools with good change management. IBM's Financial Applications Architecture group is a powerful distribution channel. Its challenges include marketing, supporting more databases and platforms (now limited to IBM), and creating international presence.

Softlab (Maestro II) This vendor offers a very good Unix, LAN server repository, and IPSE (integrated project support environment) that in theory could attract independent tools to its environment. So far it has delivered its own respectable upper CASE tools. It has major business challenges, however, including lack of a complete solution for developing application and a struggling marketing effort.

Software AG (Predict CASE and Natural) Natural is a robust 4GL for multiple platforms and is now moving quickly to supporting multiple client/server targets, a major focus for the company. Natural is excellent technology. However, the upper CASE offering of Predict CASE has not had much of an impact in the crowded marketplace, and now this vendor supports bridges from other upper CASE tools. Its major challenges are receding CASE presence (but tactical interfaces from KnowledgeWare and Intersolv help) and marketing its sound story of Natural's evolution.

Sybase (Deft and APT Workbench) Sybase provides an open development environment to link heterogeneous databases. The company's APT product supports character and Motif GUI 4GL development, the DBMS offers a strong database architecture, and Macintosh-based Deft upper CASE is a good stand-alone product. Sybase's challenges are to strengthen its 4GL for client/server, to unbundle from DBMS ties, and to integrate upper and lower CASE products.

Texas Instruments (Information Engineering Facility) This is a highly-integrated information engineering I-CASE product set, targeting relational applications on multiple platforms. It is moving quickly to targeting multiple client and server platforms from identical specifications. Its major challenges are its all-or-nothing image and making its strong rigor appeal more broadly.

Model-Prototype-Build with Multiple Vendors' Tools, But a Single Vendor's ADE Framework

A variant of the multi-vendor strategy of Section 5.3.2, mixing and matching complementary products from multiple vendors, is to constrain the selection of tools to enable adoption of a system vendor ADE at some point in the future. A number of system vendors have announced or introduced application development frameworks which consist not of individual products, but of one or more of the following: (1) a common user interface; (2) a means to pass information from one tool to another; (3) a common repository for tools; and/or (4) a common meta-model of the application development process. Examples are IBMs AD/Cycle, DEC's Cohesion, and Hewlett Packard's Softbench.

In general, these environments have not yet enjoyed much success due to the so-far minimal functionality they provide, lack of robustness in their offering, and/or the reluctance of the major CASE and other tool vendors to plug into these environments.

Conceptually, the advantages of this approach are the same as those of the multi-vendor scenario, but with the added benefit of a greater degree of loose integration. This strategy provides a focal point and commonality for a mix-and-match strategy. However, the reality is that a single repository to support diverse tools will not be robust enough for many years, if ever. Even when they mature they will lag behind the mix-and-match or I-CASE approaches in that many vendors could have conflicting interests between supporting their own environments and repositories and these system vendors.

In general, we do not believe that during the next five years system-vendor ADE's (e.g., IBM's AD/Cycle) will see significant penetration beyond their natural constituencies comprised of those committed to their platforms and software strategies.

Combinations: Bottom-Up Revolution; Top-Down Evolution

There are various hybrid approaches that may be the best blend of a long-term strategy and suboptimized tactical solutions. For example, a development organization can use an I-CASE tool in its entirety for those target environments it handles well. However, its upper CASE component coupled with a best-of-breed back-end tool can be used when the I-CASE tool does not (yet) address that target, as illustrated in Figure 5-13. For example, one organization is using Texas Instruments' IEF for planning, analysis, design, and construction of DB2 applications, but uses IEF only for planning, analysis, and logical design in combination with PowerSoft's PowerBuilder, a 4GL for Windows/SQLServer (not in IEF until 1993) at least until IEF addresses those targets (and perhaps more) due to PowerBuilder's niche strength and the then-sunk cost.

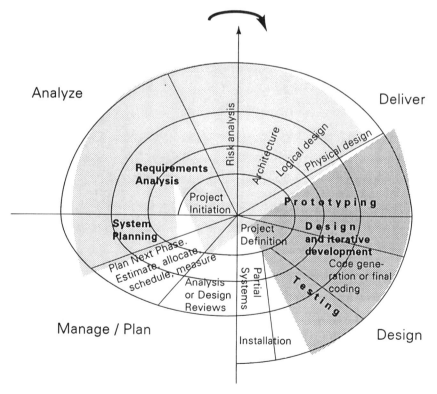

Fig. 5-13

Combinations of I-CASE Products and Specific Back-End Tools

CASE and client/server development will continue to coexist and converge by 1995 through 1997. Although there will be various point solutions for building client/server applications, some of today's proliferating small players will not survive. The nimble players will survive through niche superiority and/or alliances with larger software vendors, including CASE vendors.

5–4   Which Way Should IS Organizations Go?

In evaluating which of these strategies and specific products to pursue, organizations must first make a general self-assessment regarding their technical, methodological, investment, risk-taking, and cultural profile. Included in this assessment is a general strategic vs. tactical orientation evaluation. For example, organizations should evaluate each of the following:

- General training and proficiency;
- Strategic thinking and record of innovation;
- Ability to invest in IS;
- Overall IT plan, including platform and dependency pattern;
- Percentage of expenditure on maintenance, buy vs. build pattern; and
- Buy vs. build profile (do they mostly buy packaged applications).

In addition, development organizations should evaluate two important factors: their tolerance and experience for structure and their willingness and ability to adopt new technologies.

The first of these factors, tolerance and experience with structure and discipline, may include issues such as the following:

- Project management and metrics;
- Formal system development methodology;
- Familiarity with structured techniques and their upper CASE or I-CASE implementations; and
- History of data administration and desire for enterprise architectures.

The second factor, technology and tool adoption, may include evaluating the following:

• Desire for focused solutions with short-term payback;
• Risk tolerance and willingness to evaluate, select, and implement progressive point solutions;
• Degree of entrepreneurship; and
• Commitment to training and support of new technologies

Figure 5-14 plots these two dimensions, tolerance for structure (x-axis) against technology and tool adoption (y-axis), segmenting development organizations into four quadrants. Those in the "MIS Swamp" are those who largely still use 3GL and other traditional technology for implementation and use only an informal life cycle methodology. They

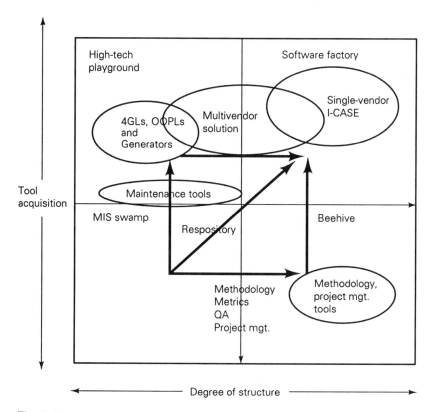

Fig. 5-14
A Development Organization Self-Assessment and Road Map

are so bogged down in maintenance of legacy systems that they spend relatively few resources on new development or re-engineering. Requirements analysis tends to be informal, and familiarity with structured analysis or design techniques, spotty. Project management, metrics, methodology, and quality assurance tend to be informal. Those in this quadrant should move "up" by employing tactical development tools, such as maintenance tools for their legacy systems and lower CASE tools for improved application development. They should begin to explore modern client/server application development tools (4GL's and generators). They should move to the "right" only to the degree that they can absorb and tolerate structure in their organization. Highly sophisticated and integrated CASE environments and the "Software Factory" of the upper right corner would likely be unattainable in one step.

Those in the "Beehive" quadrant use little modern technology for actual development, but have invested in structure, life cycle methodology, project management, and discipline. They still, however, do not make use of modern development tools found in the upper quadrants. They should move "up" and begin to use either a multi-vendor or I-CASE strategy that would improve the quality and productivity of what is now done manually.

Those in the "High-tech Playground" are already pioneering with the latest tools aimed at tactical benefits in productivity and at exploiting modern technology, such as client/server computing, for delivering competitive systems to their users. They can improve their quality and productivity as well as increase the odds of leveraging models across the enterprise, beyond one application at a time, by moving "right." This would entail a two-pronged effort: adopting a system development methodology on which the organization is trained *and* moving, only when they are ready for a more formal system development methodology, toward toward a multi-vendor, mix-and-match strategy or an I-CASE strategy if the target environments match their own.

The "Software Factory" is a goal of development organizations. It can be attained by a combination of a degree of structure and methodology appropriate for the development culture and can be supported by either a multi-vendor, mix-and-match CASE strategy or, when appropriate, an I-CASE environment by a leading vendor that supports their target environments and is compatible with their methodological culture.

The path to the "Software Factory" is not an easy one, however. The selection of appropriate tools is a small part of the effort. Like all good things in life, it takes change in people, commitment, and investment in the organization as well as modern technology.

CASE is a technology in evolution. It will remain a technology to support human activities in planning, analysis, design, prototyping, construction, testing, and maintenance of application systems. When used properly and surrounded with appropriate methodology, infrastructure, training, and management, CASE can indeed improve the quality of systems, strengthening their ability to meet rapidly changing requirements and, ultimately, their productivity.

CHAPTER 6

Database Computers

David Rabinowitz, a senior systems engineer at Teradata, has worked in the
computer industry as a systems engineer since 1968, when he joined IBM in
the United Kingdom. He has worked on a multitude of operating systems and
databases. He spent ten years with IBM in his native South Africa, before being
assigned to the IBM World Trade Systems Center in Poughkeepsie, New York.
Since then he has resided in the Boston area, and is now a consulting systems
engineer for the Large Computer Division of NCR Corporation, which
purchased Teradata Corporation, where he had worked for four and a half
years. Mr. Rabinowitz also worked for BGS Systems, teaching and consulting
on the use of the BEST/1 analytical modeling tool. He has a B.S. degree in
mathematics and mathematical statistics from the University of the
Witwatersrand in Johannesburg, South Africa.

Databases have been in the forefront
of computing advances since the early 1970's, when IMS made its way
into the working set of large IBM data processing environments. Since
then, debate has raged as to the merits of various database technologies,
with proponents of hierarchical and networked databases vociferously
arguing the respective merits and challenges of each.

However, since Dr. E. F. Codd's exploratory work on relational databases, voices of dissent have been few, and the relational model has
become firmly entrenched. As the amount of data that knowledge engineers wish to explore has exploded into the hundreds of gigabytes, the
microprocessor revolution has occurred, offering innovative developers

the opportunity to address the challenges with exciting, new, powerful, and affordable technology. Simultaneously, client/server architectures have evolved, paving the way for the "ultimate server," the database computer.

In this chapter, David Rabinowitz discusses the rationale and justification for database computers. The Teradata DBC/1012 is examined in detail as a successful implementation of such a machine. Enjoy IT.

6-1 Background and Motivation

This chapter deals with the concept and implementation of a database computer. Its very name distinguishes it from a general purpose computer, which is able to perform many functions, including that of database management.

The database computer, however, is a separate entity, dedicated only to storing, managing, accessing, aggregating, sorting, protecting, and maintaining the integrity of data on behalf of application programs running on other computers. In other words, a database computer is the ultimate server in a client/server relationship.

What are the advantages of such an environment? What are the compelling forces that make such an environment attractive? After all, this single idea spawned companies such as Britton-Lee (later Sharebase), and Teradata, at the high end of the range, and any number of SQL-based data servers at the lower end of the spectrum, including such household names as Oracle, Sybase, and Gupta. For instance, Teradata went from an idea in 1979, to a $300 million-plus company in 1991, to its acquisition of Sharebase in 1990, and ultimately, to Teradata's acquisition in 1992 by NCR. NCR itself is a giant in the computer field, with more than $6 billion in revenues, and it was acquired in 1991 by AT&T, Teradata's largest client! There seems to be a thread here...in the early 1990's, new players are appearing on the scene, such as Kendall Square Research and nCUBE.

The Recognition of Relational Database Architecture

Over the last several years, relational database technology has rapidly become the norm. The technology pioneered by Codd has multiple implementations on a variety of platforms, ranging from simple personal computers right up to the largest general purpose computers such as IBM's 3090 processing complexes. Codd postulated thirteen fundamental rules for relational databases, and most implementations comply with the majority of these, though not all. The language used to access relational databases is called **structured query language**, or **SQL** for short. There is an ANSI standard for SQL, and again, most implementations comply to a very large extent with this standard.

With this in mind, it is evident that relational database knowledge and code would, in an ideal world, be easily portable between platforms, with little or no conversion effort. This is, in fact, largely true; however, each platform offers some specific facility that may or may not be attractive to users. Reasons such as connectivity, database size, development tools, cost (to process), storing, and recovering are issues that determine what platform is appropriate for a given application.

RDBM —Prodigious Consumers of Resources

Two major issues arise when dealing with very large database implementations: the first is cost; the second has to do with the amount of data stored.

The need to store, retrieve, and analyze very large amounts of data has been recognized at the same time as relational technology has become a driving force in the industry. To say that large amounts of data means hundreds of gigabytes is, if anything, an understatement. A simple example of how these numbers can be derived is found later in this chapter.

Today's enterprise generally has only a fraction of its data available in computer-accessible media (disk, tape, optical), and as the era of knowledge engineering matures, we find that typical decision support applications enable better decisions based on the analysis of ever-greater volumes of data. So today, it is not unusual to find data bases of 20 gigabytes at the low end, to the multi-hundred gigabytes, and even more.

How does one get to such large numbers? As a simple example, let us consider a department store chain, which may have at any one time, depending on the season, nearly 25,000 stock keeping units (SKU's) in every store. The mixture of SKU's would vary from store to store, season to season, with the number of SKU's kept in a given store over the course of an entire year in the neighborhood of 40,000. Assume that analysis of daily activity at the SKU level is required (and it is!) for three months, that weekly summary activity for each SKU is kept for 65 weeks, and that there are 1,000 stores in the chain. Then the storage requirement

for just the daily history for 90 days becomes, assuming conservatively,
50 bytes per row:

$$
\begin{array}{rl}
25,000 \times & \text{(SKU)} \\
1,000 \times & \text{(STORE)} \\
50 \times & \text{(BYTES)} \\
90 & \text{(DAYS)}
\end{array}
$$

$112,500,000,000 = \textbf{112.5 gigabytes}$

Summary tables, depending on the nature of summarization (by
region, by division, by category, etc.), easily add more gigabytes to this
starting number. Note too that chains such as Kmart and Wal-Mart have
in the region of 2,000 stores, and maybe even more SKU's, and it is easy
to follow the data explosion we are witnessing.

The processing resources consumed by very large relational database decision-support applications has generally been found to be much
larger than those consumed by predecessor databases or file systems
such as IMS, IDMS, or VSAM. The flexibility offered by relational systems has been delivered, with greater or lesser success, at large cost in
traditional mainframe platforms.   As an accepted cost per MIP, a loose,
but useful metric in this study is in the $80,000-100,000 range on such a
platform. It is an ever-less costly number; but as large systems are
implemented, more and more MIP's are required.

The Micro-Processor Revolution

The advent of the microprocessor has caused the cost per MIP to be
reduced to the $15,000-20,000 range, a significant improvement over the
costs in a traditional environment. Furthermore, the availability of large
disk storage units, simply attached to the commodity microprocessors
using SCSI attachments has rendered the microprocessor a formidable
computing environment, with the ability to match power and capacity in
a balanced system at affordable costs.

The answer to the ever-increasing demand for resources seems to
be in creating a special processor, dedicated to handling only databases
—not just storing the data, but "owning" it, regulating access, assuring
integrity, and relieving the traditionally over-burdened mainframe by
off-loading database-related processing cycles onto itself. This is equivalent to the communications processors which became available in the

1970's. These were designed to off-load network-management processing from the mainframe. The mainframe received and returned only appropriately filtered and packaged messages, and applied its processing resources only to the applications needs, rather than sharing them for communications purposes. Furthermore, if the special purpose computer were able to take advantage of the microprocessor cost curve, then an additional advantage would accrue.

The Need to Share Data Across Heterogeneous Platforms

With the proliferation of users, platforms, and tools, another development has been the need to easily share data in a safe, controlled, and ordered manner. Clearly, one very desirable need is that all users work off a common base, so that when discussing results of their own specific analyses, there is a common ground for comparison!

There are many techniques for sharing data: limiting users to weekends, special requests taking weeks to turn around, giving users copies of selected data on tape or diskette to process on their own platform of choice, extracting data, and downloading over communication lines, WAN's and LAN's. Many of these solutions have their own problems. Typically when an end-user receives data two weeks after requesting it, he or she has typically forgotten why the data was requested in the first place and has derived an alternative solution or has requested yet another set of data, expected two weeks hence.

As knowledge workers, data analysts want to ask iterative questions, first defining an area of interest by a broad set of questions and then drilling down into the detail. And in addition, they want to do this from their platform of choice, using tools that are familiar to them and in which their expertise renders them productive. And the results should be available in minutes or hours, not days or weeks, depending on the volume of data under analysis and the complexity of the questions asked. Attempting to get data from a heavily utilized MVS system, for example, merely places additional stress on an already stressed environment, probably impacting "the on-lines," and making the data requester the object of ire in the operations department!

6–2 Connectivity Options for a Centralized Data Repository

In summary, it is evident that a strong demand exists for central repositories of data, *simultaneously accessible* from heterogeneous platforms. These range from large mainframes such as IBM or IBM-compatible systems running under operating systems such as MVS/XA or VM/SP or other vendors' architectures (Honeywell Bull, Unisys, Siemens) and LAN-attached systems such as Digital Equipment's VAX running VMS, UNIX-based systems on platforms as diverse as AT&T 3B2, SUN, HP9000, Amdahl's UTS, etc., right on down to Apple's Macintosh computers and MS-DOS systems running on IBM-compatible personal computers with or without Windows. The common thread is that they are all able to run tools which can generate SQL, the lingua franca of the relational world.

With all of this in mind, then, the evolution of database computers, data servers in the client/server relationship, was inevitable. (See the discussion of client/server facilities in Chapter 3 of this book.)

These servers have proliferated over the last several years, with implementations on platforms as diverse as a personal computer, right up to the Teradata Data Base Computer, the DBC/1012, capable of storing terabytes of data.

6–3 Characteristics That a Database Computer Should Offer

The characteristics of such a facility should include one or more of the following list (leveraging the microprocessor revolution and using standard, off-the-shelf components wherever possible):

1 *provide for the fundamentals of any DBMS, including data integrity, transaction integrity, controlled data access, and powerful utilities to load, archive, and recover data*

2 *offer a scalable architecture able to deliver consistent response to users as the data base volumes grow, with no artificial limits*

This is actually a twofold challenge. The first has to do with storing the data. Small databases on almost any platform offer relatively small challenges. However, as data volumes grow into the hundreds of gigabytes, the challenge becomes daunting. For instance, a single table in IBM's DB2 cannot exceed 64 gigabytes. This is because of the dependency on IBM's VSAM access method. It immediately places a burden on systems designers who may routinely encounter individual tables that exceed this size.

The second is the ability to deliver consistent response times. As data volumes grow, it is important to still be able to process the data in reasonable time frames. For instance, if a table's data volume doubles, it is reasonable to expect to traverse the data in twice the time it originally took or to be able to bring to bear, hopefully, twice the amount of resources and keep the time equal to what it was originally. Experience on most platforms does not show this to be true, especially as the number of processors that can be implemented in, say, the MVS environment is limited to only eight!

3   *have options for recovery in the event of processor and/or disk unit failure*

Most systems offer the capability to selectively "mirror" data, i.e., to store a duplicate copy of the data so that in the event of the failure of one or more disk components, processing can continue albeit in a degraded manner.

Multiprocessor complexes can sustain the loss of a processor and cause the work to be redistributed to other processors in the complex. But this begins to rule out small single processor environments as significant players in the large, database-computer arena.

4   *be affordable!*

As discussed earlier in this chapter, the affordability of a system based on microprocessors will probably be greater than that of traditional mainframe systems. Coincidentally, it is the ability to string together hundreds or thousands of microprocessors to perform complex tasks that has captured the imagination of computer scientists, rather than faster large, monolithic systems. Witness to this is the decline of the Cray enterprise and the burgeoning growth of Thinking Machines, nCUBE, and other such companies in the scientific computing arena. Doing this in the database world will be shown to have reaped rich rewards for Teradata, for instance.

5   *be able to take advantage of technological advances without compromising user investments in application software*

It is important to note that just as personal computer manufacturers transition their products from systems based on INTEL 8086 chips, through 80286, 80386, and 80486 chips without invalidating user programs, database computer manufacturers should be able to keep abreast of technology without jeopardizing their clients' investments too.

We will examine the Teradata DBC/1012 in detail, as an example of a successful database computer implementation and one that addresses all the challenges outlined above. The name of the computer is simple: DBC - Data Base Computer; the 1012 represents ten raised to the 12th power, or Tera! Hence the name of the corporation and the DBC/1012! Teradata set out to do the following:

1   create a system that was specifically designed to perform relational database processing, leveraging the microprocessor revolution and using standard, off-the-shelf components wherever possible;

2   afford the greatest amount of connectivity possible—SQL as the common language for requesting services, industry standard connectivity protocols such as IBM/370 channel architecture or TCP/IP LAN for physical communication between requestor and provider or what has come to be known as client/server.

3   offer a scalable architecture that was able to deliver a consistent response to users as the database volumes grew.

4   offer an architecture able to store many hundreds of gigabytes of data.

6–4   Architecture of a Teradata DBC/1012

We will now examine the structure of the DBC/1012 and see how it matches up to these requirements.

The DBC/1012 is comprised of five major physical components and a sixth, comprising the software required to operate and to interface to the system. The physical components are,

1   interface processors (IFP's),

2   communication processors (COP's),

3   YNET intelligent bus interconnect (YNET),

4   access module processors (AMP's), and

5   disk dtorage units (DSU's).

These are the major components that implement the system. Other components that do not warrant inspection in this document include processor and storage cabinets, power supplies, and other such items. We will examine each major component in detail (Figure 6-1).

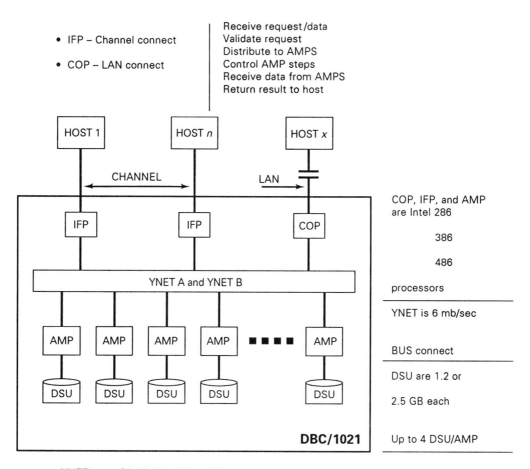

- IFP – Channel connect
- COP – LAN connect

Receive request/data
Validate request
Distribute to AMPS
Control AMP steps
Receive data from AMPS
Return result to host

HOST 1   HOST n   HOST x

CHANNEL   LAN

IFP   IFP   COP

COP, IFP, and AMP
are Intel 286

386

486

processors

YNET A and YNET B

YNET is 6 mb/sec

AMP   AMP   AMP   AMP ▪▪▪▪ AMP

BUS connect

DSU   DSU   DSU   DSU   DSU

DSU are 1.2 or

2.5 GB each

DBC/1021

Up to 4 DSU/AMP

- YNET   Distributes data and steps

           Sorts data

- AMPS   Perform data management
          Retreive/store/sort data
          Perform transaction recovery

Fig. 6-1
DBC/1012— Components and Major Functions

Interface processors (IFP's) and communication processors (COP's). These processors are discussed together because their function is similar, but not identical. The IFP's are used to channel-connect mainframes such as IBM 3090's, Siemens, UNISYS, etc. to the DBC/1012. The

COP's are used to provide an interface to local area networks and support several TCP/IP protocols.

Apart from interfacing to the outside world, the functions performed by these processors are as follows:

- receive data and SQL from the submitter;

- parse the request, checking syntax and the authorization of the user to perform the tasks specified;

- break the task in multiple steps, with as many parallel steps as possible;

- broadcast the step to the AMP's across the YNET and synchronize the execution of each step. A single step is broadcast and, when all processors signal completion of the step, the next step is broadcast. A single IFP can handle in excess of 100 discrete sessions;

- convert incoming data from its source format to ASCII mode;

- on job completion, assemble answer sets and transmit back to the host for dissemination to the originator.

In addition, a system-designated master-COP assumes responsibility for balancing work across other COP's in the DBC/1012, ensuring that an even load prevails. This task is performed in the mainframe with regard to IFP's, where the mainframe-resident Teradata Director Program (TDP) performs the load balancing task across all IFP's to which it is attached.

Note that an IFP has no disk associated with it. When the system is initiated, a buddy-AMP is assigned to each IFP and COP, and the system initiation is performed from that processor's disk.

YNET intelligent bus interconnect (YNET). The YNET is the intelligent interconnection between all the processors in the system. It is an intelligent bus, consisting of hardware and microcide, and is the subject of most of Teradata's patents. From a practical point of view, it is the medium over which messages are passed between IFP's, COP's, and AMP's as instruction steps are distributed, and over which data is transmitted to its destination. The system is always provided with two YNET's. Each has a 6-megabyte-per-second transfer rate, and if one fails the other takes over, augmenting system availability.

Access module processors (AMP's) and disk storage units (DSU's). The Teradata Operating System, a multi-tasking, multi-processing operating system, runs on every AMP. Transaction recovery, permanent journalling if specified for the table under change, transient journalling, and backing out of failed transactions, are handled by the AMP's.

The combination of AMP's and DSU's is where the parallelism of the Teradata DBC/1012 is implemented. Referring to the diagram, you will note that every AMP has a disk associated with it. In fact, each AMP may be backed by up to four DSU's. In today's implementation, this represents up to 10 gigabytes behind each AMP. A DBC/1012 may contain in excess of 1,000 processors of all types. Thus, allowing for a balance of IFP's and COP's; the theoretical limit for AMP's is in the 800 range. And if each is backed by 10 gigabytes of storage, we see a prodigious system. The MIP capability at the AMP level would be 800 × 10 (the nominal equivalent rate for INTEL 486 processors), i.e. 8,000 MIPS, and 800 × 10 gigabytes, or 8 terabytes. To date, the single biggest *installed* Teradata DBC/1012 is approximately 300 processors, still outstripping its competitors in MIPS and database size. Note too that the configuration is symmetrical at the AMP level, i.e., if an AMP has two disks, every AMP should have two disks. Like a chain, the speed and capacity of the system is determined by the slowest, smallest component.

To understand the way in which the parallelism is implemented, we must examine the way in which data is stored in the DBC/1012.

Rather than allocating data to a specific disk, the DBC/1012 is a hashed database. The data for every table is randomly distributed across all disks in the system. For example, a 1,000,000 row table on a DBC/1012 with ten AMP's would have approximately 100,000 rows on each AMP. Understanding this organization is crucial to understanding the ability of the system to manage and traverse massive amounts of data quickly.

With the understanding that every table is evenly distributed across all AMP's in the system, let us examine the mechanism for doing this. When creating a table, the user must specify a PRIMARY INDEX for the table. The PRIMARY INDEX consists of one to 16 columns that are hashed together to randomize the data, through an algorithm provided by Teradata. In fact, choosing this index is crucial to obtaining performance from the system. For example, if the column GENDER were chosen, a terrible data distribution would occur, with data stored on only two AMPs of even the largest system. And the effect of parallelism would be severely curtailed.

Now that we have the data properly distributed by choosing an appropriate PRIMARY INDEX, let us see how data is retrieved. There are several discrete cases:

1   Retrieving data rows based on equality with primary index columns.

In the case of a unique primary index, a single I/O operation will retrieve the row, if it is present in the table. In the case of a non-unique primary index, several data blocks may be retrieved to fully satisfy the request. However, in both cases, only a single AMP is involved in the operation.

2   Retrieving data based on secondary indexed columns.

In the case of a unique secondary index, two AMP's are involved in data retrieval. One I/O to retrieve the index row and one to "follow the pointer" to the primary row identified in the secondary index row. In the case of a non-unique secondary index, the secondary index subtable is built on all AMP's, and this becomes an all-AMP operation.

3   A full file scan.

Each AMP retrieves the data local to it and appropriately sorts it, if an ORDER BY clause has been included in the SQL statement. It is apparent here that the DBC/1012 can retrieve all the rows of a table much more rapidly than a serial operation. For instance, in the case outlined above, with say ten AMP's, the retrieval times would be about one tenth of that in a serial retrieval system.

The AMP's also perform data translation from ASCII to the data mode of the requesting system for data "outward bound." This must be done here, as sorting is done internally on the YNET as data is collated, and thus, data translation at the IFP level would cause an invalidly collated answer set.

Because of Teradata's hashed approach to data, the database is not stored in sequential order. Additionally, the file system is implemented in such a way that data is always rewritten to a new data block on disk, thus eliminating the need for a function like DB2's REORG, a constant irritant for DB2 installations.

In fact, the administration of the DBC/1012 is much simpler than that of a DB2 system. Like DB2, a good design is required. But thereafter, data placement, disk management, index creation, etc. are affected much more easily on the DBC/1012. No consideration for page spaces, VSAM data spaces, index spaces, STOGROUP's, and the like is required. The only two "tuning knobs" available to the user, aside from a good design, are primary and secondary index selection.

Keeping Up with Change

The DBC/1012 was originally implemented using INTEL 8086 chips. Successive models have utilized INTEL 80286, 80386, and now 80496 processors, delivering increased power at lower cost with each generation. The fundamental architecture of the system has not changed, and thus, users' investments in systems and applications have been protected.

Similarly, the disks used have progressed from 500-megabyte Winchester drives to 2.5-gigabyte drives. In this way Teradata has continued to leverage off-the-shelf, current components while delivering evermore powerful systems at greater cost efficiencies.

Scalability and Linearity

Bearing in mind the manner in which data is distributed across all the AMP's in a system, it is easy to see how Teradata is able to deliver a linearly scalable system. In conventional mainframe systems, where more than eight processors have never been successfully implemented, the portion of each additional processor added that can be applied to user tasks diminishes greatly. Thus a two-processor system delivers only 180% the capability of a single processor, a three-processor system only 260%, etc.

In the case of Teradata, however, as each processor (AMP/Disk) is added to the system, the data is redistributed so that the even distribution of data across all AMP's prevails. So now, assume we have 1,000,000 rows spread across ten AMP's, and a full file scan takes two minutes. If we wanted to have the scan complete in one minute, then adding ten AMP's would do the trick (we now have approximately 50,000 rows per AMP rather than 100,000). Conversely, if we wished to double the amount of data, but keep retrieval times the same, then adding additional AMP's would also have the same effect.

Thus, Teradata offers the ability to configure "narrow and deep," a cheaper configuration with fewer processors and less parallelism, or "shallow and wide," a more expensive performance-oriented system, to meet the needs and pockets of the users.

FALLBACK and Availability

Given that data is spread across all the AMP's in a system, it is evident that failure of an AMP processor board or disk would cause any table on the DBC/1012 to be not fully accessible. Single row retrievals of rows on AMP's that are in the system are possible, but data on a failed AMP/DSU is not.

If the failure is an AMP board and no data loss has occurred, replacing the AMP board will bring the entire system and all tables back to full availability. However, if a disk failure occurs, then the tables on the system will be missing one nth of their data, where n is the number of AMPs in the system. To deal with this situation, the DBC/1012 allows specification of a FALLBACK option for each table, as specified by the user.

In this case, a shadow copy of the data is maintained on a different AMP. The DBC/1012's operating system and file management maintain both copies of the data, and in the event of an outage of a given AMP or AMP's, is able to satisfy all data requests by utilizing the FALLBACK copy. The design is such that the likelihood of two AMP's failing in such a way that means mutual backup is unavailable is only a very remote possibility.

When FALLBACK is implemented, the system maintains a recovery journal in the event data is being updated and an AMP is out of service. When the failing component is replaced, the changes made to the backup copy are automatically applied to the primary copy. Only when full recovery is complete does the system revert to satisfying data retrieval requests from the primary copy.

FALLBACK may be implemented at any stage of a table's existence. A table may be modified to/from FALLBACK/NOFALLBACK. The table does not have to be reloaded.

6–5 The Future—NCR 3600 and 3700 Implications

What Teradata has delivered, clearly, is a very powerful, scalable system which excels in the decision support environment. It exploits the YNET for message passing. To complete the picture, a general purpose compute facility able to exploit the YNET would be a plus. This is in fact what the NCR 3600 family offers. In the same configuration as a Teradata database, NCR offers the ability to include YNET-attached UNIX-based symmetrical multiprocessors. With this capability, the following facilities are enabled:

1 merchant databases (ORACLE, SYBASE, etc.) running on powerful UNIX-based processors, oriented to OLTP and transaction processing;

2 inter-system communications on the YNET, much faster than on the LAN's hitherto used;

3 the ability for an application running on the UNIX system to access data from both the merchant database and Teradata parallel database sources; and

4 enormous flexibility and access to UNIX applications and tools.

6–6 Conclusion

The future of the massively parallel database computer seems assured, with incremental changes in already familiar architecture and with new players such as Kendall Square Research and even IBM emerging. What is considered large and cutting edge today will be "old hat" by the time this book reaches its second printing!

Massively Parallel Processing

Mr. Ed Oates, Vice President of the Advanced Products Division, Oracle where system software for massively parallel computers is being developed, was born in Los Angeles, California in 1946. During his formative years, he spent three years in Japan where his father, Robert P. Oates, participated in a joint venture between Lockheed and Kawasaki corporations. Mr. Oates took his Bachelors degree in mathematics from San Jose State College in 1968 and pursued a master's degree in cybernetic systems through 1978. His career includes software research and development at Singer Business Machines, the U.S. Army–Persinscom, Ampex Corporation, and Memorex Corporation. While in the U.S. Army, and later at Ampex, he became interested in the technology of large databases and the devices necessary to access them efficiently. In 1977, Mr. Oates, Robert Miner, and Larry Ellison founded what was to become Oracle Corporation. Oracle is currently the largest independent database management software supplier.

Mr. Kenneth Rudin graduated from Harvard University with honors in computer science. He joined Oracle Corporation upon graduation and worked as the group product manager for PL/SQL, the Oracle procedural extensions to SQL. He is currently the senior product and marketing manager for the Massively Parallel Systems Division of Oracle Corporation. He is responsible for analyzing new massively parallel machines as platforms for the Oracle Relational Database System, as well as for planning product features for these systems. He acts as an evangelist for Oracle's massively parallel systems offerings.

Massively parallel processors have historically been deployed for special purpose engineering and scientific applications such as weather modeling and image enhancement. The technology is maturing during the early 1990's so that parallel processing can be applied to commercial systems that cannot be cost-effectively implemented in any other way. The authors contend that massively parallel computers will be the mainframes of choice later in the decade and into the next century and that the impediments to commercial adoption of the technology are in the process of being removed.

This chapter explores the evolution of massively parallel processing architectures, discusses the types of applications best suited to implementation on ultra-high performance hardware, examines the cost-effectiveness of such machines for commercial applications, and analyzes the implementation of a commercial relational database manager, ORACLE, on a particular massively parallel computer, nCUBE. Enjoy IT.

7–1 What is it?

Traditional programming models rely on the serial execution of "instructions" by the underlying hardware. For example, if the problem at hand is to calculate 1,000 sums from 1,000 number pairs (for example, adding two 10 x 100 arrays together), storage for the sums will be allocated and set to zero one at a time; then each of the 1,000 number pairs, in turn, will be added to the 1,000 sums. In a **massively parallel processor (MPP)** with 1,000 processors, each processor will be responsible for one of the sums. Each processor simultaneously will allocate and zero the storage, and then add the number pair into the sum. If each of the individual processors is only one quarter as fast as the traditional processor, the potential exists for a 250-fold performance increase.

If it sounds too good to be true, it is. The problems with implementing such 1,000 processor machines are significant: The processors must communicate with one another, large amounts of data must be transferred from external storage media, and programming techniques must be devised to allow programmers to express algorithms differently than they are currently for traditional uniprocessing systems.

7–2 Why Now?

Since Ada first began programming Babbage's "Analytical Engine" in the eighteen hundreds, the search has been on for higher performance computing machinery. Until the middle of the 1980's, the problem of obtaining increased performance meant increasing the speed of the single **central processing unit (CPU)** and the associated memory and input/output systems. There were a few examples of special-purpose application of multiple processors, such as the IBM 370 Attached Processor computers, external sorting computers, and especially the ILLIAC research project.

During the 1980's, the widespread use of the inexpensive microprocessors, such as the Intel 80x86 and Motorola 68000 series, provided a new approach to achieving increased levels of performance. Work at Caltech on the Hypercube demonstrated that combining large numbers of inexpensive processors and their memories could achieve levels of performance that belied the low cost of the system. Other research projects followed, and the late 1980's saw the release of several massively parallel computer systems designed primarily for engineering and scientific applications, including the nCUBE-1, Thinking Machines CM2, and others.

The programming model for these new computers was alien to that which was familiar to traditional computer architectures. Problems needed to be divided into parts, either functionally or by data partitioning, to be operated on in parallel. The traditional model is to perform calculations one at a time in sequence; parallel programming implies that many calculations will occur simultaneously. The scientific and engineering communities were willing to transform their application programs to accommodate the new computer architectures in order to obtain the performance gains; the conversion of commercial applications was delayed because other solutions were available without reprogramming, albeit at a high cost.

During the early 1990's, single processor performance increases began to be limited by physics and cost, at the same time that microprocessors were achieving computing performance nearly the same as large mainframes. The plummeting costs of CPU's and memory led to the development of several massively parallel computers, notably nCUBE-2, CM-5, Meiko, and Intel iWarp and IPSC to name a few, which are being actively sold. Commercial software companies, like Oracle Corporation, took notice of these new computing technologies and sought to supply commercial software for them. The resulting high performance and low cost per operation point to a revolution in high performance commercial data processing. The confluence of technologies at relatively low cost is now available to enable the development of commercially viable hardware and software systems using massively parallel processing.

7–3 Roadblocks to High Performance

The traditional approach to increasing the performance level of a computing system has been to increase the speed of the central processing unit and its memory. Unfortunately, there are limits of physics and cost that inhibit unlimited performance gains.

As processing speeds increase, power consumption increases with the need for faster switching time through the hardware processing elements, and the physical size of the processing elements must decrease. Signals that propagate among the components may travel no faster than the speed of light (about one nanosecond per 30 centimeters), and actual electronic transmission speeds are several times slower than that. As processing element (gate) delays decrease to the subnanosecond range (achieved in the mid-1980's), transmission delays dominate performance calculations. As a result, processing elements are moved closer together, and the 1980's saw the rise to prominence of the single chip computer.

As the processing elements decreased in size and increased in performance (and power requirements), cooling the resulting computers became a major consideration. Chilled, moving air was not sufficient to dissipate the heat generated by some of the very high-speed computers, and exotic cooling solutions were adopted: Chilled water and Freon were two methods employed. As a result, the cost of inventing ever faster uniprocessors increased faster than the performance (Figure 7-1). Doubling the cost of a computer did not result in twice the performance.

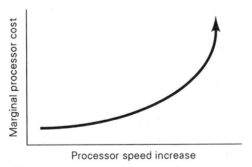

Fig. 7–1
Marginal Cost for Increased Processor Speed

Coincident with the appearance of performance limitations of mainframe computers was the proliferation of the single chip computer (microprocessor) for use in personal computers. These processors were inexpensive, and as their development continued, they became ever faster. The systems in which they were employed were not capable of mainframe performance in all areas (especially input/output and terminal handling), but the microprocessor showed the way to new levels of performance .

Sequent Computers and others sought to employ multiple microprocessors in new computer system architectures to achieve mainframe performance levels at minicomputer pricing. They were successful. The approach was to connect many processors to a common memory and input/output system and to modify the operating system software (UNIX in most cases) to disperse timesharing workloads among the many processors. This approach is known as a **tightly coupled** system with symmetric multiprocessing (Figure 7-2).

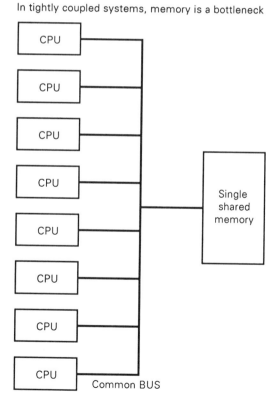

In tightly coupled systems, memory is a bottleneck

Fig. 7-2

Tightly Coupled
Systems: Fixed Memory
Bandwidth Limits
Performance

With all of the processors accessing the same memory, a new limit to performance appears: the speed and cost of memory. Complex memory sharing hardware schemes were developed, but the maximum number of processors able to be economically used appears to be around 50. Beyond that point, memory becomes a bottleneck and processors spend most of their time awaiting memory access.

Another approach to increasing performance without inordinate increase in cost is **loosely coupled** processing. Each processor has its own private memory to eliminate memory access contention, and the processors are connected via a high-speed bus (Figure 7-3). The resultant system resembles a network of independent computers. Digital Equipment Corporation produced several configurations of VAX Clusters that are loosely coupled computers. Once again, a limit to performance appeared: The interconnection among the computers was not scalable beyond several tens of processors without an inordinate increase in cost of the bus.

Each of the approaches to increased performance worked in its own way. As a means of measuring performance versus cost for a complex workload, the **Transaction Processing Council (TPC)** proposed several benchmark standards that simulate banking transactions. Oracle Corporation has run the TPC/B benchmark on each of the computer architectures, and the results are shown in Figure 7-4. Note that the best cost per transaction is achieved with a personal-computer, database-server configuration. The goal of a different computer architecture would be to achieve mainframe performance levels at PC server costs.

7–4 Massively Parallel Architecture

The loosely and tightly coupled architectures exposed two different performance roadblocks: interprocessor communication and memory contention. Massively parallel processing (MPP) attacks both of them. In addition, the cost of the overall system is reduced by the use of large numbers of identical, inexpensive components.

In a MPP computer, there are many processors (up to thousands of them), each with its own independent memory, configured to resemble the loosely coupled computer architecture. The processors then communicate with one another with a network of interconnections utilizing multiple pathways. (There are many possible interconnection topologies that have merit; we will explore only one here.) Whereas the loosely coupled computer uses a single bus that all the computing elements shared. MPP computers contain more than one per processor, but the overall number of pathways needs to be rather small to avoid great cost (Figure 7-5). Imagine a system with 1,000 processes where each must communicate directly with all of the others: 999 connections per processor times 1,000 processors is nearly one million connections.

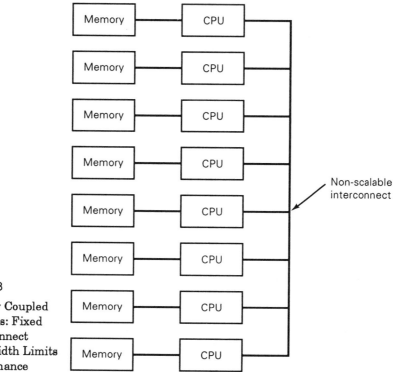

Fig. 7-3
Loosely Coupled Systems: Fixed Interconnect Bandwidth Limits Performance

One solution is to connect a processor to a defined set of "neighbors" and to provide a means of routing messages between these neighbor sets. One such interconnection topology is called hypercube architecture and is employed by the nCUBE-2 MPP Computer System. Each processing element connects directly with n other elements, where n is the order of 2^n hypercube. The nCUBE-2 allows for an order 13 hypercube: up to 8,192 processors each with 13 connections to other processing elements (nodes). To communicate with a processor with which a node is not directly connected, the message is routed by hardware though a maximum of 13 other nodes.

Computer	TPS	Computer cost	Cost/TPS
Mainframe	416	$19M	46K
Loosely coupled minicomputer	153	$2.6M	$17.2K
Tightly coupled minicomputer	319	$2.4M	$7.7K
PC LAN server	43	$112K	$2.6K

Fig. 7–4
High Performance has a High Cost Per Transaction but High Performance With a Low Cost Per Transaction is Needed

Since a very large number of processors is possible, each one need not be the ultimate in high performance. In the nCUBE-2, each processor is about 7.5 MIPS and as a result, the cost per node is the same as for PC processors. All of the processing and memory elements are identical (as are the processors for the input/output subsystems) and inexpensive. The resulting system is capable of truly staggering performance: 60,000 MIPS with aggregate communications among the nodes of 270 billion bytes per second (Figure 7-6).

MPP computers are able to take advantage of new developments in single chip processors by applying them to parallel systems as the costs of the newer processors decrease. Using the same technology, a MPP computer will always yield higher performance and lower costs than any other architecture. It is said that to improve the performance of a uniprocessor, the designer must solve physics and engineering problems; to improve the performance of a MPP computer, only engineering is involved.

7–5 Database Applicability

Traditionally, massively parallel processing computers (and other supercomputers for that matter) have been applied to scientific and engineering problems. The need for specialized programming methods and problem analysis made the adaptation of standard commercial software

difficult and expensive. In addition, most commercial software is very
input/output intensive, an area in which supercomputers did not excel.

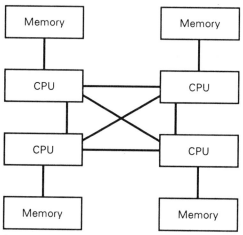

A massively parallel hardware solution
scales linearly to meet performance needs

Fig. 7-5
Massively Parallel Hardware Solution

The advent of client/server database technology in the late 1980's
enabled the application of MPP technology to commercial problems. In a
client/server configuration, the commercial application, such as a
COBOL program or transaction processing application, resides in a client computer. Traditional hardware is generally used for clients: PC's,
UNIX workstations, minicomputers, etc. The applications are generally
written by the end-user or an MIS organization where expertise focused
in the problem areas: payroll, manufacturing, and so on. The database
service resides in the server. Since the database is a specialized commercial application supplied by a software vendor with systems expertise,
such as Oracle Corporation, the adaptation of the database system to
MPP technology is economically feasible.

In order to take advantage of MPP computers, a database system
must be designed to divide the total workload over many processors.
There are essentially two different types of workloads: transaction processing and decision support. There are of course many gradations
between pure transaction systems and pure decision support application,
but we will deal with the end points for simplicity. A transaction process-

ing system performs modifications of a small number of data elements. An example is a banking application where a transaction might involve subtracting money from a checking account and inserting an audit of the operation into a history file. Decision support systems usually involve complex queries that span much of the data in a database. An example of a decision support application might be the calculation of the average salaries of each department in a company organized by job title.

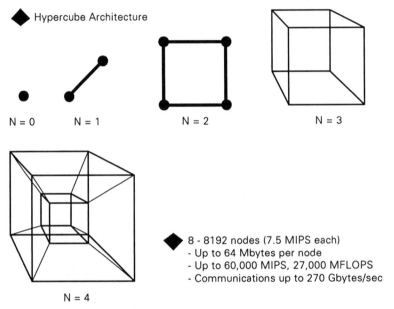

◆ Hypercube Architecture

N = 0   N = 1   N = 2   N = 3

N = 4

◆ 8 - 8192 nodes (7.5 MIPS each)
  - Up to 64 Mbytes per node
  - Up to 60,000 MIPS, 27,000 MFLOPS
  - Communications up to 270 Gbytes/sec

Fig. 7–6
Parallel Hardware Example: nCUBE 2

Transaction-oriented database system software is the simpler of the workload implementations for MPP computers. Each transaction is relatively simple, so each node of the MPP works on small units of work, and many nodes of the MPP computer could work on many transactions concurrently. The implementation requires that the database management system be able to coordinate the activities of many parallel activities on a single database, and the result will be very high overall throughput (many transactions per second) with a reasonable response time for each one. Several database management system capabilities are necessary to implement a transaction-oriented server on a MPP computer:

Multiple database instances run concurrently and independently, all accessing the same physical database. MPP computers rely on a large number of inexpensive components with minimal interconnections for their cost-effectiveness and speed. As we learned earlier, shared memories are a performance bottleneck, as would be a common shared-common-shared interconnection bus. In a MPP database server, many copies (instances) of the database management system software must execute simultaneously on different transactions with a minimum of communication among the instances. Since the object of the system is to provide transaction processing against a single database, all of the instances must share the same physical database files.

Each database instance serves multiple client applications. A system capable of thousands of transactions per second represents the work of literally tens of thousands of clients (users). The MPP database server cannot restrict each instance to a single client, but rather many tens of clients need to be served by each instance in order to create a useful system for the marketplace. It is true that if all of the clients request processing simultaneously, the individual nodes of the MPP will be overwhelmed. The usual model for a transaction processing system is that there is a significant "wait time" between transactions from any individual client, so that on average, each MPP node is processing a simple transaction from only one client.

Database instances coordinate activities via messages or data in the database. Even though each instance does not share memory with the others, from time to time requests will be made to access and possibly update the same information in the database. The instances need mechanisms to insure that each copy of the data represents its current state, and to be able to be notified when the data is modified. In addition, some changes made by instances may be "rolled back" due to requests by the client or due to some error during the transaction (for example, trying to subtract an amount greater than the current balance from an account). Other instances must always view the database in a consistent state without uncommitted changes.

Data access locks must be at a fine-grain level. It is possible to prevent database inconsistencies by locking portions of the data from access by more than one instance. Such locking must be at a fine-grain level; preferably single rows or records. If an application locks the entire database or complete tables, a bottleneck occurs where each transaction is single-threaded though the database or table locks. In a transaction processing system with thousands of clients, such bottlenecks negate the effectiveness of a MPP database server. In addition, when small portions of the data are locked to prevent concurrent updates, instances attempting to read the data must be granted access to a predictable, consistent version.

In the case study of Oracle for nCUBE below, we will examine the techniques used to satisfy each of the requirements for a successful implementation of a MPP database server for a transaction processing system. The additional requirements for decision support systems, namely the automatic distribution of operations among many processors is not addressed in the example.

An example of the type of optimization required for decision support is the parallel query. Imagine a request for information from a telephone book: Select the names and phone numbers of anyone whose address has the word "avenue" in it. The phone book is not organized with indexes on parts of addresses, so the entire book must be scanned. In a MPP computer optimized for decision support and parallel query operations, a single node could not scan the entire phone book quickly enough to provide answers in a timely fashion. So the work would be divided among many processors, each scanning ten pages only, for example. A 1,000 page phone book could be scanned by 100 processors in a very short time.

7-6 The Marketplace for Ultra-High Performance Applications

Transaction processing has traditionally been the major marketplace for ultra-high performance applications. Such systems as airline reservations, automatic teller machines, and telephone order entry represent some of the types of applications where a thousand or more transactions per second are required of the entire system. Traditionally, specialized applications running on very large mainframes were required to address the performance needs. Relational database management systems could not provide the required performance; even non-relational specialized database management systems were not up to the task (Figure 7-7). In order to achieve the ultra-high performance needed in transaction processing systems, non-database solutions such as TPF have been employed on very large-scale mainframe computers costing in the tens of millions of dollars.

Technology	Speed	Type
DB2	400 tps	Relational DBMS
ORACLE	416 tps	Relational DBMS
IMS fast path	700 tps	Non-relational DBMS
TPF	1500 tps	Non-DBMS transaction processing facility

Fig. 7–7
Performance of Various Database Management Systems

The high cost has been a barrier to entry for all but the most large-scale transaction processing applications. Systems requiring high processing rates where cost was a factor simply were not implemented. Many business applications continue to use 1960's software techniques, namely batch processing, to perform updates to the database. Such approaches lead to the familiar response to customers of insurance companies, banks, magazine subscription services, etc., that the update will take several weeks to become effective. The changed data is entered into a file where it is stored until it is time to perform the weekly, monthly, or quarterly update run. If cost-effective transaction processing systems were available, the changed data would be placed directly into the database for an instantaneous update.

Even where an organization is willing to pay the high cost for a traditional, non-database transaction processing system, optimum utilization of the data in the system is compromised. Since the data is stored in specialized files optimized for transaction processing, queries and other decision support activities require that some or all of the data be extracted into databases where the information is accessible. Even if specialized programs are written to access the data in the transaction processing format, concurrent transaction processing and query support slows down the overall performance of the system.

What is needed for a new era in high performance database management systems is the following:

- Extremely high transaction processing rates
- Concurrent transaction processing and query processing

- Industry standard application languages (SQL)

- Application portability

- Open Systems (UNIX)

- Cost-effectiveness

It would appear that database management systems for massively parallel processing computers could address all of the requirements for expanding the marketplace for ultra-high performance applications. The case study below will examine how one implementation of a relational database management system on a MPP computer addresses the needs of the marketplace, and where further work is in progress.

7–7 Case Study: Oracle for nCUBE

The Oracle Relational Database Management System is implemented on a wide variety of computer architectures and operating environments. It has been designed from its inception to permit separation of functions into different processes with interaction taking the form of messages. The major hurdle to be jumped to create an effective implementation on a MPP Computer was to eliminate the need for sharing memory when the database executed on a multiple-processor environment.

Figure 7-8 shows the three basic Oracle configurations. In the traditional computer architecture case, Oracle executes on a single processor with its memory and accesses a set of random storage (disks) as the database files. The processor memory contains a database cache that allows frequently accessed data to be obtained quickly and to minimize disk accesses. Multiple clients (users) attach to the same Oracle Server by creating a separate address space (task) for each user (Oracle Version 6) while sharing the Oracle code and common data. Oracle7 allows for a set of user tasks each of which processes requests for a number of attached clients (multi-threaded server) reducing the number of operating system processes. Performance is limited by the speed of the single processor in the system.

When the Oracle Server is moved to a **symmetric multiprocessor (SMP)** computer, exactly the same structure is used. Scalability is achieved by allowing each of the Oracle Server-user tasks (or multi-threaded servers) to execute on its own processor. When there are

Uniprocessor

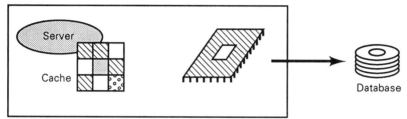

Symmetric multi-processor

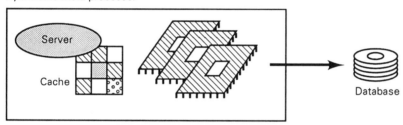

Massively parallel processor

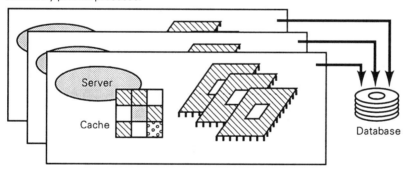

Fig. 7–8
Three Oracle Configurations

enough user tasks to occupy all of the processors, then multiple user tasks will share processors. As with the uniprocessor case, there is a single area of memory shared by all of the user tasks that contains a database cache. As the number of processors increases, contention for memory and shared hardware resources increase, as we have seen earlier. Performance is limited by the maximum number of processors that can effectively share resources before the memory becomes a bottleneck.

Oracle for nCUBE uses the MPP technology to overcome uniprocessor and SMP bottlenecks: Each processing node contains an Oracle Server that processes database requests from multiple clients (Oracle7 will utilize the multi-threaded server). All of the Oracle Servers on various nodes share the same physical database, but each has its own memory cache. User database applications execute on workstations (UNIX, Windows, Macintosh, Next, etc.) and connect to the Oracle MPP database server via a network protocol, such as **TCP/IP.**

Since each processor has its own cache of database information, a mechanism to coordinate the data and insure coherence is required. Oracle dedicates a number of nodes to a **distributed lock manager**, which is a key technology needed to successfully implement a MPP database server. Whenever an Oracle instance requires a database block to be put into its cache, a request is made to the distributed lock manager to locate that block. If it exists only on disk, it is read directly into the requesting cache. If it exists in another instance cache, but has not been modified, a copy is sent to the requesting cache, and both are marked to prevent update. If it has been modified in another cache, the block is first written to disk before being marked as read-only and sent to the requesting cache. The distributed lock manager is also notified when an instance needs to update a block marked as "read-only." Other instances with a copy in their caches are notified and the results of the update distributed when needed.

In order for the distributed lock manager to perform efficiently, the underlying hardware inter-node communications scheme must be fast and scalable. With the nCUBE architecture of hardware routing and an aggregate communications rate of 270 gigabytes per second, the Oracle for nCUBE implementation is very fast and efficient indeed. On a system with 64 nodes of 16 megabytes each, a TPC/B rate of 1,073 transactions per second has been achieved. The cost of the system was about $2.66 million, yielding $2,482 per transaction per second. The result is a system capable of providing ultra-high performance at a cost per transaction comparable to personal computer systems.

There are other techniques that allowed the Oracle Server to be transported successfully to the nCUBE computer system, but which are a standard part of the Oracle implementation. Oracle utilizes fine-grain locking to insure concurrent access by readers and writers of data (Figure 7-9). A data snapshot model is provided to guarantee that all views of data are consistent over time (Figure 7-10); and fast group commitment of database updates are used to remove input/output bottlenecks.

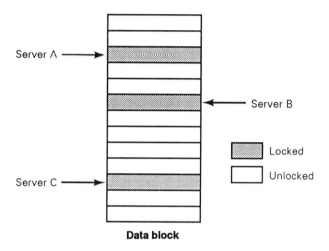

Data block

Fig. 7-9
Row Level Locking: High Parallelism Requires Finest Lock Granularity

Fine-grain locking insures that each user that needs to reserve data for exclusive use reserves only that data and nothing more. Older techniques of locking entire tables (or files) or disk data blocks are inadequate for modern database management systems. **Table level locking** was predictable enough—the program knew exactly that the effect of an update to a row of data was that the entire table was locked to its application—but prevented all update concurrency. In the banking transaction example from above, inserting a row into a history table would lock the entire history table until that transaction completed, even though another transaction competing for the history table resource would have no actual data conflicts. Transactions would be serialized on a single resource, the history table.

Block level locking provides a finer granularity so that applications only serialize if they happen to require data that resides in the same block. The problem is that multiple rows of data will exist within the same physical disk data block, so some data that is inconsequential to a particular transaction is locked. Worse yet, since data can be reorganized or moved to devices with different block sizes, identical executions of a program will behave differently. Block level locking also creates deadlock situations that are not due to programming errors, but instead, are due to coincidence. For example, if user A attempts to acquire locks on block 1 and 5 in that order, and user B attempts locks on blocks 5 and 1 in that order, neither can proceed until one of the users releases it locks. If the data that was the actual target of the locks is contained in different rows in those blocks, then there is no logical reason for the deadlock to have occurred, and the behavior of the applications will change depending upon the organization of rows into data blocks.

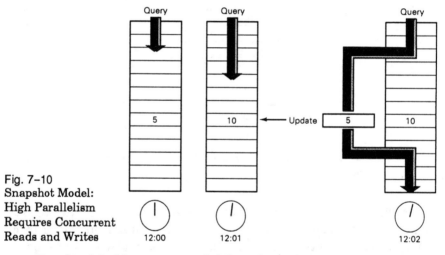

Fig. 7–10
Snapshot Model:
High Parallelism
Requires Concurrent
Reads and Writes

    Row level locking prevents bottlenecks and deadlocks. Users lock only the actual data being modified, so a bottleneck only occurs if the application is improperly designed to require all users to modify the same row of data. Deadlocks similarly will occur only due to programming errors—multiple locks should only be acquired in an agreed upon order. If they are not, deadlock is possible, but the reason is well understood and predictable.

    When a user application needs to read data from the database, it requires a consistent view of that data. A transaction may consist of the modification of many database rows in several tables. Until the user application "commits" the changes, they are not considered to be a part of the database which other user application can view. Oracle implements a snapshot model of the database for its users. Once a user application begins accessing a table, its contents are fixed and subsequent changes will not be seen unless the table access is started again. Figure 7-10 shows a query that begins scanning a table at 12:00. At 12:01 another user application updates a row in the table that has not yet been read by the first user. A snapshot of the 12:00 data is kept so that at 12:02 when the query accesses that row, it will see the table in a consistent 12:00 state. An example of the utility of the snapshot model is a query that is to calculate the total salaries of each department in a company. If that calculation starts at 12:00 and takes 20 seconds, there is a time window during which changes to the salary table can be made—it is 20 seconds long. If at 12:02 a salary update program begins to change some salaries, the query must not see any of those changes during its run for its results to be meaningful. The summary report indicates that it contains calculations valid at 12:00. It is not meaningful to document that the results may or may not be valid; department 1 is valid at 12:00, department 2 at 12:02, and department 3 at some unknown combination!

The prevention of input/output bottlenecks is also critical to any high performance system. A serious potential bottleneck occurs on database logging devices where data must be written from memory during a "commit" operation. A commit occurs when a user application indicates that its modifications are complete and should be made a permanent part of the database. The modified data must be moved from volatile memory to a permanent storage device such as a disk. The Oracle Server optimizes the commit process by grouping the changes from multiple transactions into the same physical input/output operation, as well as by striping the data across multiple devices. When the changes are written into log files, the commit is complete. At a later time, the actual database is updated from the memory caches. If the database management system is stopped before the database files can be updated, the log file is used to reconstruct the database changes when the system is next started.

The first Oracle for nCUBE system was demonstrated in 1991 and yielded record high levels of performance and capacity: 1,073 transactions per second with a 100 billion byte database at a cost of $2,482 per transaction per second. A small nCUBE configuration was used for the demonstration—only 64 nodes. Since the nCUBE-2 has a potential configuration of 8,192 nodes, even greater performance can be expected in the future. The demonstration system only addresses the issue of transaction throughput. Future development will address decreased response time to allow for the system to be used for simultaneous transaction processing and decision support applications.

7–8 The Future: The New Mainframes?

Today's mainframes deliver high performance at a very high cost: Oracle has achieved 416 transactions per second at a cost of $46,000 per transaction. The initial demonstration of Oracle for nCUBE has achieved 1,073 transactions per second at a cost of $2,482 per transaction. The cost of increased performance on the mainframe is likely to increase the cost of transactions, since they are nearly at the limits of technology right now. It is much more likely that massively parallel processing computers will emerge as the replacement for computer systems at the very high end of commercial processing. The form will be different from existing mainframes: User applications will execute on remote computers such as minicomputers, workstations, and PC's, with the mainframe providing database, electronic mail, and other applications services.

The notion that all future computing will migrate to workstations is naive. The problem is managing one of the most valuable corporate assets, data, as it is dispersed geographically onto individual desktops. How does the corporate entity ensure that all of the data is accurate, secure, and recoverable in the event of disaster? One thousand PC's may have the processing power and storage of a single MPP computer, but the management problem is much more complex. Corporate data will reside in centralized servers managed by professional staffs of operators, database administrators, network administrators, and the like. Applications will reside on the desktop (or palmtop or shirt pocket!), and departmental data may reside on smaller servers.

Developing Strategic Business Systems Using Object Technology

Dr. Jerrold Grochow is Vice President and Chief Technology Officer at American Management Systems, Inc., an information systems development and consulting firm. As senior member of the Corporate Technology Group, he supervises the introduction of new technologies into the firms business practices. He has been a consultant on object technology to IBM and is on the Board of Directors of Knowledge Systems Corporation, an object technology consulting firm.

Previous chapters discussed pragmatic skills in developing an enterprise model, distributed and client/server computing, object database technology and application, CASE and application development technologies, database computers, and massively parallel processing. From the IT professional's viewpoint, an important question to ask for each of these emerging technologies is what to do with it?

As an IS executive, for example, should you ignore the technology? Ask your technology scanning staff to keep an eye on the development, but do nothing? Start a pilot project? Or recommend your CEO to make a major commitment to this technology because of its strategic importance to the organization? How do you go about doing this and where do you start?

In this chapter, Jerry Grochow discusses issues involved in developing strategic business systems using object technology. Jerry is in a unique position to address this problem because of his experience in supervising the introduction of new technologies into AMS's business practice and his expertise in object technology. Enjoy IT.

8-1   Introduction

Over the past several years, the thunder of object orientation has become louder and louder. We are bombarded with articles, speeches, and pronouncements on the use of object technology as the savior of our industry. We are inundated with advertisements and product literature on the latest books, languages, and tools to make object design and development painless. We are exhorted to "think like an object, act like an object, be an object." And somehow this will make all the problems of computer system development disappear.

Unfortunately, a great deal of this cacophony is rehashing old ground for those of us in the information systems part of the industry (alias business systems, management information systems, etc.). We have heard it all before. "Use structured techniques and your systems will be maintainable." "Use 4GL's and you will eliminate the application backlog." "Use CASE tools and you will improve productivity 50-100%" "Object technology will deliver on all the promises that other technologies didn't." Yes, and the check is in the mail.

If object technology is really going to help us, we need to address the "real" problems in designing and developing "strategic business systems." When you are trying to figure out how to extend the life of existing systems of more than a million lines of COBOL code (mostly undocumented) running as a stand-alone system on a mainframe computer, the issue is not whether C++ is object-oriented enough or which dialect of Smalltalk to use. The real issues in object technology are

- will it scale?
- can it be managed?
- will it perform?

In other words, the fundamental issues have to do with whether object technology will provide value to the IS manager in the form of robust tools and methods for creating heavy-duty systems. The IS manager is searching for new methods, but they have to apply to the large scale, high volume situations that must be faced every day in the world of business systems. With hundreds (or thousands) of on-line users making split second decisions regarding millions of dollars, the brokerage house IS manager cannot explain a strange lull in system response because the environment is "garbage collecting." With nightly production schedules that cannot be slipped without risking a federal audit, the bank IS manager cannot say that the new object-oriented system doesn't handle batch processing so well. With database sizes measured in terabytes, the insurance company IS manager cannot be excused because the object-oriented database can't store an object that spans physical volumes.

The world of the IS manager is more demanding than many realize. It requires saying in advance how long it is going to take to develop a new system and being within shooting distance of that estimate when the results are in. It often constrains solutions by requiring the use of equipment and people it has already (no—we can't "shoot all the COBOL programmers," as one industry executive once suggested). And it *must* find new technologies that are going to help it out of the mess it is in.

So, the question is whether object technology is *the* technology and if so, how we can introduce it to the million or so programmers and analysts who call the IS organization their home. Of course, one could argue that object technology was never meant for creating large scale business applications. Isn't it most applicable to the creation of complex user interfaces and workstation-based applications? Certainly, the concepts of object-oriented design are as applicable to difficult business problems as they are to difficult technical problems and complex user interfaces.

For an IS manager, the question becomes, what should I do now in regard to object technology? At AMS, as well as at a number of other companies, we are actively engaged in bringing object technology up to industrial strength for use in strategic business systems. Many organizations are starting pilot projects to assess the state of the technology for themselves. Others are taking the plunge based on what information there is (and a great deal of faith). Everywhere, people are moving to understand, to embrace, to enhance this technology. There are many difficult problems, but they are being studied and addressed in a way that will make object technology more useful.

8–2 Strategic Business Systems and Object Technology

I define a strategic business system as one that is integral to the day-to-day operation of a large organization. Today, such systems are typically characterized as monolithic, COBOL-based, mainframe-oriented. More and more, however, they are being **downsized** to networks and distributed architectures. They are systems where data integrity is paramount and where many-hour-long batch processing runs are common. Their face is changing from text to graphics, but underneath, they are still the same behemoths that are necessary to run today's large organizations.

A strategic business system's portfolio may encompass hundreds of systems with total code in the tens of millions of lines. The limiting factor in improving IS, therefore, is often the management processes we have or are capable of developing. Design management, configuration management, and versioning are qualitatively different with a project team of 100 people than with a team of ten or only one. When we are dealing with such projects, the management processes cannot be left to chance or informal methods. They need to be standardized, documented, and supported by appropriate automated tools. Such tools barely exist today for projects employing structured and information engineering methods, let alone for projects using object technology.

So far, the vendors of object technology are giving us, the users of object technology, only pieces of a complex puzzle, without our being able to see what the completed picture will look like—or even if the pieces will all fit together without any holes! Each vendor has its niche, each book its topic, each speaker his or her axe to grind. But will it all work when we try to develop strategic business systems for today's large organizations?

The answer so far is that we don't really know. With only one or two visible examples (and those implemented several years ago using specially developed tools, techniques, and languages), several issues fundamental to the IS world have not been adequately addressed, namely scalability, manageability, and performance.

In a general sense, the entire field of **software engineering** has evolved as the response to these issues. Software engineering provides the systematic approaches and standards that enable us to develop large systems, manage large projects, and achieve acceptable performance. Without this discipline, we produce spaghetti code that costs a lot to maintain (or becomes unmaintainable) and is unable to meet the changing needs of the organizations it is supposed to support. I hope that we have not forgotten this in the rush to develop new systems by "iterative development," to create reusable software based on object libraries, or to get to market first with new methods, tools, and languages.

Object programming without object engineering will lead to just as much chaos as any other technique.

8–3 Software Engineering for Object Technology

For the past 25 years, our industry has been laboring to turn itself into a profession worthy of being called software engineering. Over that time, many aspects of a discipline of software engineering have been explored. The key ones that need to be addressed for object technology are:

1 A defined life cycle (phases and tasks)
2 Methods and techniques for performing those tasks
3 Tools and languages
4 A **design repository**
5 Estimating methods for development effort and cost
6 Estimating methods for operating costs of systems
7 Training and educational curricula

The referenced article by Norman Plant provides a list of requirements for many of these areas, but I want to address a few more specifically in terms of the three fundamental issues of scalability, manageability, and performance.

Life Cycle

A life cycle for developing large, object-oriented information systems must allow for the orderly formulation of system requirements, translation of those requirements into tested high performance software, and integration of components into libraries that can be used in other systems.

Most practitioners of object technology talk about *methods* for designing and developing systems, but not about the life cycle. Rebecca Wirfs-Brock's article lays out her ideas for such an object-oriented system life cycle. With a few added components, her proposal sounds suspiciously like the development life cycles being followed by most organizations today. Perhaps this is because a life cycle designed to produce an industrial strength system is by its nature more structured than one designed to develop a prototype or even a small-scale system. Her life cycle begins with the process of developing an overall concept and design for the system before getting into the iterative, object-oriented programming cycle. It ends with explicit "cleanup" and "generalization for broader utility" (as life cycle phases) as necessary post-implementation steps. In short, she attempts to fit the iterative prototyping structure of the object-oriented development environment to the life cycle of industrial strength systems based on reusable components.

The concept of a life cycle is extremely important for both manageability and scalability of object technology. By focusing on the life cycle and its various phases, rather than just on individual development techniques, we are forced to look at how an object "matures," i.e., how it progresses through various design and developmental steps and how it (sometimes) ends up in a reusable object library. Without this overarching set of ideas, we can easily end up with objects that are ill-conceived and just as troublesome to maintain as our most unstructured 3GL code.

Methods and Techniques

Within the context of the life cycle, methods and techniques must be specified for how to go about the processes of design, development, and implementation of object-oriented systems.

You have only to go to your local technical bookstore to see the number of object-oriented design methods that have been proposed. While there are similarities, each has its own approach. Some are "pure" methods (relying only on object models), while some are hybrids (combining object models with dataflow models, entity-relationship models, or the like). Very few have been validated, particularly as they pertain to large systems. This is currently a major source of confusion to organizations attempting to move into the object arena. Allowing each project team to make its own selection (as some organizations are currently doing, reminiscent of the days prior to structured design) is a sure way of losing management control.

Methods and techniques also imply documentation. And documentation, to be readily understandable, needs to have a standardized form. Experience to date seems to show that object-oriented systems have an even larger requirement for documentation and comments in the code than 3GL-based systems (perhaps because there is as yet no standard for other documentation). Most of us know the importance of reading in English what the original programmer thought he or she was doing and why. The object technology goal of reuse actually brings with it a higher standard for documentation quality. If systems based on objects are indeed going to be highly maintainable, there has to be some standard for object documentation as well.

Tools and Languages

Software engineering tools and programming languages provide the medium for applying methods and techniques toward the production of operational systems. This applies to programming tools, design tools, testing tools, configuration management tools, etc. (Computer-aided software engineering, CASE, refers to the use of automated tools in performing software engineering tasks. While it has come to be used in relation to structured techniques and information engineering, the term CASE applies equally well here.) Large business systems will exist for 20 years or more. We need tools and languages that will be effective during development and during the 90-95% percent of the system life cycle that occurs after the system goes into production.

For 25 years, IS systems have been coded primarily in COBOL. There was, for a while, a flurry of activity in PL/1, but it never really caught on. (I wonder what we can learn from the fact that the one highly publicized object-based business system in existence today was implemented in PL/1.) Now we are being asked to switch to C++ or Smalltalk, languages whose richness is constrained not so much in their syntax as in the class libraries that are really part of the "language environment." Studying the base classes is really "learning the language" and we are not much better off there than we were 10 or 15 years ago with COBOL: programmers and designers have to study the specific dialect and the class libraries of the particular implementation they want to use. (Different versions of Smalltalk come with between 100 and 250 base classes. C++ versions generally come with only a few or no base classes; but there are many such libraries available from third party suppliers.)

Having a consistent set of base classes across the different implementations of Smalltalk and C++ will make it a lot easier to develop a cadre of experienced object developers. If the differences remain significant for too much longer, this factor will impede the transition to object technology by making it too difficult to move people from one environment to another. And if there is no agreement, it is likely that differences will arise from project to project in the same organization—again creating an unmanageable situation.

The biggest tool challenge for object technology, however, may be creating the kind of "object library browser" that will integrate indexing, documentation, and code in a way that truly makes large class hierarchies accessible. Granted that there is a significant compactness of code in object-oriented programming languages, and granted that significant reuse will also account for reductions in lines of code, but by how much? Even at a ten-to-one reduction from today's systems, providing equivalent functionality will mean systems with thousands of objects and tens of thousands of methods. Since a large portion of what it means to use object technology is to understand the class hierarchy of the system, and thus, to understand what can be reused, how will we approach design and development of such massive systems? At what point will dis-economies begin to set in? A 100 object system can be understood in detail by a single person; but what about a 1,000 object system, or a 10,000 object system? This, of course, assumes that we will be able to figure out how to document and index objects in a meaningful way when we have thousands of objects. The solution of this problem is a requirement to ensuring scalability of object technology.

Other tools also need to be scalable. One of the configuration management tools we have been using to help control a Smalltalk development effort gets high marks for capabilities, but seems to have been designed with a different sized project in mind. Each application defined to the tool is limited to about 50 object classes. When you have more than about five people working together, the disk files get so large that you have to reorganize the database every other day. The idea is good, but this type of tool will need a major overhaul in features as well as performance to support a project ten times this size.

Design Repository

A design repository provides a generalized model and a database for the information that must be stored about a system as a basis for future enhancement and maintenance. It provides a common facility for tool developers to store the information their tools create and for tools users (i.e., application developers) to access this information.

Object-based systems will need this type of repository as much, if not more, than traditionally developed systems. The use of object technology does not relieve us of the need to access a wide array of information as we perform maintenance and enhancement. In fact, the fundamental ideas of reusability demand it. The object hierarchy itself contains some of the information that one would store in a design repository, although it is not sufficient and is not in a form that can be easily accessed. Saying that object systems are "self-documenting" is just ignoring the issue.

IBM and other CASE tool vendors have been having major problems in trying to agree on a repository design and architecture for traditionally developed application systems. They are now trying to tackle the introduction of object technology as an add-on to other unresolved issues. In this, as in other areas, the progression of object technology will be hindered by the general problems facing our industry for which we do not yet have good solutions.

Estimating Methods

Estimating development and operational costs is integral to the justification of new systems development. Methods are needed for creating such estimates before object technology will be fully accepted.

As part of our work at AMS, we have been trying to learn from the experience of others in estimating the time and cost of developing object-oriented systems. Unfortunately, the best summary of this experience is, estimate as you would have using traditional techniques. Using object-oriented technology will take less (time, effort, resources).

This may be good for a laugh, but it hardly supports a major paradigm shift. Managers want to see quantified estimates of system development cost and effort. Before they will go out and commit to major changes in the way they develop systems, they will need something more than a very uncertain "it will take less time." (From the additional perspective of a consulting firm attempting to bid system development jobs, I also need something more to tell a potential client than "it will be better," particularly if I want to be paid for my consultation!)

Training and Education

It almost goes without saying that courses, workshops, and other information to educate analysts, designers, programmers, and managers are required to ensure the successful introduction of the life cycle, methods, techniques, tools, and languages of object technology.

There seem to be two suggestions regarding training and education in object technology: the "forget everything you know" approach and the "objects build on what you know" approach. I am not sure that these divergent viewpoints will ever be reconciled, but I submit that it is difficult for most people to forget everything they know.

To the extent that object technology presents a major paradigm shift, we have to help people integrate these new ideas into their existing mental models of systems. This is significantly more difficult than simply teaching someone a new programming language. And as an industry, we haven't had such great success even at that. The people teaching "Object Technology for COBOL Developers" will need more than a week to interact with their students if the message is going to stick.

8–4 Ready for Prime Time?

So the 64-dollar question is whether object technology is ready for the prime time of developing large scale strategic business systems. At the current rate of change in the technology, the tools and languages should be ready in about 12 to 18 months, although there will be continuing issues of scalability and performance. At the rate of change of management processes, however, it may be a lot longer before the tools and languages can be widely and effectively applied in the IS environment (I am not counting three people doing a pilot project as wide use or COBOL programs written in Smalltalk as effective use).

We have a chicken-egg problem working here: We can't get to large application systems until we have a certain infrastructure available (related to life cycle, methods, tools, languages, and management) that will provide a foundation for a successful project, and we can't get that until we try some things to see what works. Obviously, some organizations are taking a giant step (perhaps a "leap of faith") and moving from small scale testing of concepts to large scale implementation. Since most large organizations are risk-averse, however, they will need to see significant activity in the areas I have discussed before moving out of the pilot project stage. In fact, prudent IS managers will already have moved at least to this stage to help their organizations understand what the issues mean in their own environments. In some sense, what we really need is an "iterative prototyping" approach to the introduction of object-oriented infrastructure so that organizations can move forward with minimal risk of heading down a dead end.

While we cannot have all the answers before we start, we should be working on them and willing to talk about the results. Strategic business systems deal with some hard problems. That's where object technology should be able to give our industry the greatest payoff. And if it does, there will be more than enough benefit to go around.

8–5 Acknowledgments

Material in this chapter was adapted from an article in the September, 1992, issue of *Hotline on Object Technology*. The author would like to thank Milt Hess, Andy Baer, and Fred Forman for their helpful comments and suggestions.

8–6 References

Grochow, Jerrold M. "Developing Strategic Business Systems Using Object Technology," *Hotline on Object Technology* Vol. 3, No. 11, September, 1992.

Plant, Norman. "What large scale IT users want from OO suppliers?" *Hotline on Object Technology*, Vol. 3, No. 7, May 1992

Taylor, David A. *Object-Oriented Technology: A Manager's Guide*, Addison-Wesley, 1990.

Taylor, David A. *Object-Oriented Information Systems: Planning and Implementation*, John Wiley and Sons, 1992.

Wirfs-Brock, Rebecca. "The Phases of an Object-Oriented Application," *Smalltalk Report*, Vol. 1, No. 5, February, 1992.

Visual Information Access Systems

David Friend, Chairman of Pilot Executive Software, founded Pilot Software in 1983. Pilot introduced the first commercial executive information system (EIS) in 1984, and Mr. Friend has often been cited as the father of the EIS industry. Mr. Friend has written dozens of articles on EIS and is a regular speaker at trade shows and industry conferences. In 1991 he was featured on the cover of *Datamation* magazine.

In 1991, Mr. Friend engineered Pilot's acquisition of the software arm of Thorn EMI, TECS, which gave Pilot a strong presence in the DSS market and direct operations in most European countries. Today Pilot's worldwide operations employ approximately 300 people.

Prior to Pilot, Mr. Friend founded Computer Pictures Corp., one of the first companies in the business graphics software market. He authored the company's flagship product called Trend Spotter. Mr. Friend served as Chairman of Computer Pictures until its acquisition by Cullinet Software, Inc. in 1982.

Prior to Computer Pictures, Mr. Friend was President of ARP Instruments, Inc., which was one of the first manufacturers of music synthesizers. ARP was the synthesizer of choice for many of the world's most famous rock bands and jazz musicians, and Mr. Friend became well known as a pioneer in the electronic musical instrument industry.

Mr. Friend holds bachelor's degrees in music and engineering from Yale University where he was a Scholar of the House. He was a David Sarnoff Fellow at Princeton University's Graduate School of Engineering. He is currently a trustee of Berklee College of Music and the Boston Chamber Music Society and is a former trustee of the New England Conservatory of Music.

We have presented many emerging technologies that can be used to design and develop application systems. Application systems, however, are only a means to delivering data to the end-user. From the user's viewpoint, it is data needed to facilitate activities, not application software. It would do users little good if an application system was designed through an ER modeling approach, using CASE tools, storing data in an object database machine which has massively parallel processing capability, but running on a client workstation that cannot display data retrieved from the server in a friendly manner.

From the IT professionals viewpoint, a critical question to ask is how to put data into the hands of the user in an easy manner. In this chapter, David Friend answers this question through what he calls "visual information access systems." David is in a unique position to address this problem because of his experience in developing executive information systems. Enjoy IT.

9-1 Introduction

The most striking effect of the computer era has been the amount of information that has been collected and stored—information on what you buy, how much you earn, where you travel, what you watch on TV, where you live, and so forth. It is estimated that in the past decade, more recorded information has been generated than in the entire history of mankind.

What is equally striking is that our society has become completely dependent upon this rich store of data for economic growth. Virtually every business process is dependent on the availability of computer-based data. For example, you can't market a product without computerized customer and prospect lists. When you buy a bar-coded product, a computerized price list feeds the cash register. You can't advertise a product without computer-based statistics on demographics, media, and costs. You can't design a new product without computerized parts lists, design tools, and project management. And so on.

Anyone who works in information systems is aware of the magnitude of our stores of detailed information and the accelerating pace of information acquisition. In fact, there is a very good argument to be made that the pace of data acquisition has far outstripped our ability to use it effectively. All this new data is a gold mine waiting to be exploited. The problem, it seems, is not so much how to get data into a computer, but how to get it out in a meaningful and useful way.

Getting information out of a computer is the province of reporting systems. Traditionally, reporting systems have been paper-based. However, with the quantity and level of detail available in computer databases, paper is no longer an appropriate medium. There are simply too much data, updated too frequently, with too many useful ways of looking at the data for paper to be a viable medium for reporting. So a new breed of reporting system is emerging which allows users to work directly with computer-based information. It is what Microsoft's Bill Gates refers to "as information at your fingertips." It is a new way of thinking about information access and the technologies that are implied. We call it **visual information access (VIA)** (Figure 9-1).

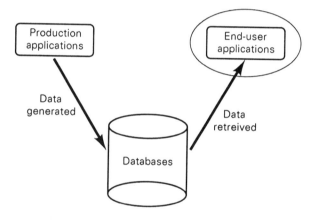

Fig. 9–1

Visual information access systems are more concerned with how we retrieve and view data than how data are acquired or stored, with the proviso that specialized data servers may be needed to provide adequate response time for live access.

9–2 What is Visual Information Access?

At a very general level, most computer software programs fall into three categories: those used to get data into a database, those used to get data out of a database, and database programs themselves. For the most part, data is collected through automated processes (such as cash registers, production line bar-code readers, ATM's, etc.) or through manual data entry programs (transcribed from insurance claims forms, sales orders, purchase orders, etc.). The databases themselves have changed over the years from being largely customized file systems that are part of the application to generalized (mostly relational) databases that are purchased separately from the applications. We'll be focusing on getting data out of the database and, to some extent, the database technology itself.

The business of getting data out of a database falls into two general categories:

1   Service-related queries (such as accessing your credit card balance)

2   Management reporting

In recent years, most service-related queries are performed on-line using specialized software which is highly tuned to the specific service. An example would be computerized telephone directory assistance. Management reporting, on the other hand, has basically been done with paper. In fact, a class of software called "report writers" has evolved to help developers more efficiently produce paper reports. Visual information access (VIA) systems are evolving as the on-screen successors to paper-based reporting systems.

9–3 The Problem with Paper

The problem with paper-based reporting stems from the fact that the automated collection of data from supermarket scanners, automated production facilities, use of credit cards, etc., coupled with the dramatically lower cost of processing such data has turned paper output into a severe bottleneck. Higher speed printers and more paper will not solve the problem. Over the past five years, the amount of computer-generated paper has increased 14% per year, to a total of nearly 600,000,000,000 pages in 1991. Meanwhile recent surveys have shown that the usefulness of such printout is declining: Approximately 98% of the pages printed are never looked at and essentially go from printer to trash can without ever seeing the light of day. There is so much data to look at and so many possible ways to aggregate and view the data that no amount of printout can ever anticipate even a fraction of the users' needs.

Another problem is speed. Most business processes run on a day to day basis. While paper-based reports were fine for most monthly financial statements, the logistics of printing and distributing a large number of reports on a daily basis are daunting. In a world of accelerating processes, faster deliveries, lower inventories, and highly competitive services, data distribution that relies on paper is too slow.

The only solution to this problem is to give the users themselves the power to link directly to data using electronic means. As the infrastructure of PC's, networks, and servers becomes as ubiquitous as the in-box, mail truck, and trash can, information workers at all levels of the organization will be turning to their PC's rather than traditional paper reports for the information they need to do their jobs. Rather than using report writers to churn out paper-based reports, they will be using VIA tools to design specialized human interfaces to the live databases.

There are fundamental differences between report writers and visual information access systems. For one thing, paper-based reports are canned images of data, as opposed to live numbers. VIA is not simply a matter of transferring paper-style reports to the computer screen. Rather, such on-screen reporting deals with live interactions with the underlying data and the ability of users to immediately alter their view of the data in a nearly infinite number of ways. Visual information access is a combination of database access technology, data transformation, visual data representation, and data navigation techniques.

9-4 The Three Pillars of VIA

There are three essential components to a visual information access system (Figure 9-2). First, the one which most people immediately identify with VIA, is the GUI *front-end*. This component is the "visual" in VIA. It is also the component that ultimately defines what kind of applications can and cannot be built from a human interface standpoint. It is also the part of the system that typically requires the most programming and development effort.

The second most obvious component of any VIA system is the *back-end* data server. In most cases today, this back end server is an SQL relational database, such as Oracle, DB2, SQL Server, Ingres, etc. While relational databases are good, general purpose data stores which can accomplish nearly anything in batch mode, they do not provide adequate speed for many types of live reporting applications. Hence, VIA brings about a need for different, more specialized data servers that are more tailored to particular types of data and queries.

Finally, there is frequently a need for some sort of computational engine that sits between the database server and the GUI. The Gartner Group refers to this class of software as *"middleware"* for reasons which are obvious from Figure 9-2. The need for middleware is not appreciated by many people attempting to build VIA systems today.

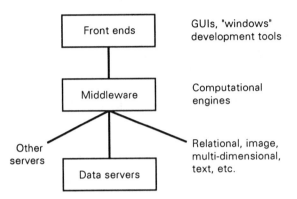

Fig. 9-2

The "Three Pillars" of *Visual Information Access* systems are based on an open-architecture which allows software modules to be snapped together to form complete systems.

9-5 The Need for Middleware

Since the need for middleware is probably the most poorly understood aspect of VIA, lets examine this first. To begin with, *some* applications can be built without middleware (Figure 9-3). Such applications are typically those which require little or no transformation of the raw data and which use the underlying database in a way that offers adequate response time. For example, the speed of an SQL relational database can usually be expressed in terms of an approximate number of records accessed per second. For example, Oracle running on one of our VAX's was recently clocked at about 120 records per second.

Fig. 9-3

Some reporting systems can be built by simply putting a GUI front-end onto a relational data server. However, the GUI still needs to be "data driven" and to use dynamic menus to maintain independence of application and database.

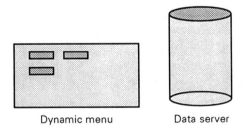

Dynamic menu   Data server

An application which only needs to retrieve one or two records per screen will work quite nicely. An application which requires that 10,000 records be retrieved and aggregated for each screen will be too slow to be usable. An example of an application which might work fine would be a human resources application in which the user is locating and retrieving individual records on individual employees. Where such an application might get into trouble would be if the application were able to allow users to ask questions such as, "let me see the total salaries and FICA taxes for all employees except executives." If there are 10,000 employees, this kind of query might be unacceptably slow.

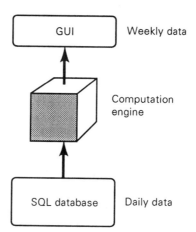

Fig. 9–4
If data is stored daily and the user wishes to see data in a weekly format, a "middleware" computation engine is needed to make the conversion.

Speed is not the only reason that one needs middleware (Figure 9-4). Consider a simple and highly plausible situation where sales data is stored on a daily basis and the user wishes to see the data displayed on his or her screen in weekly form. If your only tools are an SQL database and a GUI front-end, where are you going to convert the days to weeks? Periodicity conversions are not as trivial as you might think because they need extensive knowledge of the calendar; they need to know about holidays, fiscal years, calendar years, 4-4-5 accounting periods, leap years, and so forth. Furthermore, all data don't convert the same way. To get weekly sales, you add up the days. To get weekly inventory, you don't add up the days—you take inventory at the end of the period, or perhaps an average over the period in question. It turns out that there are over a dozen different common rules for time-series data aggregation. The periodicity conversion program in one of Pilot's products cost over \$2 million to develop, so I have a good appreciation for the complexities of what appears to be a simple problem.

Another example of an application where middleware would probably be required might be anything where forecasting is required. For example, suppose a company has a database with daily sales data and the user wishes to see not only the daily actual numbers, but also a statistical forecast showing where he will be at the end of the month versus forecast. Statistical forecasting is not something that is easily done with either SQL or most front-end products. Again what is required is a computational engine (middleware) which extracts data from the database, computes the statistical forecasts, and then passes all the data along to the front-end for display.

9–6 Front-end GUI's

Front-end GUI's generally fall into three categories:

1   General purpose "Windows application tools"
2   Friendly SQL interfaces
3   Visual Information Access tools

Visual Information Access tools, such as Pilot's LightShip, are specifically designed to create end-user applications which access information in a semi-structured way. For example, I use a VIA application which allows me to look at current sales activity by product and sales region and compare these numbers against forecast and pipeline. While the data in this application is stored in an SQL database, my "view" of this data has nothing to do with SQL or relational data structures. I am simply presented with a screen that allows me to navigate from one view of data to another by pointing and clicking with my mouse. I never see the words "field," "record," or "select" or any other database terminology—just terms which are of specific meaning to my company's sales organization. My VIA tools have been used to create a unique application which insulates me from the structure of the underlying database.

More general purpose Windows development tools, such as Microsoft's *Visual Basic*, Borland's *Object Vision*, Asymmetrix's *Toolbook*, and so forth, can usually be made to deliver VIA-like functionality. However, all of these tools require learning a programming language and require significantly more development effort. In some cases, because of the general purpose nature of the product, certain functions will run unacceptably slowly and maintenance will be too costly.

All of these tools are "object-oriented." The difference between a VIA tool whose purpose is limited to reporting applications and general purpose Windows development tools is in the kinds of objects utilized to build an application. For example, one of the most basic capabilities of any reporting tool is the ability to display a properly formatted table of numbers.

	Actual	Budget	Variance
Sales	$13,420.01	$13,200.00	$220.01
Expenses	$10,204.00	$100,000.00	$204.00
Net Profit	$3,224.01	$3,200.00	$24.01

A properly formatted table of numbers is a basic part of any reporting system. A VIA tool ought to include a "document object" that can produce such tables with minimum development effort.

In a programming product like Visual Basic, the developer has no "table object" which automatically knows how to deal with arrays of numbers, so all of this must be created by writing many lines of computer code. A VIA tool, on the other hand, ought to include a table object which can be simply connected to a source of data using "point and click" methodology. Maintenance is also effected by the different kinds of tools. Changing the dollar signs to deutsche-mark signs, for instance, should be as simple as clicking on the table and changing the chart object characteristics. With a programming language development tool, the table is programmed using string manipulation, and the programmer would have to find all the instances of dollar signs and replace them. He would also have to change all the uses of commas and periods which are used differently when expressing values in deutsche marks.

Another example of native VIA capabilities should be the ability to read the contents of a cell on the screen. For example, a logical way to allow a user to see the details of "Sales," "Expenses," or "Net Profits" in the previous table would be to allow the user to simply point to the word on the screen and click the mouse. A VIA tool should be able to read the word you are pointing at and allow that word to be used in the next query to the database. Most general purpose Windows development tools will only feed back the X-Y coordinates of the mouse. It requires you to write the code to figure out what word the user is pointing at.

A third example is basic business graphs, such as bar charts or line charts. If graphical objects exist at all in general purpose Windows tools, they will be primitives such as rectangles, lines, circles, and so forth. Again, a great deal of effort is required to turn these primitives into an attractively designed bar chart with properly spaced scaling and so forth. A VIA tool, on the other hand, ought to support a "chart object" which can be visually linked to a table of numbers. Creating a bar chart in a VIA tool is considered basic reporting functionality and ought to take no more than a few minutes to set up (Figure 9-5).

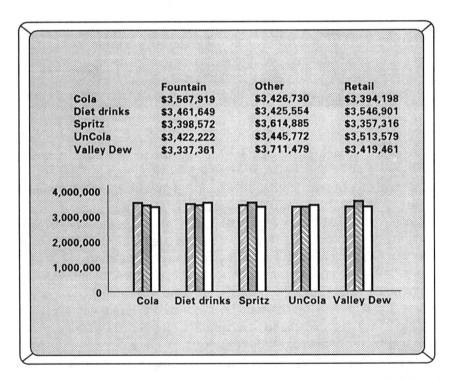

Fig. 9-5

In this example from Pilot's *LightShip,* a report screen is composed of just three simple objects: 1) a TEXT object for the heading, 2), a DOC-UMENT object for the data table, and 3), a CHART object for the bar chart which is linked to the DOCUMENT.

"Friendly query tools" such as Cognos' *Power Play* or Pioneer Software's *Q+E* represent the third major category of GUI front-ends. These tools are specifically oriented toward allowing non-technical users to formulate SQL queries without having to know the SQL syntax. These SQL query generators can make a useful adjunct to other GUI front-ends which have more application building capabilities.

9–7 Back-End Database Servers

Relational databases are good general purpose tools for storing and retrieving simple numerical data and short text strings. They are particularly useful where the inherent structure of the data maps nicely to the row and column format of a relational table. The classic example of a good use of a relational table is a human resources database with one record per employee. A good relational database can locate and retrieve an employee record in a few hundredths of a second.

Some data, however, are inherently structured in a way that maps awkwardly to a relational database. Sales and marketing data are the most obvious multi-dimensional data. For example, a major retailer uses an SQL database to collect daily sales data from 1,200 retail stores. They carry 30,000 different products and wish to store 3 years worth of daily sales data in order to facilitate year-to-year comparisons. In third normal form, the SQL table looks like this:

PRODUCT	STORE	DAY	SALES	PRICE
Prod A	A	1	2,310	15
Prod A	A	2	130	15
Prod A	A	3	0	15
Prod B	A	1	4,312	6
Prod B	A	2	0	6
Prod B	A	3	0	6
Prod A	B	1	145	15
Prod A	B	2	1,340	15
Prod A	B	3	0	15
		etc.		

A typical relational database containing 3rd Normal Form Data. 1,200 stores, 30,000 products, and 3 years of daily data results in a database with 36 billion records.

With 1,200 stores, 30,000 products, and approximately 1,000 days of historical information, this database contains 36,000,000,000 records. If a user of this database wished to total up sales for any one store for a week, the query would require that 30,000 × 7 or 210,000 records be retrieved and aggregated. Using DB2 on a typical IBM mainframe, this query would take approximately 1,000 seconds, or roughly 16 minutes.

Another problem with this particular database is that not every product is sold in every store on every day—there are a lot of zeros (this is known as "sparse data"). Also, the price of each product tends to repeat day after day. Rather than repeat, it would be more efficient if the database only needed to store price change events. A database which dealt efficiently with all the zeros and the redundant price data could store the same information in a fraction of the disk space.

The right way to store this kind of data is in a multi-dimensional data server. A multi-dimensional database is an n-dimensional cube of data which is designed to perform row and column arithmetic at spread-sheet speeds (Figure 9-6).

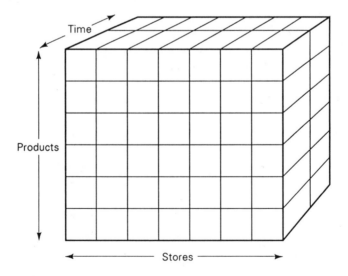

Fig. 9–6

The same data can be stored in an array of 1,200 stores by 30,000 products by 1,095 daily data points. Row and column arithmetic can be performed at spreadsheet speeds.

A multi-dimensional data server is a much better "fit" for this data. Now the user can perform row and column arithmetic at spreadsheet speeds, and it would be reasonable to expect that our 16 minute query could be sped up by at least one order of magnitude. This could mean the difference between a usable VIA application and one which is too slow to be usable.

There are other kinds of data structures that lend themselves to other specialized data servers. For example, many applications require access to text information, rather than numerical data. For such applications, a data server that can do a high-speed, full text search might be essential. Other applications need to store and retrieve images, maps, or diagrams. Still others need to be able to access voice or full motion video. The point is that data warehousing is one thing, but live data access is another. A database to support production transactional processing may be entirely different from the server in which the data is staged for live access and analysis.

9–8 Conclusion

The world is quickly getting used to the idea of turning to a computer screen rather than a stack of paper for day to day information needs. Live data reporting presents a new set of technological challenges and is promoting the creation of many new products. VIA tools will soon be an integral part of nearly every significant database application. As you migrate to this new way of providing reporting, the most important fact to keep in mind is that most reporting systems in the past have been based on batch processing. To make the leap to VIA, you have to think about more than a friendly front end to your SQL databases.

10

Toward Total Data Quality Management (TDQM)

Richard Y. Wang, Assistant Professor of Information Technologies, MIT Sloan School of Management and editor of this book, received his Ph.D. degree with a concentration in Information Technologies from MIT's Sloan School of Management. He has published extensively in the fields of database management systems, connectivity among information systems, and data quality management.

Professor Wang teaches a number of IT related courses at the graduate level, including one that provides a broad coverage of trends and perspectives in the computer industry. He is a principal investigator of several information technology related research projects. Most recently, he initiated a research program in Total Data Quality Management (TDQM). TDQM research investigates issues involved in data quality from both the technical and managerial perspectives.

Professor Wang is very active in professional services. He serves as a review for many research journals, conferences, and grant proposals. Most recently, he organized the annual workshop on Information Technologies and Systems (WITS), which brings IT researchers and practitioners together to exchange ideas and results.

Henry B. Kon, Pd.D. candidate, MIT Sloan School of Management, is actively investigating issues related to data quality. Prior to joining MIT, he worked in the IT area for over ten years with experience in the semiconductor, insurance, banking, medical products, transportation, and imaging and database technology development industries.

His education includes an undergraduate degree in electrical and biomedical engineering from Rutgers University, a graduate degree in computer science from New York University's Courant Institute of Mathematical Sciences, and he is now on his way towards the completion of his doctorate at MIT. His other interests include heterogeneous databases, software engineering, imaging, networking, and the application and management of information technologies to facilitate organizational solutions.

As we discussed in the previous chapters, the last decade has brought significant advancements in the research and application of IT in such areas as client/server and distributed computing, object-based approaches, and CASE. We are now better equipped than ever to quickly develop systems that deliver data from a variety of sources in a variety of formats. In the process, data has moved from being a "poor cousin" of the application program to being the core component of applications design, and data has become a product in its own right. This trend is becoming increasingly evident when one thinks of such new terms as information warehouse[1], national information infrastructure, and information marketplace.[2]

In Chapter 9, David Friend discussed how to put data in the hands of the user through visual information access systems.   An important question for the IS manager to follow up is, how good is that data? Bad data leads to bad decisions and unintended actions. If the end result of an information system is to deliver information, then a final measure of the success of an information system should be the quality of its data.

In this chapter, we discuss the following topics: (1) the impacts of data quality, (2) an analogy between product manufacturing and data manufacturing, (3) a framework for total data quality management, and (4) an approach to data quality management in an organizational setting. Enjoy IT.

10–1   Social and Managerial Impacts of Data Quality

Organizations across industries are increasingly integrating their business processes across functional, product, and geographic lines. As a result, many business activities require access to a variety of information systems within the company as well as access to data outside the organization. Unfortunately, these databases may contain poor quality data. *The Wall Street Journal* recently reported:

> Thanks to computers, huge databases brimming with information are at our fingertips, just waiting to be tapped. They can be mined to find sales prospects among existing customers; they can be analyzed to unearth costly corporate habits; they can be manipulated to divine

1. Information Warehouse Framework", *IBM Programming Announcement*. September 11, 1991

2. Dertuzos, Michael. "Building the Information Marketplace", *Technology Review*. January 1991.

future trends. Just one problem: Those huge databases may be full of junk.... In a world where people are moving to total quality management, one of the critical areas is data.[3]

Overall, poor quality data can have substantial impacts from both a social and a managerial perspective. In the next section we highlight the social ramifications and discuss three managerial perspectives of data quality: customer service, managerial support, and productivity.

Social Impacts: Privacy and Security

Errors in credit reporting are one of the most striking examples of the social consequences of poor quality data. The credit industry not only collects financial data on individuals, but also compiles employment records. In addition to the denial of credit, an error on a personal report can cause employment problems. One congressional witness testified that "he lost his job when he was reported as having a criminal record... a record that really belonged to a man with a similar name."[4] In light of such testimonies, congress is pushing for legislation to require that the credit industry retain accurate data no matter where the data originated.[5]

More generally, data is generated and used on a variety of potentially sensitive topics on individuals and organizations including data on medical, financial, employment, consumption, and legal activities. The organizations creating and using this data may include government agencies, insurance companies, banks, marketing, financial organizations, and countless others. The collectors, users, and subjects of this data may all have an interest in the quality of this data.

Managerial Impacts: Customer Service, Managerial Support, Productivity

In our effort to assess the managerial and economic impacts of data quality in corporate environments, we interviewed employees from many organizations, including the following which we will call Worldwide Shipping, Bullish Securities, and Comfortable Flight. Three areas where

3. Database Are Plagued By Reign of Error," *The Wall Street Journal.* May 26, 1992
4. *The Washington Post.* June 9, 1991
5. *Business Week International.* July 20,1991

data quality affects corporate profits for these organizations are illustrated below.

Customer Service. When higher data quality results in better customer service, there can be a direct positive impact on the bottom line. For example, Worldwide Shipping is one of the largest providers of international ocean freight services. Under the old way of doing business, collection methods for data on cargo and equipment inventories were highly labor-intensive and error-prone. Inaccuracies in the data were commonplace, often causing shipments to be sent to the wrong destination and sometimes to be lost altogether, resulting in unhappy customers, investigative efforts to locate lost goods, and rerouting.

In the late 1980's, among other quality control programs, Worldwide began installing radio frequency-based tracking mechanisms in their shipping ports to keep track of their containers, chassis, and trucks. The tracking mechanisms are much like bar-code scanners in that each container (i.e., "box" that sits on a truck's trailer) can be uniquely and reliably identified as it moves through checkpoints, with real-time transaction database updates.

The end result is that Worldwide can now provide up to the second and exact data to its customers about the location and, thus, the delivery schedules for their goods. Many customers consider this a critical factor in choosing Worldwide as their shipping vendor.

Managerial Support. Because it is strategic to an organizations success, the managerial decision-making arena is an area where data quality can impact the bottom line. With the proliferation of management support systems[6], more data will originate from databases both within and across organizational boundaries.

Bullish Securities, a major New York investment bank, illustrates the value of data in such systems. Recently, the bank implemented a risk management system to gather information documenting its securities positions. With complete and timely data, the system serves as a tool which executives use to monitor the firm's exposure to various market risks. However, when critical data was mismanaged, the system left the bank vulnerable to major losses. For example, during a recent incident, data availability and problems in timeliness caused the risk manage-

6. Rockart, J.F. and Short, J.E. "IT in the 1990's: Managing Organizational Interdependence." *Sloan Management Review.* Sloan School of Management, MIT 1989: 30 (2).

ment system to fail to alert management of a large interest rate exposure. When interest rates changed dramatically, Bullish was caught unaware and absorbed a net loss totaling more than $250 million.

Productivity. Productivity can be increased where low quality data causes lost revenues, unproductive re-work, downtime, redundant data entry, and the cost of data inspection. Comfortable Flight, a large U.S. airline company, inadvertently corrupted its database of passenger reservations while installing some new software that turned out to have bugs. Programmers fixed the software, but they didn't correct the false reservations it had made. As a result, planes for several months were taking off partly empty because of phantom bookings, impacting the bottom line significantly. More attention to the handling of the database could have prevented such a problem.

The above examples illustrate that data quality can affect both our personal and organizational lives. We now move on to describe the analogy between product manufacturing and data manufacturing.

10-2   From Product Manufacturing to Data Manufacturing

Organizations have learned that in order to deliver a quality product or service, they need to implement quality programs. Many corporations have devoted significant time and energy in a variety of quality initiatives such as inter-functional teams, reliability engineering, and statistical quality control. Much work on quality management for corporate productivity has been conducted in the field of manufacturing. Few organizations, however, have the processes, skills, or systems in place for managing the quality of their data.

It is interesting to note that fundamental analogies exist between quality issues in a manufacturing environment and those in an information systems environment. Manufacturing can be viewed as a processing system that acts on input material to produce output material. Analogously, an information system can be viewed as a processing system acting on input data to produce output data. Figure 10-1 illustrates this analogy.

From this, we can borrow principles of quality management established for product manufacturing to data manufacturing. For example, product manufacturing concepts such as customer satisfaction, conformance to specification, and zero-defect product can each be applied to data manufacturing.

	Product manufacturing	Data manufacturing
Input	Raw materials	Input data
Process	Manufacturing line	Information systems

Fig. 10-1
The analogy between product and data manufacturing

In general, manufacturing-related activities consist of two parts. One is the *design and implementation* of the manufacturing line, including engineering analysis, engineering specifications, and the implementation and deployment of hardware and software. This is typically performed by a manufacturing design and engineering group. The second is the *production and distribution* of the product. Typically, the people responsible for production inherit the line from or work with the designers and engineers, and put the line to use. Product quality is a function of both of these, the manufacturing machinery as well as the methods and skills applied at production time.

These two concepts have exact analogs in the data manufacturing domain, discussed next.

The Data Systems Life Cycle

Before we begin to think about the improvement of data quality, we need to develop a basic conceptual framework. We use our manufacturing analogy to consider two domains of activity. The first is the *design and implementation* of the information system, the second is the *production and distribution* of the data. We refer to these as the data systems life cycle and the data product value chain.

The *Data Systems Life Cycle* (Figure 10-2(a)) focuses on the activities that go into the design, development, testing, and deployment to the user community of the information system. Because the data that results from an information system is a function of all of these activities, each one must be considered a potential target area for data quality improvement. Consider the following three examples of quality issues related to the data systems life cycle: (1) the data designed into the system is not the data required by the users (requirements analysis); (2) the testing of software and database functionality is incomplete and corrupted data results (software QA); (3) the user community is inadequately trained in the input and retrieval of data from the system (training).

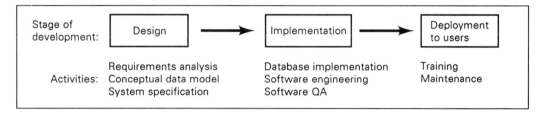

Fig. 10–2(a)
The Data Systems Life Cycle (The Data Manufacturing System)

The Data Product Value Chain

The data product value chain (Figure 10-2(b)) highlights different aspects of data production. This value chain represents a three-way division of labor involving the handling of data.

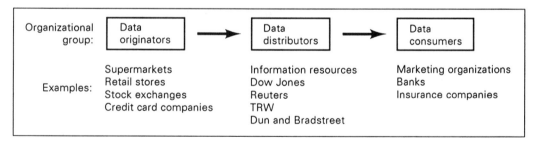

Fig. 10-2(b)
The Data Product Value Chain (Data Production)

Data originators generate data having value to others; for example, supermarkets collect and resell point-of-sale data. Data distributors purchase data from the originators and resell it to consuming organizations; for example, Information Resources, Inc. (IRI) purchases point-of-sale data from supermarkets, analyzes and processes it, and then resells it to consumer marketing firms such as General Mills. Finally, consuming organizations are those which acquire data generated externally. For example, banks buy credit data from distributors such as TRW and Dun & Bradstreet.

With the exception of distributors, most companies do not belong solely to one group or another. In fact, most organizations are vertically integrated with respect to data flows, with different departments each performing different functions. For example, a marketing organization may consume data (e.g., on customer buying) generated by the finance organization. As a result of vertical integration, most IS organizations have responsibility for each function: data origination, internal distribution, and consumption of both internally and externally generated data.

In summary, data manufacturing consists of two components: the data manufacturing system and the data production process. The data manufacturing system corresponds to the data systems life cycle and the data production process corresponds to the data product value chain.

In the next section we introduce a framework for total data quality management (TDQM). This framework outlines the scope of issues and concepts related to quality data as a product and data quality improvement as an organizational process.

10–3   A Framework for Total Data Quality Management

Quality control and management have become competitive necessities for most businesses today, and there is a rich experience on the topic of quality that dates back several decades. Approaches range from technical, such as statistical process control, to managerial, such as quality circles. An analogous experience base is needed for data quality. But how do we reduce the myriad of complex issues around data quality into manageable concepts and tractable solutions? We introduce a TDQM framework, shown in Figure 10-3, to deal with these issues.

This framework includes two primary interrelated dimensions:

- three components of the continuous data quality enhancement process: *measurement*, *analysis*, and *improvement*, and

- three perspectives on which to base solutions: *economics*, *technology*, and *organizations*.

It suggests that at the highest level, data quality efforts can be motivated by needs for quality business operations. Different steps of the business value chain may have different types of data requirements. The next two sections describe these dimensions in more detail.

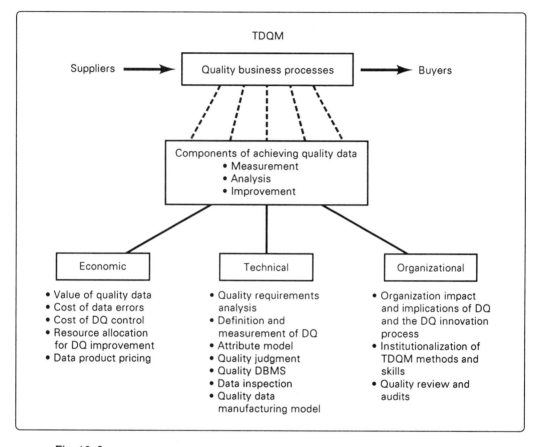

Fig. 10-3
The TDQM Schematic— a Perspective of Data Quality

Continuous Measurement, Analysis, and Improvement

The three components of the quality enhancement process are *measurement* and definition of data quality, *analysis* of the economic impact on the business based on data quality, and *improvement* of data quality through both technical and managerial solutions. They are diagrammed in Figure 10-4, and are discussed in more detail below.

Measurement of Data Quality. Although the notion of data quality sounds intuitive, most notions of "data quality" in current practice are not well defined. Most people, when asked about data quality, respond

with such terms as accuracy and timeliness, but when asked for definitions of these terms come to realize the subtlety of the concepts involved.
A consensus and clear definition of data quality is needed.

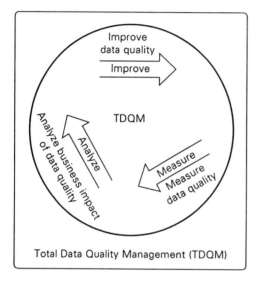

Fig. 10-4
The MAI Perspective of Data Quality

Our studies have revealed that data consumers use multiple dimensions when they think about data quality, such as accuracy, believability,
relevance, timeliness, and completeness.[7] In fact, even the most obvious
dimension, Accuracy, does not have a sufficiently robust definition. Thus
any attempt to *create* quality data is limited by our lack of *understanding*
of its basic ingredients. The measurement component addresses issues of
data quality definition, measurement, and derivations.

Analysis of Data Quality Impact on Business. This component
addresses the value chain relationship between *high quality* data and
the successful operation of the business, and alternatively, how *low quality* data impacts the business.

For example, in a transportation company it was determined that
poor data quality and usage was the cause of 77% of the delivery misses

7. Guarrascio, L.M. and Wang, R.Y., "Dimensions of Data Quality: Beyond Accuracy."
   (CISL-91-06) Composite Information Systems Laboratory, Sloan School of Management,
   MIT, June 1991.

which in turn was the major reason for an estimated loss of about $1 billion in sales, based on lost market share. Analysis techniques relate data quality to key business parameters, such as sales, customer satisfaction, and profitability.

Improvement of Data Quality. This component addresses various methods for improving data quality. These methods can be grouped into three interrelated categories:

- business redesign,

- data quality motivation, and

- the use of new technologies.

Business redesign attempts to simplify and streamline the operation to minimize the opportunity for data errors to occur. Data quality motivation focuses on how rewards, benefits, and perceptions may encourage improved data handling by members of the organization. New technologies focus on improving procedures for data capture and processing through techniques such as data entry in remote or mobile situations, direct inter-computer communications, and computer-assisted quality control. For example, in the transportation company example, radio frequency-based data entry devices (for equipment and cargo inventories data capture) were introduced in moving vehicles which scanned up and down the container yards. This introduced both a new technology and a business redesign, resulting in more accurate and timely data.

In the next section we describe the second dimension which focuses on perspectives, rather than activities related to data quality enhancement.

Economic, Technical, and Organizational Perspectives

The second dimension focuses less on how to implement a data quality enhancement process, and more on defining perspectives relevant to its analysis. Next we describe how each of these perspectives, economic, technical, and organizational, are related to data quality.

The *economic* perspective deals with issues of valuation such as how much would it cost to achieve quality data, how much it is worth, and how to allocate resources for data quality. Under constrained resources, clearly not all data quality problems or opportunities can be simultaneously addressed.

The *technology* perspective deals with defining and measuring data quality as well as systems and methods for the enhancement of data quality. This is a fairly broad component in that there are applications for technologies at virtually every point on the data systems life cycle and the data product value chain. For example, tools that support data quality requirements analysis, statistical process control for data quality, and advanced data acquisition devices can be used in various capacities. These tools will facilitate the data quality administration function.

The *organizational* perspective deals with the implications of data quality on the social fabric of the firm. It considers issues related to the motivation and responses of both individuals and groups towards organizational change and the proper handling of data. This may include the process of developing organizational commitment to data quality, the technology infrastructure development, modifications of incentives towards data handling, and the overall institutionalization of methods for enhancing data quality.

We have discussed the analogy between product manufacturing and data manufacturing, outlined relevant perspectives (economics, technology, and organization) and components (measurement, analysis, and improvement) of data quality enhancement that we believe are fundamental to TDQM.

The concepts we have developed so far in this chapter do not address improvement of data quality in an organizational setting. After going through the exercise of defining relevant aspects of data quality, there are questions that come to mind: *Where from here? What should change in my organization today? Who will carry out these changes?* Below we provide a managerial perspective to address these questions.

10–4   Managing Data Quality

Implementing a data quality improvement program requires significant organizational change as well as the adoption of new management techniques and technologies. Following Tribus, an authority on the implementation of Demming's quality management principles, we group the required organizational changes into five categories:

1   Clearly articulate a data quality vision in business terms.

2   Establish central responsibility for data quality within IS groups and functional groups interacting with IS.

3   Educate project and systems managers.

4   Teach new data quality skills to the entire IS organization.

5   Institutionalize continuous data quality improvement.

Each of these is discussed individually in the next five subsections.

Clearly Articulate a Data Quality Vision

In order to improve quality, one must first set quality standards. Such standards should be expressed by users in business terms. For example, Mayflower Bank, a large U.S. bank, states in a Data Administration Task Force Report, "customer service and decision making will be unconstrained by the availability, accessibility, or accuracy of data held in automated form on any strategic platform."

Since leadership is crucial in the early stages of any quality improvement program, the data quality vision must be clearly identified with top level management in IS. The chief information officer (CIO) must make data quality a priority for the entire organization.

Establish Central Responsibility for Data Quality Within IS

Once a vision has been articulated, the organization needs to establish responsibility for data quality. Ultimately, this responsibility rests with the CIO, but another person, reporting directly to the CIO, needs to be given day-to-day responsibility for data quality. Some organizations proclaim that quality is "everybody's responsibility," but in practice this often leads to confusion and inaction. For these reasons, a data administrator (DA) must be given responsibility and authority for assuring data quality explicitly.

Where the database administrator (DBA) tends to be systems-oriented, the DA should be more managerial and analytical. The DA is responsible for making sure that data resources are managed to meet business needs. For larger organizations, the DA should head a data administration staff which serves as a center of expertise on the application of quality management within the IS organization.

In most organizations today, data administration is restricted to a fairly low level function concerned primarily with the development of data models. In the future, organizations will need to enhance the power and prestige of data administration in order to provide a credible and effective center of responsibility for data quality management.

We broadly consider three aspects of the data quality improvement process: breakthroughs, iterative improvement, and maintenance. These represent the complexity of the data quality-related innovation as well as the level of effort and change entailed by the improvement effort. Figure 10-5 indicates that the data administrator has responsibilities spread across breakthroughs and iterative improvements.

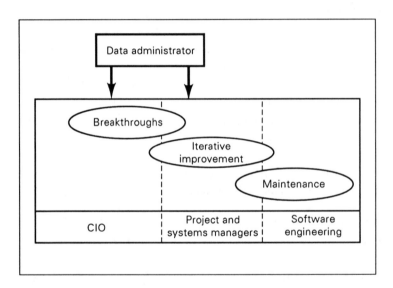

Fig. 10-5

Allocation of Responsibility for Data Quality Improvements

In the area of breakthroughs, the data administrator coordinates work with the CIO and senior level management to identify systems redesign projects and new technologies which could have a large impact on the organization's management of data quality. In terms of less radical, iterative improvements, the data administrator serves as a central source of information and guidance which project and systems managers can access regarding data quality matters. Maintenance involves more traditional activities associated with data applications, where attention to data quality would be applied to the installed base of systems.

Our case studies illustrate the variety of approaches organizations are taking to assigning responsibility for data quality. For example, Mayflower Bank outlined a breakthrough technological initiative centered around the creation of a data administrator position. The data administrator will be responsible for the development and installation of a *data delivery utility architecture* for corporate data. As the corporation's official source of data, this system's primary function is to serve as a regulated, central repository for data storage and standards enforcement. Updating and accessing stored data will occur via a set of coordinated technologies designed to ensure data quality.

In a contrasting example, Materials Manufacturing, a multinational corporation, has chosen not to centralize data quality administration, and is instead pushing responsibility back to the sources of the data. This is in line with their corporate goals of ensuring quality at the source, minimizing inspection processes, and corporate movements towards distributed systems.

Thus, we see centralization and decentralization as two fundamentally different approaches to data quality improvement. Each may carry its own rewards and pitfalls and must be considered in the context of a given data quality improvement effort. A hybrid approach may be the most reasonable in the short term given the immaturity of data warehouse technology as well as rapid change in the areas of in client/server and distributed computing.

Educate Project and Systems Managers

Once central responsibility for data quality management has been established, the stage is set to begin educating those people in the organization who will take charge of improvements in data quality. Within IS, these are the project and systems managers. These managers must learn the relationship between quality and productivity so that they consider investing the time and resources appropriate to improving data quality. Beyond this, they must learn specific methods of data quality improvement that are relevant to their projects or systems. For project development managers, this means learning to view data quality as a fundamental objective. For systems managers, it means learning to apply quality principles to monitor and improve data-handling systems.

Teach New Data Quality Skills to the Entire IS Organization

Responsibility for the successful implementation and maintenance of quality programs belongs to the entire organization. Hence, the entire IS organization may need new skills in order to put new programs into place.

In general, data quality responsibilities will fall into one or more of the following three categories: inspection and data entry, process control, and systems design. Below we discuss the three categories of data quality responsibility and the relevant skills required for each.

Inspection and Data Entry. Inspection and data entry involve responsibility for the accuracy of data as it is transcribed into a system or at interim points during processing of the data by the system. Current practice for data inspection remains mostly manual, although interactive and forms-based user interfaces can be used to filter out or detect errors. Mayflower Bank has established corporate policies on data entry urging that

- data should be entered into machine form only once (e.g., not copied from computer to paper to computer),

- data should be obtained as close as possible to the point of data origin, and

- newly entered data should be subject to automated edits, consistency checks, and audits as appropriate.

Process Control. Process control involves maintaining and monitoring the performance of systems with respect to data quality management. In addition to statistical quality control, the training required here involves the use of auditability tools for tracking down the source of data quality problems. In one data quality survey, over 50% of respondents expressed difficulty in tracking down the sources of data quality problems.[8] In addition, people with process control responsibilities frequently need training in procedures for the uploading and downloading of data. Mayflower determined that any uploading of data to the mainframe should require the same editing and consistency checks required of newly entered data.

8. Hansen, M. and Wang, R.Y., "Managing Data Quality: A Critical Issue for the Decade to Come" *(CISL-90-05) Composite Information Systems Laboratory*, Sloan School of Management, MIT, December 1990.

Systems Design. Finally, systems design involves building new systems or upgrading existing applications with data quality management as a primary design goal. In this area there are a host of tools and techniques which professional IS developers should learn in order to design systems which are compatible with data quality goals (e.g., CASE tools, data modeling, intelligent user interface design, data warehouses, and auditing tools).

For example, with respect to systems design, Mayflower is in the process of developing and installing a data warehouse. Achieving this will require corporate IS to define which data is needed from the divisions, how often to upload it, and where it should reside. In this manner, the data warehouse addresses interpretability, availability, and timeliness as well as accuracy.

(Note that inspection and data entry would fall under the data product value chain; systems design would fall under the data systems life cycle; and process control may fall under both.)

Institutionalize Continuous Data Quality Improvement

Once the entire organization has received the necessary training and data quality improvement plans have been put into action, it is necessary for top management to ensure that the data quality improvement process becomes institutionalized. For example, regular meetings, presentations, and reporting structures should be established to track the organization's progress in meeting data quality goals. Additionally, data quality improvement projects need to become part of the budgetary process.

Operationalizing Data Quality Management

In order to define continuous improvement projects, organizations should focus on *critical success factors* in order to identify operational objectives critical to the successful management of data quality. Based on interviews and surveys, five critical success factors have been identified: (1) certify existing corporate data; (2) standardize data definitions; (3) certify external data sources; (4) control internal data; and (5) provide data auditability.

Figure 10-6 illustrates the systems and data sources these five critical success factors impact. *Certifying existing corporate data* implies providing a guarantee that the corporate data, depicted in the center, satisfies the quality requirements of existing applications. *Standardizing data definitions* ensures that all data flows (indicated by arrows) among systems adhering to the standard can be implemented in a straightforward manner. *Certifying external data sources* involves ensuring that the sources depicted in the outer ring have acceptably low error rates. Similarly, *controlling internal data* implies certifying all of the applications depicted in the inner circle, as well as their interfaces with the corporate data. Finally, providing *data auditability* implies that when data quality problems are detected in the corporate data, they can be traced to the source, whether it be internal or external.

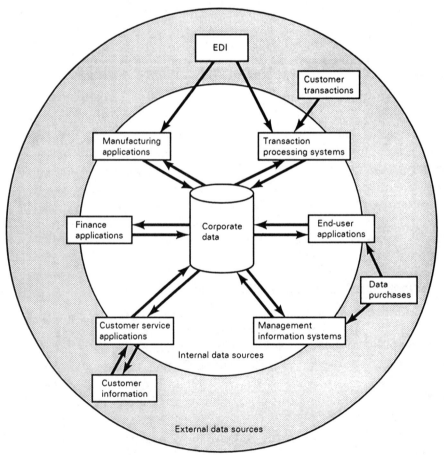

Fig. 10–6
External and Internal Sources for Data Quality Management

10–5   Concluding Remarks

In this chapter, we have discussed several issues. First we introduced the concept of data quality, providing broad definitions of the term and discussing impacts and motivation for the issue.

Next we presented a fundamental analogy between product manufacturing and data manufacturing that leads to the data aystems life cycle and the data product value chain as a means of describing the range of activity involved in data production. We provided a framework for total data quality management describing activities related to continuous data quality measurement, analysis, and improvement from economic, technical, and organizational perspectives. Finally, we discussed the improvement of data quality in an organizational setting.

Following the analogy between manufacturing and information systems, we have argued that there is a significant amount of economic benefit to be gained if data quality can be managed effectively. The issues involved range from technical to managerial. They may depend on the nature of the data itself, the application of the data, the information systems involved, and the related organizational and economic superstructures around the information systems.

We are actively conducting research along the following directions: How do we define and measure data quality? What kinds of information technologies can be developed to certify data and to provide data auditability? What kinds of operations management techniques can be applied to develop a foundation for data quality management? Should data originators, data distributors, and data consumers manage data quality problems differently, or is there a single underlying issue? What is the relationship between data quality and corresponding data characteristics? These inquiries will help develop a body of knowledge for data quality management — a critical issue for the decade to come.

Perspectives on the IT Industry

We have presented trends in the IT industry. In this part of the book, we present perspectives of different communities of the IT industry. First, the media's perspective is presented through the lens of Computerworld and The Wall Street Journal in Chapters 11-12. Paul Gillin, Executive Editor of Computerworld, tells the story behind the stories reported by Computerworld and Bill Bulkeley, a veteran staff reporter of The Wall Street Journal, shows how to read The Journal.

Next, in Chapter 13, we present the investor's perspective through the lens of Wall Street. This perspective is presented by Rick Sherlund, Vice President and Senior Analyst in the Investment Research Department at Goldman, Sachs & Co. Rick is frequently quoted by The Wall Street Journal and interviewed by the Nightly Business Report (NBR) on issues related to the software industry. The consultant's perspective is presented in Chapter 14 by Peter DiGiammarino, one of the top executives of AMS, and Charles Rossotti, Chairman, President, and Chief Executive of AMS. They present a model that helps define the market served and the services provided by AMS and other IT consulting firms.

The CIO's perspective is presented in Chapter 15 by Michael Zucchini, who is an executive vice president and CIO of Fleet Financial Group. In communicating the perspective of the CIO, Michael chooses to focus on the financial services industry and to frame his insights in the context of a practical, day-to-day reality in the banking business, where the role of the CIO has become critical in the age of consolidation.

The conclusion is presented in Chapter 16 by Stuart Madnick, who is the John Norris Maguire Professor of Information Technology and Leaders for Manufacturing Professor of Management Science at the MIT Sloan School of Management. In his view, most businesses large and small around the world, are facing twin crises in the business environment and information technology. How they respond to these crises will determine the winners and the losers. This concluding chapter offers a vision on how to "put IT all together before it falls apart." Enjoy IT.

The Media's Perspective: *Computerworld*

Paul Gillin, Executive Editor of *Computerworld*, has ten years of experience as a writer and editor in the computer industry, including five years as executive editor of *Computerworld*, a respected weekly newspaper for information system management. He oversees the operations of the newspaper's 57-person staff and is responsible for setting editorial direction.

Gillin has covered all aspects of corporate computing from microcomputers to corporate information systems. He is a frequent speaker at user group meetings and on college campuses as well as on radio and TV. He is also on the advisory boards of several major computer industry trade shows.

Prior to joining *Computerworld* in his current position, he was executive news editor of *Digital Review*, where he helped manage that publication's conversion from magazine to newspaper format. He was also a senior editor at *PC Week*. He began his career in computer journalism at *Computerworld* in 1982, where he covered large systems software and worked to establish that paper's first PC section. He holds a B.S. in journalism from Boston University.

W e read IT-related trade publications as part of our professional activities. The media plays an influential role in the dynamics of the IT industry, and whoever understands the media will clearly have a competitive edge over those who do not. The important things to know about the media include how reporters write stories, how journal editors select stories to print, and how the reader should read between the lines. In this chapter, Paul Gillin tell us the stories behind the story. Enjoy IT.

11–1 Introduction

Every Monday morning, four milk crates full of mail weighing about 120 pounds are delivered to *Computerworld's* editorial department in Framingham, Massachusetts. It will be the first of three deliveries that day.

At about the same time, the daily newspapers arrive, brimming with business news. They must be scoured, and relevant stories passed along to reporters for follow-up. Early in the week, between 20 and 30 computer trade publications arrive, adding another 3,000 pages of computer-related reading matter.

At 10:30, a dozen Federal Express packages are delivered, most of them from computer technology firms. The *Business Wire* news service has been in action for about two hours. By the end of the day it will have emitted a five-inch-thick stack of neatly perforated information.

During the day, information will continue to pour in. One of our networking editors will conclude a half-hour phone interview to find that she has received eight phone-mail messages during the call. The fax machine will be busy constantly; it's not unusual for 60 pages of faxes to arrive overnight. And MCIMail and Compuserve will add their share of electronic chatter: letters from readers, press releases, and assorted other bits of industry news.

Welcome to the newsroom at a major computer publication. It's a scene that is played out at high-tech publishers and business newspapers around the world every day. The sheer volume of information arriving in our offices could keep one person busy almost full time just parceling it out to reporters. Sifting through it and deciding what to act on and what to ignore can involve literally thousands of decisions in a single day. And if our editors miss an important story they have to be prepared to explain how it happened and why it won't happen again

When I started covering the IT industry at *Computerworld* in 1982 you could count the number of significant publications in the field on the fingers of both hands. There were two weekly newspapers, one bi-weekly tabloid, and a handful of monthlies. Most were dedicated to data processing management or highly specialized technical topics like software development.

Today, computer publishing is one of the largest special-interest publishing categories in the world. By my own count, there are at least a dozen weekly computer publications, about as many bi-weeklies, and countless monthly magazines. The *Standard Rate and Data Service* guide to business publications lists more than 200 computer titles in such specialty areas as portable computing, Hewlett-Packard systems, or imaging technology. *Computerworld's* parent company, International Data Group, publishes more than 150 newspapers and magazines around the world devoted solely to information technology. In addition, major daily publications like *The Wall Street Journal*, *The New York Times*, and *USA Today* devote substantial resources and editorial space to high-technology news.

Why such an explosion of activity in so little time?

Because in less than ten years, computing has become so much a part of the fabric of American business, education, and home life that it has created a seemingly unquenchable thirst for information about products, applications, and trends. As applications of computers have become more specialized, information needs have also become narrower. There are computing magazines for bankers, doctors, accountants, teachers, librarians, engineers, physicists, and federal government employees. If you're interested in information about buying and using PC's, you could read magazines literally around the clock and still not keep up.

Information overload has become one of the thorniest problems facing IT professionals. A typical Fortune 500 IS manager's office is strewn with trade publications, more than anyone can hope to read in a busy week. Information overload consistently ranks among the top concerns of IS managers as evidenced by our own readership studies. Faced with cost-cutting pressure from top management, end-user demands for more information access and the quickening march of technology, many IT people feel helpless in the struggle to keep up with the pace of change in their profession. Most don't even try. Successful IS managers limit their reading to those publications that they trust and which have the best understanding of their needs. It's the only way to cope.

11–2 The Understanding Gap

With so much printed and electronic information available from so many different sources, you would assume that every angle has been covered. But in reality, media coverage of IT is quite narrow. Much of it concentrates on the products and political jostling of the industry's biggest players with relatively little attention to the bigger picture of how computers are changing the way we live and work. This isn't surprising: As I noted at the outset of this chapter, just keeping up with change in this frantic industry is difficult enough.

But change is occurring. The media stands at a turning point in its ability to understand and communicate both the promise and problems that IT presents to society. As IT has grown from a cottage industry into a $150 billion money machine in just a few years, the media has increasingly had to balance the difficulty of understanding complex technology with the need to cover it intelligently.

Throughout the 1960's and 70's there was little general media coverage of IT. Computers were back-room monsters managed by teams of nameless technicians who specialized in obscure technologies. IT had little direct impact on our lives and received correspondingly little media attention.

With the advent of the personal computer and dramatic advances in ease of use during the 1980's, the computer became a more important part of out lives. The media took interest. Unfortunately, computing is not easy to understand. The mind cannot comprehend the size of a trillion-byte database or the concept of operations occurring at the speed of light. The fact that such advances were possible led to a spate of "gee whiz" technology coverage during the early and mid-80's. Reporters dazzled by product demonstrations often didn't think to ask what practical value a new product might have or even if the vendor had the wherewithal to develop and ship the product on time. As a result, coverage focused on the technology, not its practical value. Sometimes things get out of hand. In 1984, a startup company called Ovation Technologies received extensive and enthusiastic media coverage for a product it never finished. At one point, the company even issued a press release describing the product as a market industry leader despite the fact that it didn't exist. When Ovation fell, it fell hard. The experience sobered many of us in the press, who realized that amid all the hoopla, we had failed to ask the fundamental question: Did Ovation work?

Media coverage of IT has improved greatly since then, but it still tends to focus disproportionately on advanced technologies and hot companies at the expense of the larger societal issues. Some reasons:

1   *The industry has been a financial high-flyer that has made a lot of people a lot of money.* Industry success stories are intriguing because the winners can rise so far so fast. As a result, people like Microsoft billionaire Bill Gates have been covered as curiosities—circus side-

show attractions—rather than as leaders of a revolution in the workplace. How have Microsoft's products changed the way Americans work? Is the company addressing the fundamental problem of American productivity? What are Microsoft's relations like with its customers? It's hard to tell from the distracting media focus on Gates and Microsoft's success.

The computer industry's personalities are fascinating. The field tends to attract extremely bright (and often quirky) people who work at the frontiers of new technology. Their technical and financial achievements, often at a very early age, make for great human interest reading, and that is what the media thrives on.

2   *Computer technology is still incomprehensible to the average person.* This is no fault of the reader or reporter. Rather, the IT industry has wrapped itself in a cloak of jargon and self-congratulatory technobabble that distracts attention from more meaningful issues. Thus we have plenty of stories on the race to build faster machines, but comparatively little coverage of the terrible incompatibility problems that face IT professionals trying to connect their systems together. The hardware story plays well to a reader with limited technical knowledge: It's easy to understand that one machine is faster than another. And few readers have the time or patience to learn about why different flavors of UNIX won't play together. The media covers the hardware performance wars because the issues are relatively simple. And the industry, which would rather not face up to the thornier implementation problems that vex every IT professional, is happy to have it that way.

3   *Computer companies have great PR.* They play the media like a violin, stoking the appetite for "gee-whiz" technology, but downplaying questions about its practical use. As a result, technologies like fiber-optic communications, CD-ROM, videotext, on-line consumer databases, pen computing, and virtual reality generate huge amounts of coverage despite limited commercial demand. These technologies aren't necessarily failures, but their glitzy facade creates excitement that's out of proportion. I am often amazed by how unprepared high-tech companies are to promote the successes of their customers. They are so focused on product that they pay little attention to value.

The media needs to shake loose from this tendency to be blinded by high technology. Fortunately, there are encouraging signs. The turning point may well have come in November, 1988, when a smart, young Cornell University graduate student sent out a mischievous "worm" program on the Internet research computer network. Robert Tappan Morris didn't expect his prank to cause any damage, but because of his own coding error, the program began to copy itself madly over the network. Within a few hours, over 6,000 computers on the Internet had been shut down by the worm and other users were scrambling frantically to intercept the program before it struck their machines.

The media covered the Internet worm extensively and intelligently. The fiasco pointed out computer vulnerability to sabotage and demonstrated that significant productive time could be disrupted by technology problems. For once, computers became a news story not for their technical marvels, but because of their shortcomings.

The Michelangelo virus hysteria of March, 1992 carried that theme forward. There is no question that fears of a massive computer virus-infection on March 6 were blown far out of proportion and that the media played a big role in fanning the flames. But Michelangelo was potentially a very serious problem, and media attention no doubt saved many users from losing weeks or months worth of work. Like the Internet worm, this story was significant because it drew attention to how important computers have become in our lives and how that reliance carries with it a certain amount of risk.

These are just two notable examples of how the media is building awareness of IT as a life style and not just a technology issue. There are many more. Increased coverage of security breaches by hackers, high-tech successes and failures in the Persian Gulf, abuses of consumer credit information by credit bureaus, privacy issues, and the risks and rewards of demographic target marketing are some other stories that have received close attention from the general media. IT is coming to be seen not as a cure-all, but as an advance in human development that also presents a very imposing set of problems. However, the media has only scratched the surface in documenting what those problems are and how we can cope with them.

11–3 Understanding the Computer Press

If you're an IT professional, you will probably come to rely heavily on the computer trade press for information relevant to your job. Trade publications exist to help you work smarter. They hope that if they're successful at that, you will read them regularly. Then they can sell advertisers on the merits of putting their messages in front of your nose as you leaf through the pages.

The following pages should give you some insight into how the computer trade press works and how you can get more out of what you read. I won't attempt to cover the general or business media in much detail; I've done little work in those areas and they fulfill a very different role from the computer trades. Rather, use these remarks to make decisions about which publications to trust and which to avoid.

The task of choosing which publications to read can seem overwhelming, but it doesn't have to be. Computer publications fall into three basic categories: industry-specific, functional, and technology-specific. High-level IS managers generally try to read at least one key publication in each category. Each type of computing publication has a unique set of characteristics.

Industry-specific These publications focus on computer use in your company's main line of business. Examples include *Bank Systems & Technology*, *Managing Automation*, *Computers in Libraries*, and *Federal Computer Week*. Editorial tends to be less technical than what you'll find in functional or technology-specific books. Articles are oriented toward business issues, personalities, and innovative uses of computers by businesses in your field. This is also an excellent place to keep track of product developments that relate directly to your business.

Functional This highly competitive category addresses interests common to a specific professional function within IT. Examples include *Computerworld* (IS management), *Network World* (network management), *Infoworld* (end-user computing management), *Computer Reseller News* (computer dealers), and *Software Magazine* (software developers). Within each major function, there are often two or more news-oriented tabloid weeklies who compete vigorously and several feature-rich monthly magazines.

Functional publications are doing their jobs well if they help you do your job better. Editorial covers major new products, technical and strategic issues relating to your job function, career development advice, and news about what your peers are doing in other companies.

Technology-specific   Probably the largest category by circulation, technology-specific publications address machines and what makes them tick. Examples include *PC Magazine, Macworld, PC World*, and *Sunworld*. PC publications are by far the biggest, with circulations of up to 800,000. These publications compete to give readers the greatest amount of information about the greatest number of products. This is the most technical publishing group, often relying on extensive lab testing and benchmarking and vast new product listings. You can get lost in these magazines. They frequently exceed 400 pages in size.

There is sometimes considerable crossover between technology-specific and functional publications. *Digital News*, for example, is aimed at managers of Digital Equipment Corp. computers. Since many companies use DEC as their data processing standard, *Digital News* also contains a healthy amount of management information and news about non-DEC issues, such as open systems and internetworking. A VAX systems manager might satisfy his information needs by reading the weekly *Computerworld* for information about the IS management field in general, the fortnightly *Digital News* for an update on DEC and the large DEC third party market, and *DEC Professional* for technical information specific to VAX technology. He might also subscribe to an industry-specific technology magazine as well as to a daily business paper that keeps him abreast of breaking news. Thus, with five publications, his information needs are pretty well covered.

11–4 How One Computer Publication Covers IT

Computerworld has covered corporate information systems since 1967. It is one of the largest and—according to numerous readership studies—most respected publications in the field. Over the years we have experimented with many different ways of approaching our job and settled on a few rules that work. While every trade publication goes about its business differently, most of the news-weeklies follow a set of guidelines that are pretty consistent from one publication to another. Understanding how we work may help you get more out of the publications you read.

Audience

Computerworld is a functional newspaper for information systems managers and those who aspire to be information systems managers. Our audience has remained basically the same for 25 years, although the interests and information needs of IS managers have changed radically over time. The key to our success is understanding the needs of our target readers thoroughly and building that understanding into every story. Focus is the key to success in business, and the same principle holds true in publishing. When a publication fails, chances are it has lost touch with its readers, or its readers have ceased to exist as an identifiable group. We have many ways of keeping in contact with our readers.

1 ***Readership Studies***   Every three months we send out 2,000 surveys at random to people on our subscriber list. We get between 650 and 800 responses. We ask a series of questions about our readers' jobs, professional interests, and reading habits. The results of these surveys play a decisive role in shaping our editorial coverage. For example, in 1990 we detected a decisive shift toward reader interest in technology-specific publications and cost-justification issues. We responded by expanding our technical sections and adding buyer-oriented features. Later readership studies showed that the steps we took had successfully addressed these changing reader concerns. If you subscribe to a trade publication, chances are good you'll get one of these surveys at some point. I urge you to fill it out. It makes a difference.

2 ***Focus Groups***   As useful as quantitative research is, sometimes it's useful just to listen to people talk. That's why we use focus groups. Led by a professional moderator, these small groups of eight to ten readers provide us valuable gut-level feedback on how they like *Computerworld* as it is and how they react to any proposed changes. It's rare that we make any major change to the paper without bouncing it off at least a couple of focus groups.

3 ***Direct Reader Contact***   We have 57 people on our editorial staff of whom about 40 actively write and edit stories. Writers are required to contact IS managers in the process of reporting every significant news or feature story. Generally, the people contacted are users of a specific product or customers of a company that is in the story. This practice is a key "reality check" that keeps writers think-

ing of reader needs in every story they report. In addition, we expect our writers to travel extensively, attending trade shows and management conferences and visiting individual users. The user site visit is a staple at *Computerworld* because it puts writers into a reader's home territory where they can get a much better sense of the day-to-day pressures that affect our audience.

4 ***Other Quantitative Research*** We spend over $200,000 a year conducting user surveys on a wide variety of topics ranging from buying plans to product satisfaction to management issues. The results of these surveys appear as news or feature stories and keep us in constant contact with user concerns in specific areas.

Beats

Our reporters work on "beats," meaning that they are responsible for covering news, issues, and trends in specific technology areas. We have never found a substitute for technology beats. The reality is that the IS field is technology-driven and readers tend to be interested in specific product categories.

We divide the IT world into three basic categories: systems, software, and networking. Within each category there can be subcategories, such as PC's, workstations, minicomputers, mainframes, and supercomputers in the systems area or PC applications and PC operating systems within software.

Breaking the world down into categories allows us to more easily assign beats according to a reporter's background. For example, a writer who has experience watching the PC applications software area can transfer some of those skills to minicomputer applications because many of the concepts are the same. Similarly, one reporter may cover both local area network and host-centric network management because the technology is basically the same. Only the scale is different.

Some reporters are assigned to cover certain companies in whole or in part. For example, Microsoft is such an influential company that it justifies having two reporters assigned to it, one on the systems software side and the other watching applications. Meanwhile, the Microsoft systems software reporter also covers IBM's OS/2 business, because that is a very direct Microsoft competitor.

Finally, we have other reporters dedicated to covering issues and news relating to IS management. This is the very heart of our reader-focused coverage and requires an unusual set of skills. Management reporters are assigned to watch the comings and goings of the top IS managers in the country, to look for stories about companies as users of IT, and to track the issues that weigh most heavily on our readers' minds. It is a very difficult beat: The news is often bad (so-and-so was fired or his department was outsourced), users are reluctant to discuss IS projects they consider strategic, and there are few sources of quick and easy information such as PR agencies or corporate communications departments. For these reasons, we tend to move our most senior people into management coverage. A solid grounding in technology prepares people well for writing about its application.

Staff

For the same reason that lawyers are poor advertising copywriters, engineers make lousy reporters. The creative skills needed to seek out and piece together information on a short deadline are very different from the more methodical process of building complete and fully tested systems. With this in mind, we look for strong communications and reportorial skills in our staff and put less emphasis on high-tech background. Although computing experience is a plus, the fact is that most of our reporters have learned about technology principally from writing about it on the job

This works for us, but wouldn't necessarily work for other publications. We are a big-picture newspaper in the world of computer trade publications, and our emphasis is on news. It's less important for one of our reporters to understand how a processor chip works than it is to understand that it does work and analyze what that means for customers. Technical information can be gathered from talking to engineers, but you do not have to be an engineer yourself to gather it.

In contrast, a writer for a more technical publication like *Sunworld* would have to be able to get down to the programming code level to write effectively about some of the topics that magazine approaches. This works for a technical audience; it doesn't work for readers who want a quick scan of the week's top news.

What's News

At the beginning of this chapter, I described the crush of information that arrives at our offices every day. Our editors must make snap judgments on each piece of information that comes in the mail, over the wires, or on the telephone. It is a process that quickly becomes instinctive. There's simply no time to consider the nuances of every news item.

To expedite their decisions, editors intuitively apply some basic criteria to each item.

1   *Is it relevant to our readers?* Between 80% and 90% of all information can be discarded on this basis alone. This is by far the most important question to ask and it answers the toughest question of all, whether the news will even get into the paper.

2   *Is it timely?* Every piece of information has time value. Some, like a company's earnings report or the release of a new product, need to be communicated to readers as quickly as possible. Others can be handed over to editors in the less time-dependent sections of the paper for use in feature stories or news follow-ups.

3   *Is the company a major player?* News from big companies impacts many more readers than news from startups or marginal players. The big players correspondingly attract more attention.

4   *Is it unexpected?* To the annoyance of most businesses, their bad news gets more press coverage than their good news. Why is that? Simply stated, news happens when something changes. When a company does what it is supposed to do—make a product, sell it, and make a profit—it is continuing on a course it has already set. No surprises. On the other hand, when a company fails to achieve what it plans to achieve, that failure is news precisely because failure is not in the plan. News can be made on the positive side: unusually strong earnings or a large number of customer orders for a new product. But bad news is more disruptive to a company and its customers and receives more attention.

5   *Is it exclusive?* Information that comes in the mail or over the wires is only a fraction of what appears in the paper every week. In the brutally competitive news reporting field, success is also a function of exclusivity. If an editor can be certain that her reporter has a piece of information exclusively, and if it meets all the above criteria, that story may well be headed for page one.

There are several kinds of exclusivity. The most common is product-related, and many publications such as *Infoworld* and *PC Week* excel at "scooping" each other on new product plans of the major players. This obsession with secrecy causes much hand-wringing by vendor executives, who think the need to control leaks compromises the development process. But it is a fact of the business that publications compete aggressively to find out exactly what those executives have up their sleeves.

A more subtle exclusive is the kind that snatches a trend or story that otherwise would have been ignored or might never have been covered. For example, in early 1992, *Computerworld* published a series of reports on customer dissatisfaction with the pricing and support policies of major software vendors. The stories were based on extensive interviews with customers, and led some of the largest software vendors to revamp those policies. Had the story not been reported, it probably would have passed unnoticed and the changes delayed or never made at all. But the fact that the trend was uncovered made it an exclusive news story in its own right.

News Reporting

The fundamentals of reporting on the IT industry have changed dramatically in recent years as a result of competition both within the trade press and from daily newspapers. Ten years ago, trade reporting basically answered the questions of "who, what, when, where, why, and how" because the trades were the only media covering the industry. Today, daily newspapers do an excellent job of reporting the "five W's" and the function of weeklies and monthlies is increasingly to interpret the news and relate it to their readers.

For example, in 1991 *The Wall Street Journal* broke the first new about IBM's and Apple's plans to jointly develop products. In the ensuing months, further details came to light as the business and trade press competed to sketch in the final picture. By the time the formal announcement was made in July, 1991 and the press conference staged in September, the news about the alliance was old. But trade publications continued to find many new and interesting angles for their specific audiences. They analyzed which vendors would win and lose from the deal, established time-lines by which to measure the alliance's success, and helped readers decide how to take the partnership into consideration in making their own buying decisions. Both IBM-Apple and the press lapsed into silence for a while after development work began, but expect news emerging from the labs to quickly go under the microscope as the media competes to establish reader relevance.

While the scope of news reporting has changed as the industry has become more competitive, the fundamentals have not. Reporters still do much of their work on the telephone or on location, talking to the key players and nailing down facts. Each bit of information must be filtered for its significance to the reader and assigned a corresponding place in the story—the Apple-IBM agreement, for example, had little significance for mainframe data center operators. The story is usually then bounced off a number of sources who serve as reality checks—people who know the reader perspective exceedingly well or who are themselves informed readers. This input is critical because it helps editors determine real-life relevancy. An announcement that is made with great fanfare by the vendors, but which meets with a yawn from readers is likely to get low placement.

11–5 Caveat Emptor

Up until now, I've presented a fairly optimistic view of media coverage of IT. But the news is not all good, and you, the reader, are not always uppermost in the editor's mind, as you should be. The business press in general and the trade press in particular still face some serious challenges to presenting the full spectrum of issues in IT that affect our personal and professional lives.

One shortcoming of both the general and business press is the "gee-whiz" attitude toward high technology that I alluded to earlier. Many general media outlets are still unequipped to cover technology knowledgeably. Newspapers and wire services tend to assign reporters with a general business background to report major events in the computer industry. These reporters usually have little background in the field and must start their reporting from ground zero, literally asking questions like "what is an operating system?" (Believe me, I've spoken to many of these reporters myself.) This is no bad reflection on the journalists themselves, but it is stupid of editors to think that a reporter who has covered banking or the stock market for two years can suddenly write intelligently about a new supercomputer. Dazzled by the technical wizardry, spoon fed by the PR departments, and ill-equipped to broach complex issues, these junior reporters often end up doing just what the vendors want them to do: marvel at the technology.

One important exception to this trend is *The Wall Street Journal.* The paper, which had virtually no computer coverage ten years ago, now devotes substantial resources to covering high-tech industries intelligently and fairly. It devotes at least a half-dozen reporters to the computer industry and it has broken ground in reporting on serious issues like technology's threat to personal privacy, the sometimes questionable productivity benefits of computer investments, and the self-indulgent politics that the industry elite play with each other. It is a role model for the business press.

The trade media suffers from a more subtle, but considerably more dangerous weakness in its vulnerability to pressure from special interests. This is caused by a unique contradiction: It must report critically on companies who advertise and, thus, ultimately sign the paychecks. Most major publications are pretty good about keeping church and state separate, at least as a policy. But abuse is common among even the most established players.

This pressure to stroke advertisers can lead to editorial coverage that contradicts the needs of readers. For example, one leading PC magazine published a review of a leading word processing package written by a consultant who had written the product's documentation under contract to the vendor. Can someone with a vested interest in a product's success even hope to evaluate it fairly? Absolutely not. Another leading PC weekly published a substantial editorial supplement on groupware sponsored entirely by the leading vendor of groupware products. The articles gushed about the value of the vendor's products to users and the supplement closed with a two page question-and-answer interview with the vendor's CEO. The package was not only misleading, it was downright contemptuous of the publication's readers for it did not even attempt to cover the vendor's competitors or evaluate the product critically. A well-recognized columnist later quit this publication, charging that he was pressured to write favorably about another major advertiser.

Both of these publications are successful and highly respected in their fields; but the relentless advertiser pressure that is a fact of life in the trade media caused them to lose sight of their fundamental responsibility to readers and serve the interests of the wrong audience. This is particularly true at "controlled" publications, or those distributed free of charge. They derive all of their revenue from advertising, making the responsibility to the vendor even more intense.

At smaller publications the pressure is even worse. There, the loss of a single major advertiser can be a death blow, and when that advertiser says jump, the publisher is hard-pressed not to listen. Sometimes bylined articles are submitted by vendors and published verbatim. Or friendly stories about vendors will appear in the same issue in which a major ad campaign is running. The problem with kowtowing to advertisers is that it calls into question the value of the entire editorial product. More fundamentally, it does not serve the interests of the readers, and that is the core value that publication must uphold.

I am not suggesting that computer trade publications don't serve their audience honestly or keep a wall between advertising and editorial. Most of them try their hardest to be fair. But the pressure is there and sometimes it overcomes even the best of them.

Consequently, my advice to IT professionals is to read critically. Seek your own reality checks of important information by checking other publications. Be skeptical about grand claims or talk of breakthroughs. And always regard publications as just one arrow in your quiver of information sources. Trade shows, user groups, newsletters, vendor briefings, and hands-on product demonstrations all have significant value. The media can tell you a lot about the information technology industry, but it shouldn't make your decisions for you.

The Media's Perspective:
The Wall Street Journal

William Bulkeley, a staff reporter of *The Wall Street Journal,* joined *The Journal* in 1972. He developed, planned, and wrote a broad range of stories, expanding *The Journal's* coverage of technology and computers. Mr. Bulkeley has worked in several of *The Wall Street Journal's* bureaus: Dallas, where he covered oil and agriculture, Detroit, where he covered autos, Los Angeles, where he covered housing and finance, and, most recently, Boston, where he has focused on technology and information systems as well as acting as substitute editor on *The Wall Street Journal* Page One staff.

He has had stories reprinted in *The Best of The Wall Street Journal*, *The American Character*, *This Abundant Land*, and has co-authored the book, *American Dynasties* (about American families that grew out of *The Wall Street Journal* series).

As a teacher, Mr. Bulkeley has lectured for the Harvard Extension Program, acted as a writing coach for *Software Magazine*, judged the news writing awards for the Computer Press Association, and is currently a lecturer for Simmons College Graduate School of Communications in business journalism.

In 1992, Mr. Bulkeley became a columnist, inaugurating and writing the Information Age column in *The Journal*.

Before joining *The Wall Street Journal*, Mr. Bulkeley graduated from Yale University in 1972, cum laude, where he was also the managing editor of the *Yale Daily News*.

If you are looking for news in *The Wall Street Journal* about specific companies, then you should go to page B2 of Section 2 first. If you see a story in *The Journal* gets a two-column headline, then it means that it is "something cataclysmic like the start of the Persian Gulf War." Complementing Chapter 11, in this chapter Bill Bulkeley summarizes how to read *The Wall Street Journal* effectively. Enjoy IT.

12-1 Effective Use of *The Wall Street Journal*

Lots of periodicals cover the computer industry every week. Lots of newspapers cover the world every day. The closest you can come to daily coverage of the computer industry is *The Wall Street Journal.*

The Journal's primary interest is covering the most important stories in the worlds of business, economics, and investment each day. Because the computer industry is such a big part of the economic world, the *WSJ* covers many of its twists and turns.

Reading the *WSJ* solely for computer news can be frustrating. Stories can appear on the front page, on page 3, in the second section, and in the stock market briefs. Stories can also pop up unexpectedly throughout the paper. It can bewilder the unsuspecting reader; but there are rational ways for the information processing executive to look for news.

The Journal's basic editorial direction was defined by Bernerd Kilgore, one of the legendary figures of American journalism. As early as the 1940's—before television networks existed—Kilgore divined that investors and business people from coast to coast were interested in the same news. He often said that the businesspersons in Portland, Maine, and Portland, Oregon, needed the same information. He felt the same way about grain processors and steel makers, and he would have felt the same way about computer makers, if they had been around at the time.

The result is that the *WSJ* is edited for business people, broadly defined. While investors are a big part of the audience, managers, technologists, human resources professionals, and CEO's are part of the mix as well. The editors try to highlight stories that interest the most people. Stories of interest to smaller audiences are played at lesser importance. One big difficulty is deciding whether something that helps a big group a little is more important than one that hurts a smaller group a lot. Does a story about possible capital gains cuts outweigh a story that Hewlett-Packard's earnings have plummeted? Those are the decisions that *Journal* editors make every day, and their decisions can be seen by the placement of stories.

Anyone who looks at the front page of the *WSJ* knows it's a different kind of paper. For one thing, there aren't any photographs. Sometimes there are some line drawings or charts, but that's it.

Even more fundamental: *The Journal* doesn't play news stories on its front page. Generally, the prime places on Page One—the left and right columns—are reserved for major feature stories. Column six is for the major economic or business feature, and column one is for a feature on politics, foreign affairs, or social issues. In the middle of the page is a more light-hearted feature on topics ranging from the panic that sets in when Bostonians confront snow to tourists who visit Northern Ireland for fun.

The Journal normally plays its biggest news stories on page 2 and page 3. Only major news developments supplant features in column six. Only something cataclysmic like the start of the Persian Gulf War gets a two-column headline, *The Journal's* equivalent of a six-column banner.

The way to tell what news *The Journal's* editors think is most important is to read the What's News columns on Page One. Columns two and three of *The Journal's* Page One list in order of importance the most significant business stories and general interest stories of each day. Each brief summary also includes a "refer line" telling the reader what page the full story of the event is on. All the business stories and most of the general stories have refer lines.

It's tough to read *The Journal* without reference to the What's News columns, because the compartmentalization of the paper means that some important computer stories are on page 3, others on the second front and still others on the technology page and the market pages. *The Journal* also provides an index of companies mentioned in stories on page 2 of the second section. That reference is a handy way to follow news of a particular company or check on whether a story ran. However, checking for every computer company every day is a daunting task.

The Journal's editor's most important guideline for judging news worthiness is dollar value. The more dollars, the more important a story is. A $1 billion contract for General Electric is more important than a $900 million contract for General Dynamics. Under *Journal* guidelines, contracts smaller than $10 million aren't even written up.

If a story runs, but the price isn't included, that usually means the reporter has received guidance that the transaction involved is bigger than $10 million.

A related guideline is market impact. News about stocks with big market "caps" (short for capitalization, or shares outstanding times market price) is more important than news about stocks with small caps.

Most important, news is what is unexpected. If a company announces strong earnings and the stock doesn't move, it is normally because analysts have been told to expect those earnings by the company, and they have passed on word to their clients. Only if news exceeds expectations, or more dramatically, confounds expectations, will the stock go up or down. Often editors decide against doing a story because the stock doesn't move after an announcement.

Big stories about big-cap computer companies will usually show up on page 3 or 4 of *The Journal*. Otherwise, editors try to place them on the technology page of the second section.

The second section, called Marketplace, is the most likely section for computer stories to appear. The front of the second section often has at least one computer-related story. On Thursday the lef- hand column is on Personal Technology and often includes product evaluations and descriptions of new hardware. Every few weeks, that left-hand slot has brief items on new technologies.

Inside the Marketplace section, there is a technology page that carries some major stories and many minor ones about the computer industry. Medical stories also appear on the technology page. On Tuesdays the technology page includes a weekly column called Information Age that covers the way technology affects people in their work and daily lives. Technical developments, new products, and financial information about smaller companies usually appear in other stories on the technology page.

The other place in the paper to check for computer news is the OTC Focus on page C6 in the Money & Investing section. Technology stocks are the most important issues in the over-the-counter market, and the column often briefly summarizes corporate developments that cause stocks to rise or fall.

Regrettably, there isn't any guarantee that every computer-related story is in one of those places. Sometimes management changes are handled on the Who's News pages. *The Journal* writes about changes of chairman or president for all companies. For the largest companies—those in the Fortune 500 listings—it covers changes in boards of directors and vice presidents as well.

Sometimes legal issues appear in the legal pages, although major issues of software copyright usually go on the technology page. And because of space constraints or late-breaking stories, some technology stories may be scattered in the first or third sections of the paper.

Someday everybody will be able to afford electronic filters that scan the Dow Jones News Retrieval Database for the latest stories on topics a reader needs. But for now, reading *The Wall Street Journal* with discretion can keep a reader reasonably up to date on the information world.•

CHAPTER 13

The Investor's Perspective: Analyzing the IT Industry

Rick Sherlund is a Vice President and Senior Analyst in the Investment Research Department at Goldman, Sachs & Co. Rick attended Cornell University, receiving a Bachelor of Science degree, with honors, in 1977 and a Master of Business Administration in 1978. After graduating, Rick worked with Arthur Anderson & Co. in Los Angeles and is a Certified Public Accountant in the State of California.

Rick joined Goldman Sachs & Co. in 1982 and has been rated the number one Wall Street analyst following the Software and Computer Services industry for the past several years by Institutional Investor magazine. While at Goldman Sachs, Rick has been closely involved with the firm's merger and investment banking activities, including the initial public offerings of Microsoft, Borland, and Sybase.

Rick is a founding officer and past President of the Software and Computer Services Industry Analyst Group, a member of the New York Society of Securities Analysts, and the American Institute of Certified Public Accountants. Rick's hobbies include fly fishing, squash, and white water kayaking.

The Wall Street Journal, September 9, 1992

By William M. Bulkeley (Staff Reporter)

CAMBRIDGE, MASS. -- **Lotus Development Corp.**, facing a loss of leadership in its core spreadsheet business, cut the suggested retail price of 1-2-3 for Windows to $495.... In over-the-counter trading late yesterday, Lotus stock was quoted at $16.50, down $1. Indeed, analysts say that Lotus' leadership in the overall spreadsheet market is in jeopardy for the first time.... **Richard Sherlund**, an analyst with Goldman Sachs, says he thinks Lotus will retain a lead in the spreadsheet market, but he thinks Lotus' market share measured in dollars will fall below 50% for the first time. He says that Lotus' spreadsheet market share is likely to fall to 46% this year from 54% while Microsoft's share will rise to 43% from 36%.

How did Rick Sherlund analyze the PC software market? Why would *Institutional Investor* magazine rate him as the number one Wall Street analyst following the software and computer services industry for the past several years? In this chapter, Rick explains the role of the analyst and efficient markets, and implications of industry trends in investment considerations. Enjoy IT.

13–1   The Role of the Analyst and Efficient Markets

The role of the securities analyst is to gather and assess all publicly available information that could affect a company or its industry and to communicate significant conclusions to investors so that the underlying stock price appropriately and efficiently reflects the most up-to-date assessment of earnings expectations and risks. The analyst is the primary mechanism for achieving efficient capital markets–assuring that stock prices reflect all publicly available information.

The market provides the analyst and investor with a real-time barometer of investor sentiment—a measure of how investors view the risks and rewards of a stock based on current assessments of currently available public information. Analysts are highly competitive in the pursuit of information that could positively or negatively impact a stock. The analyst is much like an investigative reporter, constantly in pursuit of incremental new information or insights.

Conceptually, the analyst's role is straightforward. In practice, analysts and investors strive to achieve superior returns from the market by attempting to anticipate stock-impacting information (typically relating to a company's earnings potential or risk profile), in an environment of uncertainty. Analysts must use their industry expertise in conjunction with impartial and uncertain information to draw subjective assessments. The subjective nature of investment analysis creates many differing points of view. It is these differing opinions that fuel the dynamics and volatility of the market.

The market price of a stock is a constantly fluctuating measure of the level of investor sentiment; an equilibrium price defining the level at which the most pessimistic assessment among the sellers (the lowest asking price) is equal to the most bullish assessment among the buyers (the highest bid price).

13–2   Investment Considerations

Software and computer service company stocks are valued as growth stocks. Valuation is primarily a function of the rate of earnings growth and the degree of confidence investors have in a company's ability to achieve forecast earnings growth. Traditional measures of value—price to book and price to revenues—are only relevant in assessing downside risk, which is substantial if growth expectations are unfulfilled.

Traditional asset-based measures of valuation would lead investors to favor distressed companies, managements of which have failed to position them for successful long-term growth, and would discourage investors from owning the most promising growth companies. Microsoft, for example, became a public company in March 1986 with stock selling at about five times book value and four times revenues (much too expensive for traditional "value" investors), but it has since appreciated more than forty-fold in price due to robust revenue and earnings growth.

The downside risk to which investors are exposed in this sector is equally great, however, given the absence of a "value" underpinning. Oracle stock is an example of this risk, having declined in price from $26 per share in early 1990 to a low of $5 six months later.

Computer service companies in general have more stable, predictable growth rates than software companies because of the recurring revenue streams inherent in providing an ongoing service to clients. These companies are relatively "low tech"—using proven technology to deliver cost-effective services. As a result, computer service stocks generally sell at higher multiples relative to their growth rates than the "higher tech" software companies, which typically have greater uncertainty about the long-term success of their product technology and the sustainability of their growth. Investing in the software sector requires greater analysis of the underlying technology trends than is necessary for the service sector.

In assessing technology changes, we note that evolutionary advancements are typically healthy for the market and tend to stimulate the industry's continued growth while preserving the status quo of competing companies' relative market share. Investors must be more concerned about technological discontinuities—innovations that are not upwardly compatible with existing technology and have the potential to radically alter market share in favor of upstart new companies that are not hindered by economic necessities of preserving a revenue stream tied to older technology and supporting an intransigent, installed user base.

The effect of technology trends is typically controversial, as are the judgments about a market's real growth potential. Investor assessments of a technology company's growth potential and the effects of technological innovation on the market (at least at the early stage of innovation) are inherently subjective. The dynamic nature of technology markets and necessarily subjective assessments by investors contribute to the high share price volatility in this sector.

The risk of technological discontinuities suggests that investors should not invest based on an assumed long-term sustainable earnings growth rate, which requires extrapolation of existing trends beyond the period of reasonable visibility. The appropriate investor time horizon may be as long as several years associated with a major wave of new technology (such as the movement to the client/server model of computing or the introduction of a new generation of Windows-based PC software—both of which are discussed later) or as short as the several quarter period of rapidly accelerating growth associated with a new product cycle.

When assessing the fundamentals of a software company, it is most important to ascertain that management is technical, possessing the vision to position the company to take advantage of the emerging trends and demonstrating the capability of delivering a steady stream of new products and product updates. The most successful software companies appear to be driven by a strong management visionary who imparts to the organization, often with evangelical zeal, a sense of urgency in fulfilling a technical vision. The organization takes on personality attributes of its leader, who is usually well focused in product development, aggressive in pursuit of advancing the technology, and has an almost neurotic, instinctive fear of complacency. A mature, well-seasoned chief operating officer and chief financial officer are required to complement the role of the visionary (who is typically the founder), since the visionary may not have the aptitude, or interest, to "mind the store."

Product acquisitions are often synergistic in the software industry, but frequent product or company acquisitions may also be viewed as a weakness in management's vision and ability to build new products in anticipation of emerging industry trends and market demand.

Product cycles are also more important to software vendors than computer service companies. Product cycles are more important in determining earnings momentum than is the overall economic environment or even overall underlying industry demand. For example, Microsoft has long reported 50% revenue growth, benefiting from a strong new product cycle for Windows and Windows-based applications. This has even occurred during a period of declining domestic GDP and in a period in which underlying worldwide personal computer (PC) unit demand increased only about 5%–10%.

Successful new product introductions generally lead to accelerated earnings momentum and, consequently, multiple expansion in software stocks. We refer to this early stage of the product cycle as the "sweet spot," when investor psychology begins to turn more optimistic, the likelihood of a positive earnings surprise is the greatest and the likelihood of negative earnings surprise is reduced. During this early phase of a new product cycle, revenues tend to accelerate faster than expenses (particularly those expenses that are headcount related), and margins therefore expand, providing a cushion against a possible earnings disappointment. Earnings disappointments are typically more evident when earnings momentum is decelerating and margins are contracting.

In assessing a company's risks of a negative earnings surprise (which frequently results in an immediate one-third loss of market value), investors need to consider management's own earnings visibility. In the PC software sector, products are generally shipped gradually over the quarter so management's visibility is generally pretty good. Today, there appears to be little end-of-quarter "channel stuffing"—pushing products out to distributors at the end of the quarter to benefit that quarter's revenues. Distributors are also easily surveyed (at least in the U.S. market) by investors for an independent assessment of current demand.

Mainframe and minicomputer software vendors are generally more difficult to monitor. For many such companies, the sales cycle is long, and the direct sales force is accustomed to offering aggressive price incentives and payment terms at the end of the quarter in order to meet sales quotas; this results in nervous anticipation by management and investors, who are awaiting evidence that big-ticket (and very high incremental margin) sales actually closed during the quarter. Eventually, all "end-of-quarter bookers" have a shortfall. Investors must then struggle to ascertain whether this is an indication of a one-quarter problem (which is unusual) or evidence of a more secular decline in fundamentals.

It is interesting to note that PC software stocks (as well as technology stocks in general) have a distinct seasonal pattern of relative underperformance during the summer months, which we have referred to as the "June Effect." Seasonally slow sales during the summer months have historically caused investor anxieties to rise as evidence mounts of slowing demand and second-tier companies with slower underlying growth begin to show anecdotal evidence of declining fundamentals. Investors have traditionally been unable to determine whether the summer slowdown is indeed seasonal or whether they are witnessing a secular deterioration in demand. The seasonally weak summer months are followed by the seasonally strongest months of September-December, a period in which the stocks have tended to rebound, outperforming the market.

A final point on valuation: We note that much of the stock price volatility in this sector is a function of constantly shifting investor psychology. The perception of a greater risk to the attainability of current earnings estimates or the sustainability of longer-term earnings growth rates is quickly reflected in a lower share price. Conversely, news of an upcoming new product introduction, which might benefit earnings momentum, can be very beneficial. There is also a high level of unsubstantiated speculation that contributes to investor apprehensions and share price volatility in this sector, all of which contributes to a tendency of investors to "sit close to the exit."

13–3   Implications of Industry Trends

We review briefly the implications of two of the most pervasive industry trends—the market's rapid adoption of Windows as a graphical user interface for PC's and the emergence of client/server computing.

New Generation of PC Software

The market's growing adoption of Windows as a PC graphical user interface (GUI) is resulting in a strong acceleration in demand for PC software, fueling a replacement cycle of current-generation character mode software with a new generation of Windows-based graphical interface products.

PC software demand has historically been driven by sales of new PC's, currently selling at about 22 million units per year (IBM and compatible DOS-based PC's). The introduction of a new generation of graphical interface-based PC software should create incremental demand from the installed base of about 120 million PC users who may upgrade their software to the emerging new generation of Windows products. The principal market is likely to be an estimated 35 million 386SX-, 386DX-, and

486-based PC's capable of running Windows. Also, the somewhat larger market of 40 million 80286-based PC's (that can run Windows but, we believe, will be likely to subsequently upgrade to 386-based computers for better performance) represents a larger, but perhaps slower-to-upgrade, market opportunity.

The industry benefits resulting from the introduction of significant new technology—GUI products—is analogous to the replacement cycles enjoyed in other industries, such as the television industry. Demand for televisions accelerated sharply following the introduction of color in the early 1960's as a replacement for monochrome, and again in the late 1960's and early 1970's, when transistors replaced vacuum tubes, making it possible for portable televisions to proliferate.

The main beneficiary of the replacement cycle to a new generation of PC GUIs is Microsoft, which provides Windows and has the broadest range of Windows-based applications on the market. The decision of Microsoft's PC software competitors not to support Windows (until well after Microsoft) provided Microsoft with a considerable lead in delivering a broad family of Windows-based application products. This is a lead that Microsoft hopes will enable it to retain a high market share in what should be a very high-growth Windows-application market as its competitors belatedly begin to introduce Windows products.

Windows is likely to fuel upgrade cycles for all PC software vendors. It also represents a risk to the entrenched market share leaders, however. Windows provides a discontinuity in the market, the point of vulnerability when a contender has an opportunity to capture market share as the user evaluates which new generation product to upgrade to.

Lotus is at risk in its traditional spreadsheet market to a loss of share to Microsoft and Borland International, but it hopes for a share of WordPerfect and Microsoft's word processing market following its acquisition of Samna (Ami Pro, a Windows-based wordprocessor), and strong growth in its Notes and CC:Mail products.

Software Publishing is also exposed to competitive market share erosion as a number of large vendors have used the introduction of Windows as a platform to introduce competitive new presentation graphics products.

We believe Microsoft and Borland are best positioned to benefit from the market adoption of a new generation of Windows software.

The biggest technological risk to Microsoft is probably the upcoming introduction of a new object-oriented operating system (Pink) from Apple and IBM. Whether these two partners will be successful in delivering a next generation operating system that represents a technological discontinuity is highly controversial, given that Microsoft is also adding object-oriented extensions to Windows. Microsoft's approach is unlikely to be as technically elegant as Pink (which is architected "from the ground up" as an object-oriented operating system) but may be sufficient to maintain industry dominance given the enormous advantage of upward compatibility for a very large installed base. Microsoft's challenge, if Pink is successfully developed and meets current Apple and IBM technical expectations, will be to successfully bridge the technology gap that could otherwise represent a very serious technical discontinuity for Microsoft's operating system and Windows application business.

Our estimates of the size of the PC software market and market share positions are shown in Figure 13-1 and Tables 13-1 and 13-2.

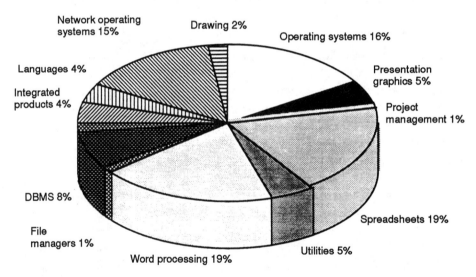

Fig. 13-1
Worldwide PC Software Vendor Revenues, Calendar 1991

13-4 Emergence of Client/Server Computing

With advancements in price performance of PC's and workstations, and the parallel advancements in networking technology, it has become more cost effective to distribute processing, applications, application

Table 13–1   PC Software Market Principal Products
Worldwide Software Vendor Revenues, Calendar 1990–1991 (millions)

	1990		1991	
Spreadsheets	$755	18%	$1,050	19%
Word processing	827	19%	1,033	19%
Operating systems	515	12%	855	15%
Network operating systems	710	17%	824	15%
Database management systems	367	9%	450	8%
Languages	159	4%	240	4%
Presentation graphics	225	5%	252	5%
Utilities	185	4%	250	5%
Integrated products	212	5%	218	4%
Desktop publishing	103	2%	115	2%
Drawing	63	1%	102	2%
Project management	46	1%	51	1%
File managers	37	1%	42	1%
	$4,204	100%	$5,482	100%

Goldman, Sachs & Co. estimates and IDC.

development tools, and data storage across a network of mini- and microprocessor-based servers (typically, Sun, DEC, other minicomputer or UNIX microprocessor-based systems that provide central data management) and clients (desktop PC's or workstations that handle the user interface and local data manipulation).

Independent relational database management system (RDBMS) vendors (Oracle, Sybase, Ingres, and Informix) have broadly targeted their products for the emergence of this new distributed model of computing, referred to as the client/server model.

The emergence of client/server computing is a pervasive industry trend. The traditional model of centralized corporate data processing, which enabled mainframe hardware and software vendors to prosper in the 1970's and 1980's, is becoming economically obsolete for new application development, in our opinion. Networks of interconnected microprocessor-based systems (with powerful PC and workstation client machines

Table 13–2   Market Share Analysis

| | Word Processing | | | | | |
| | 1989 | | 1990 | | 1991 | |
	Revenue	Market Share	Revenue	Market Share	Revenue	Market Share
Word Perfect	$250	45%	$450	54%	$500	48%
Microsoft	100	18%	180	22%	350	34%
IBM Display Write	80	14%	80	10%	70	7%
Lotus	10	2%	15	2%	35	3%
Word Star	35	6%	37	4%	33	3%
Ashton-Tate/Bor-land	30	5%	25	3%	10	1%
Software Publish-ing	10	2%	10	1%	10	1%
Other	40	7%	30	4%	25	2%
	$555	**100%**	**$827**	**100%**	**$1,033**	**100%**

| | Spreadsheets—Revenue | | | | | |
| | 1989 | | 1990 | | 1991 | |
	Revenue	Market Share	Revenue	Market Share	Revenue	Market Share
Lotus	$400	82%	$515	68%	$575	55%
Microsoft	60	12%	145	19%	335	32%
Borland	15	3%	65	9%	115	11%
Other	10	2%	30	4%	25	2%
	$485	**100%**	**$755**	**100%**	**$1,050**	**100%**

Table 13–2 (Cont.)   Market Share Analysis

	Spreadsheets—Units					
	1989		**1990**		**1991**	
	Units	**Market Share**	**Units**	**Market Share**	**Units**	**Market Share**
Lotus 1-2-3	1,270,000	55%	1,600,000	50%	1,900,000	43%
Microsoft Excel	260,000	11%	440,000	14%	1,100,00	25%
Microsoft Multiplan	200,000	9%	250,000	8%	150,000	3%
Borland Quattro Pro	150,000	7%	620,000	19%	1,100,00	25%
CA SuperCalc	300,000	13%	225,000	7%	150,000	3%
Other	115,000	5%	65,000	2%	60,000	1%
	2,295,000	**100%**	**3,200,000**	**100%**	**4,460,000**	**100%**

Revenues and units are for IBM and compatible PC's, exclusive of Apple Macintosh and other operating systems platforms. Unit sales include competitive upgrades (i.e., a 1-2-3 user "upgrading" to Quattro Pro for $129), but exclude updates (i.e., a 1-2-3 Release 2.2 user updating to 1-2-3 Release 2.3). OEM units are also included. Revenues are total spreadsheet-related revenues and include updates and upgrades.

	PC Database Management					
	1989		**1990**		**1991**	
	Revenue	**Market Share**	**Revenue**	**Market Share**	**Revenue**	**Market Share**
Ashton-Tate[a]	$180	55%	$170	46%	$175	39%
Borland[a]	40	12%	67	18%	95	21%
		⇒ 67%		⇒64%		⇒60%
Fox Software	15	5%	20	5%	40	9%
Nantucket	25	8%	25	7%	30	7%
Data Ease	15	5%	17	5%	25	6%
Micro Rim	20	6%	18	5%	15	3%
Other	30	9%	50	14%	70	16%
	$325	**100%**	**$367**	**100%**	**$450**	**100%**

a. Borland and Ashton-Tate merged in October 1991.

Table 13–2 (Cont.) Market Share Analysis

	Presentation Graphics					
	1989		1990		1991	
	Revenue	Market Share	Revenue	Market Share	Revenue	Market Share
Software Publishing	$68	47%	$110	49%	$115	46%
Lotus	45	31%	60	27%	70	28%
Microsoft	0	0%	15	7%	18	7%
Micrografx	5	3%	10	4%	12	5%
Ashton-Tate	3	2%	5	2%	4	2%
Aldus	0	0%	0	0%	3	1%
Other	25	17%	25	11%	30	12%
	$146	100%	$225	100%	$252	100%

	Languages					
	1989		1990		1991	
	Revenue	Market Share	Revenue	Market Share	Revenue	Market Share
Microsoft	$60	60%	$65	55%	$70	44%
Borland	30	17%	42	20%	89	29%
Microfocus	25	14%	30	14%	50	16%
Zortech/Symantec	4	2%	7	3%	11	4%
Other	10	6%	30	7%	25	7%
	$129	100%	$159	100%	$240	100%

Table 13–2 (Cont.)   Market Share Analysis

	Spreadsheets—Units			
	1990		1991	
	Revenue	Market Share	Revenue	Market Share
Network Operating Systems				
Novell	$450	63%	$544	66%
Banyan	50	7%	75	9%
IBM	50	7%	65	8%
3Com	50	7%	10	1%
Tops	10	1%	5	1%
Other	100	14%	125	15%
	$129	**100%**	**$824**	**100%**

	PC Database Management			
	1990		1991	
	Revenue	Market Share	Revenue	Market Share
Operating Systems				
MSFT (DOS and OS/2)	$235	46%	$395	46%
Windows 3.0	210	41%	360	42%
Xenix/UNIX	50	10%	75	9%
Other	20	4%	25	3%
	$515	**100%**	**$855**	**100%**

Table 13–2 (Cont.)   Market Share Analysis

Integrated Products

| | 1990 | | 1991 | |
	Revenue	Market Share	Revenue	Market Share
Lotus	$60	28%	$60	28%
Microsoft	40	19%	55	25%
Enable	30	14%	30	14%
Software Products	22	10%	28	13%
Spinnaker	15	7%	15	7%
Ashton-Tate/Borland	25	12%	10	7%
Informix	10	5%	10	5%
Other	10	5%	10	5%
	$212	**100%**	**$218**	**100%**

Utilities

| | 1990 | | 1991 | |
	Revenue	Market Share	Revenue	Market Share
Norton/Symantec	$50	27%	$95	38%
Central Point	55	30%	75	30%
Fifth Generation	40	22%	40	16%
Other	40	22%	40	16%
	$185	**100%**	**$250**	**100%**

Desktop Publishing

| | 1990 | | 1991 | |
	Revenue	Market Share	Revenue	Market Share
Aldus	$49	48%	$50	43%
Ventura	34	33%	28	24%
Interleaf	2	1%	10	9%
Spinnaker First Publisher	5	5%	5	4%
Other	13	13%	22	19%
	$103	**100%**	**$115**	**100%**

Table 13–2 (Cont.)   Market Share Analysis

Drawing

	1990		1991	
	Revenue	Market Share	Revenue	Market Share
Corel	$25	40%	$50	49%
Micrografx	13	21%	25	25%
CSC-Arts and Letters	11	17%	13	13%
GEM	8	13%	4	4%
Other	6	10%	10	10%
	$63	**100%**	**$102**	**100%**

Project Managers

	1990		1991	
	Revenue	Market Share	Revenue	Market Share
Microsoft	$20	43%	$25	49%
Symantec	17	37%	20	39%
Computer Associates	4	9%	3	6%
Software Publishing	2	4%	1	2%
Other	3	7%	2	4%
	$46	**100%**	**$51**	**100%**

File Managers

	1990		1991	
	Revenue	Market Share	Revenue	Market Share
Symantec Q&A	$18	43%	$20	48%
Software Publishing Pro File	10	27%	7	17%
Ashton-Tate/Borland	1	3%	3	7%
Other	10	27%	12	29%
	$37	**100%**	**$42**	**100%**

networked to more powerful microprocessor-based servers running database management, applications, and communications software) are now able to offer superior distributed processing power and are more economical than the traditional centralized mainframe-based model of computing. The new distributed computing architecture (the client/server model) is now emerging, designed to embrace the superior price/performance of microprocessor-based systems, enabling users to offload processing to more cost-effective machines and take advantage of an innovative new generation of programming tools.

The new servers and workstations (now approaching 100 MIPS) offer performance that is well in excess of the uniprocessor performance of high-end DEC and IBM mainframes for a fraction of the cost. Multiprocessor products from Sequent, Pyramid, and a growing list of others offer peak performance that is several times that of IBM's highest performance mainframes for about one-tenth the price. In addition to the hardware price consideration, an equally compelling factor is the advantage of migrating away from proprietary hardware and operating systems to more open systems, where a greater choice of vendors and breadth of innovative new generation programming tools exist. (The price/performance improvements in microprocessor-based systems is so rapid that the point of technical irony has been reached; for example, a new 75-MIPS client workstation may be interconnected to an existing far less powerful 40-MIPS mainframe server.)

It is believed that there is more than $2 trillion invested in mainframe hardware and software by corporate MIS departments, a mitigating factor in the demise of the mainframe environment. However, for new application development, the client/server model offers a compelling alternative. The infrastructure of systems software, networking, data access and storage, data security, and other communications and support facilities built around the mainframe is now becoming available on microprocessor-based client/server systems. This will facilitate the movement of data and applications off the mainframe, and the dollars spent by data processing departments will increasingly shift to vendors of this more economical and less-proprietary platform of computing. On the client (PC or workstation) side, graphical interfaces, 32-bit virtual memory multitasking operating systems, and object-oriented and visual programming tools are outpacing innovation on the mainframe in user and programmer ease of use, efficiency, and ergonomics.

The transition from higher-priced proprietary minicomputers to lower-priced multi-user and network-based servers depresses revenue growth for the RDBMS vendors since lower up-front software license fees are typically associated with these lower-priced systems. The RDBMS vendors have historically priced their software by the size (class) of machine for which the software is used. For example, for a large multi-user minicomputer, the RDBMS competitors have recently begun to price their software based on the number of users. There are typically few users on a system initially, the period when an organization is using the RDBMS and programming tools to develop applications. At a later date, these applications are deployed across a wide number of users. Under user-based pricing, a greater portion of the revenue from these systems is, therefore, generated later as applications are deployed and the system is expanded.

In general, the downward cascading of hardware pricing has mixed implications for the RDBMS vendors. Declining hardware prices stimulate demand and cause a greater portion of large corporate MIS spending to be directed to client/server computing solutions. Lower pricing per system, however, must be made up by a greater volume as applications are deployed across a network, and organizations must become accustomed to the shift to per-user pricing.

The RDBMS market is estimated at about $2.0 billion in 1991. IBM dominates the mainframe segment with DB2, which has about a 85%-90% market share. DEC has about a 25% market share on the DEC VAX platform and is gaining some share as a result of bundling in (without additional cost) a run-time (execute only, no development environment) version of its Rdb RDBMS. Oracle probably has about a 50% market share in the DEC VAX market and Sybase 5%–10%.

Among the four leading independent RDBMS vendors, Oracle has about a 66% share of total revenues (including RDBMS, tools, service, and support) for 1991 versus 13% for Ingres, 11% for Informix, and 10% for Sybase (Table 13-3). Sybase is growing much faster than its competitors, however, gaining about two percentage points of market share over the past year, while Oracle has lost about four percentage points. (The extent of Oracle's market share decline may be exaggerated by the inflated revenues in 1990, resulting from a jump in large multi-million-dollar site licenses, which are no longer as prevalent.)

The dramatic slowdown in overall RDBMS industry growth over the past two years (Table 13-3) reflects the transition from higher-priced

Table 13–3 Total Revenues for Independent RDBMS Vendors (millions)[a]

	1989[b]					1990					1991				
	March	June	Sept.	Dec.	Total	March	June	Sept.	Dec.	Total	March	June	Sept.	Dec.	Total
Oracle	$139.3	$196.0	$165.9	$194.1	$695.3	238.0	$318.4	$214.8	$256.6	$1,027.8	$269.5	$287.1	$244.7	$283.9	$1,085.2
Ingres	27.8	47.2	28.9	39.5	143.4	39.5	46.3	33.1	44.4	163.3	49.4	61.0	42.0	62.5	214.9
Informix	26.4	28.6	31.6	36.7	123.3	32.4	36.5	38.0	39.2	146.1	37.8	39.8	48.3	52.0	177.9
Sybase	8.9	13.0	15.1	20.4	57.4	16.5	23.0	29.2	34.3	103.3	32.2	36.1	41.0	51.0	160.3
Total	$202.3	$284.8	$241.5	$290.7	$1,019.4	$326.4	$424.2	$315.1	$374.5	$1,440.2	$388.9	$424.0	$376.0	$449.4	$1,638.3

a. 1989 revenues were not restated by Informix, although subsequent periods have been.

b. For Informix, Goldman, Sachs & Co. estimates of restated revenues for change in revenue recognition accounting.

Dramatic Deceleration in Industry Revenue Growth

	1990					1991				
	March	June	Sept.	Dec.	Total	March	June	Sept.	Dec.	Total
Oracle	70.9%	62.4%	29.5%	32.2%	47.8%	13.2%	-9.8%	13.9%	10.6%	5.6%
Ingres	42.1%	-1.9%	14.5%	12.4%	13.9%	25.1%	31.7%	26.9%	40.8%	31.6%
Informix	23.0%	27.8%	20.2%	6.8%	18.5%	16.7%	9.0%	27.1%	32.7%	21.8%
Sybase	85.4%	76.9%	93.4%	68.1%	79.4%	95.2%	57.0%	40.4%	48.7%	55.6%
Total	61.3%	48.9%	30.5%	28.8%	41.3%	19.1%	0.0%	19.3%	20.0%	13.8%

minicomputers to lower-priced multi-user and network-based servers and the related lower up-front software licenses (as discussed earlier), a slowdown as new client/server technology is evaluated as an alternative to traditional minicomputers, a more difficult economy, and probably a less-frantic quest for market share given the constraints of over lever- aged balance sheets in this sector resulting from liberal accounts receiv- able terms that were used as a competitive weapon over the past several years. The transition to UNIX-based systems creates a near-term depres- sant on revenue growth for RDBMS vendors but the market trends appear very favorable over the longer term as an increasing percentage of data processing budgets shift from traditional mainframe solutions to client/server computing.

The Consultant's Perspective

Peter F. DiGiammarino, is one of the top executives of American Management
Systems (AMS), a management consulting and system development firm
serving clients from offices around the world. With 3,200 employees and 1991
revenues of $285 million, AMS is one of the world's largest providers of
integrated systems consulting, development, and application software
products.

Mr. DiGiammarino leads AMS's practice of providing management consulting and
systems development services to commercial banks and diversified financial
service companies in North America and Europe. His focus is on creatively
applying technology to achieve breakthrough improvements in performance
and quality service levels through a combination of industry expertise, proven
methods and procedures, and extraordinary depth of technological
competence. His specialty is working with business executives to maximize
the value of technology in pursuit of their business objectives, whether they
seek to offer new or improved products and services, to expand markets, to
increase productivity, or to otherwise improve bottom-line performance. His
current responsibilities range over 400 AMS professionals located in five
regional offices in the U.S. and three in Europe serving the largest banks and
non-bank retail lenders, including: American Express, Bank of America, Bank
One, and Barclays.

A native of Lexington, Massachusetts, Mr. DiGiammarino joined American
Management Systems in 1977 after earning an M.S. degree in management
from MIT's Sloan School of Management. In 1975 he received a B.S. degree,
with honors, from the University of Massachusetts at Amherst, where he
completed an interdisciplinary major in computer science, economics, and
mathematics.

Charles Rossotti is chairman, president, and chief executive of AMS, a company he
helped to found in 1970. Specializing in applying computer technology to
solving the complex management problems of large organizations, AMS
serves large financial institutions, energy and telecommunications firms,
aerospace companies, government agencies, universities, and other large

corporations. The firm is publicly held and is traded on the NASDAQ market. AMS was started as a new venture in 1970. Mr. Rossotti has been involved in all aspects of the creation and management of the business, including financial, marketing, product development, and general management.

In addition to the AMS Board, Mr. Rossotti serves on the board of directors of NationsBank Corporation, Intersolv, Inc., and Caterair International, and he is a member of the Council on Foreign Relations.

Mr. Rossotti received his Bachelor of Arts degree, magna cum laude from Georgetown University in 1962. In 1964, he earned an M.B.A. with high distinction from the Harvard Business School.

Mr. Rossotti was born in New York City. He is married and has two children, and he enjoys tennis, running, and sailing.

Whether you are pursuing a career as an entrepreneur, starting your own consulting business, or (as an IS manager) trying to leverage the services provided by consultants, it pays to understand the consultant's perspective. What is the nature of the consulting business? How do they view IT? What kind of services do they provide? As leading consultants, Charles Rossotti and Peter DiGiammarino are in a unique position to shed light on this subject. Enjoy IT.

14–1 Target market

This chapter presents a model that helps define the market served and the services provided by AMS and other IT consulting firms. It helps to think about this model at two levels. The first addresses the market that is potentially accessible over a mid-to-long term time horizon, given our current general business skills, resources, and interests. The second level refers to the market that is available to us in the immediate-to-near term, given our specific areas of expertise and resources. An analogy is the car business. If we were a manufacturer of cars, the worldwide market for all kinds of cars would be the potentially accessible market in the long run; but the immediate market might be limited to the size and price range of cars we currently make and the countries where we currently have distribution channels. For convenience, we call the first level our general market and the second level our market segments.

General Market

Even though the boundaries of our general market are not as sharply defined as those of the car business, it is quite possible to make some clear distinctions that separate our market from our non-markets.

We note that the definition and analysis of our target market is critically linked to the range of services we think we are qualified to provide. We evolve a definition of our business by starting with a top-level view of the potential market. By making a succession of distinctions that rule in or rule out the component parts, based on what we do, who does it, and how it is done, we derive a fairly unambiguous definition of our general market.

The complete model for defining our general market is displayed in Figure 14-1. Box A, at the top, connotes all spending by all organizations on any aspect of information technology. This begins the definition of AMS's market by asserting that what we do is related to the use of information technology by organizations. That is, almost everything we do is directly related to information technology, and we do not sell to individual consumers.

A large part of this top box includes the market for providing technology capacity to organizations. This is shown in box B1, and includes hardware, systems software, tools, and communications. This is not part of AMS's market. Box B2 comprises resources used to manage, operate, and maintain systems and processes that are already in place. These resources can be either inside staff or outside services, otherwise known as outsourcing or facilities management, as shown in boxes C1 and C2. This is not our domain either.

This leads us to box B3, which references the production of new or improved systems and processes, our primary domain. Resources addressing this market are used to plan, select, and decide on where and how to invest in improved systems and processes, to design, implement, and acquire new or improved systems and processes, and finally, to implement and roll out new systems. This work can be done by inside staff or by using outside services and software packages, or, as is most often the case, by a combination of these. Almost all of the work we do falls into this general category. Recent studies indicate that the market represented by box B3 seems to be growing faster than overall IT spending.

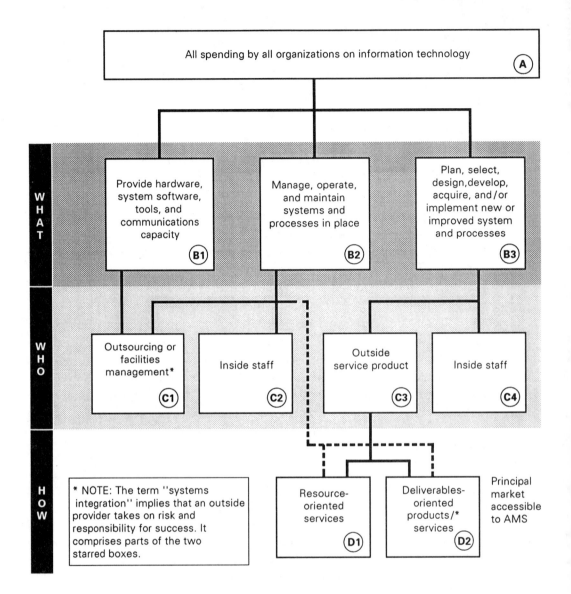

Fig. 14-1
Top-down view of general Information Technology market

Now we move down the hierarchy to box C4 which comprises resources devoted to new or improved systems and processes that are provided by outside servicers. The total spending in this box is small relative to the total in box B3, because most of this work is still performed by in-house resources. However, we have observed that this mix appears to be changing as organizations shift more work outside; so spending in box C4 is growing faster than spending in box B3.

Finally we arrive at one last and vital distinction in defining the market, and that is the distinction between services that are resource-oriented and those that are deliverables-oriented. Both kinds of services advance the general purpose of helping the using organization achieve new or improved systems or processes, so they are part of the box B3 hierarchy. Resource-oriented services, box D1, commonly known as contract programming or body shopping, consists of providing skilled resources; the commitment of the provider is limited to the providing of the skills promised. But in the deliverables-oriented services, box D2, the service provider assumes a commitment to the success of the end result and assumes responsibility for managing the resources for this purpose. While this responsibility is often shared with internal client staff, the responsibility is very real. Most of AMS's domain is in deliverables-oriented products and services, box D2. It is worth mentioning that although most of the spending on outside services in boxes D1 and D2 is driven by the need for new or improved systems and processes, some is driven by the need for the maintenance of existing systems, hence, the dotted lines from B2. In addition, market trends clearly indicate that demand for deliverables-oriented services is growing faster than demand for resource-oriented services.

This model also helps to define the elusive term "systems integrator." Historically, this term referred to firms, such as defense contractors, who put together diverse components of technology. Today, the term refers to a contractor who takes some of the risk and responsibility for the end result of a technology-oriented project or program, much as a construction contractor takes responsibility for a building project. Hence, systems integration comprises part of box C1, for outsourcing of existing systems and processes, and part of box D2, deliverables-oriented projects to provide new or improved systems and processes. Either of these may or may not include the provision of hardware. The main idea is that the contractor takes responsibility for an end result rather than just providing resources or components. While this is a key element of much of what we do, it is not a useful definition of our general market because it includes many services (e.g., outsourcing) that are not part of our primary market and excludes some that are (e.g., planning and consulting).

Bringing all this together allows us to arrive at a general definition of AMS's primary market. Our market comprises products and services for clients who need new or improved systems or processes. Kinds of services include those used by clients to plan and to decide on new or improved systems and processes and to select appropriate technology;

services to design, develop, or acquire systems; and services and products to implement systems. Our primary emphasis is on that part of the market that uses services on a deliverables-oriented basis, with AMS taking responsibility for, and managing the resources needed to achieve, a defined result for the client. A secondary part of AMS's market is for services that support ongoing operations of systems that AMS has provided or that we have helped a client develop or implement.

Broadly stated, AMS exists to advance the performance of our clients through effective use of information technology. To be successful this requires both general skills (or core competencies) which are long-lasting and broadly applicable, and specialized skills and assets which are applicable to particular market segments within the general market.

The general skills that define our core competencies are examined below.

Business/technology analysis Defining client business problems in useful terms; identifying appropriate technology; formulating and analyzing appropriate options; accumulating and providing business and functional expertise in important areas; balancing and assessing risks; proposing plans; developing business system concepts; consulting with decision-makers; analyzing business cases; assessing management and organizational implications; communicating in written and presentational form; and helping clients decide what decisions to make and actions to take.

Complex business systems development and implementation Defining appropriate scope for a system; making trade-offs; developing robust application architecture; selecting appropriate development tools and techniques; managing client relationship needed for a successful project; high productivity design and development work; project and team management; making correct personnel assignments; team motivation; managing the evolution of the business in a planned, organized manner; dealing in special issues of large projects including participating in complex data conversions; performance issues, training programs, testing, interfaces, operational environments and processes; doing everything necessary to make project successful; preparing proposals and negotiating contracts.

Developing, supporting, and implementing complex reusable applications software systems Encompasses many of same skills as business system development, but with added dimensions; common architecture and foundation software; generality and flexibility; handling multiple technology environments; managing development partner-client relationships and business relationships; managing releases; methodology for product-based systems projects; product support.

Business development Identification of business opportunities; establishing and building client relationships and networks; connecting with high levels in client organization; using references; creating image; winning "share of mind"; shaping RFP's; writing winning proposals; managing competitive proposal process; getting "follow-on" business; creative business proposals and deals; using alliances and partnerships with other industry participants; managing overall client relationships for complex clients; effective contract negotiations; creative pricing; establishing our value.

Market Segments

While the boundaries of the general market accessible to AMS are very broad and loosely contoured, the boundaries of particular market segments can be exceedingly specific. In fact, one could consider almost every opportunity to do a new piece of business with a client as a uniquely defined market segment that can be distinguished from every other opportunity in quite precise ways.

If we think of any particular client opportunity as a decision to invest AMS marketing resources, based on a few characteristics we can intuitively and quickly judge the likelihood of success. For example, suppose a large county government near our headquarters in Virginia, where we were already engaged, asked us to provide a financial management systems based on one of our packaged software products in a technology environment we regularly support. We would almost certainly view this as a highly promising opportunity for AMS. By contrast, if a medium-sized auto parts manufacturing company in Mexico invited us to propose to provide a bill of materials system on a Univac computer, we would probably regret spending the cost of postage on a letter declining the invitation.

While these examples represent extremes, they help reveal five primary variables which, in combination, define very specific identifiable market segments for the general services we provide. These are

- client size,
- client accessibility by AMS,
- industry/business function,
- client technology preferences and orientations, and
- client culture, location, and language.

In Figure 14-2, we consider the boundaries of the general market accessible to AMS, resting on our long term core competencies. Within the general market are segments in which our competitiveness depends on where we stand on the five attributes. While the core competencies, and hence our general market, do not change except very slowly over time, our competitiveness in specific segments changes constantly based on investments we and our competitors make in developing functional and technical expertise, software, client relationships, and deployment of staff. Each of these attributes operates in a somewhat different way to influence our competitiveness in a market segment.

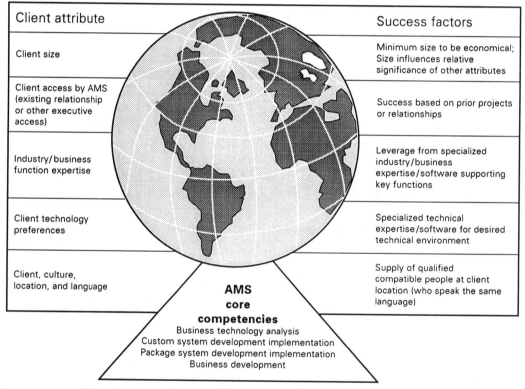

Client attribute	Success factors
Client size	Minimum size to be economical; Size influences relative significance of other attributes
Client access by AMS (existing relationship or other executive access)	Success based on prior projects or relationships
Industry/business function expertise	Leverage from specialized industry/business expertise/software supporting key functions
Client technology preferences	Specialized technical expertise/software for desired technical environment
Client, culture, location, and language	Supply of qualified compatible people at client location (who speak the same language)

AMS core competencies
Business technology analysis
Custom system development implementation
Package system development implementation
Business development

Fig. 14–2
Model for defining market segments within the general market: general market accessible to AMS

Client size is important in two ways. First, there is a minimum size for a client that is economical for us to serve, given the way we do business and the kind of services we provide. Because of the high cost of marketing to a new client, we ordinarily cannot afford to target clients that do not have the potential to invest a substantial amount of money with us. In addition, the high cost of our services means that only fairly large clients can afford to do much work with us unless we happen to have a packaged software product that fit their need pretty tightly. The second consideration with regard to client size, is that size influences the relative importance of the other attributes. In general, the largest clients put more emphasis on technology expertise and previous relationships (i.e., client access), and somewhat less emphasis on very specific industry/functional expertise, and even less emphasis on tightly fitting software packages. This is true because large clients often consider their business practices and systems needs to be unique or at least significantly different from other firms, even in the same industry.

Client access by AMS is an important variable in many situations. Clients with whom we have strong relationships, especially those who have had successful experiences with us, are more likely to do business with us than those who have not. This helps explain why over 80% of our revenue in any year comes from clients we have worked with in the prior year. Furthermore, the importance of networking and developing strong personal ties, especially at very senior levels, is suggested by this success factor.

Industry and business functional knowledge is also an important variable in defining market segments. Experience in a vertical industry builds credibility with a client, helps in communicating with a client, helps in being efficient in doing quality work for the client, and helps in understanding the business practices of the client. For all these reasons, we are more competitive in pursuing an opportunity with banking, telecomm, local government, or federal government clients, where we have well-developed practices, than with a hospital since we have not accumulated a critical mass of experience in health care. Expertise in a particular functional area of an industry, such as loan origination in banking or cellular billing in telecomm, is an even more specific version of industry knowledge, and offering a packaged software system that supports a particular business function within an industry is an even more highly leveraged form of asset.

As we get more specific in the spectrum of industry/functional expertise and software, however, we potentially narrow our appeal to clients who view themselves as special or unique within an industry, unless we position this asset correctly. Furthermore, if we become too focused on very specific knowledge or offerings, we may become blind to more general opportunities to serve clients who know us principally because of our industry or business functional knowledge.

Client technology preference is important as a defining variable in most situations. For more established technologies, having a demonstrated level of expertise (or, if our software is involved, being able to support the preferred environment) is usually a minimum requirement, but is not a distinguishing competitive factor. In newer technologies, such as Unix and Imaging, technology expertise can be a distinguishing competitive factor. However, newer technologies eventually become established and, hence, are not a long term competitive asset. We also find that organizations who view technology as an important part of their corporate strategy are more likely to be interested in long term relationships with us.

Finally client culture, location, and language are grouped together as an important variable. Our ability to supply qualified people where the client needs them and who speak the language the client speaks, is both a minimum requirement and a competitive economic factor. There is a minimum need to have enough people at the client, speaking its language and operating comfortably in its culture, to complete a project successfully. But, even if the minimum need is met, our competitive position is greatly influenced by the cost of deploying people and the depth of local presence, both physically and in terms of culture and language. These considerations, however, are not absolute, as they are weighed against the client's options along the other key variables. This explains, for example, why we are able to get new clients in countries where we have never done business and have little or no presence, e.g., our first project in Belgium. The software and industry knowledge overrides the locational variable. However, the locational variable limits the scope of work we are able to do competitively to that which is directly related to our functional knowledge or product. This locational variable operates, although less powerfully, in the U.S. We are able to do more business with Bell Atlantic in the Washington, D.C. area, where we have many qualified people deployed, than we could if Bell Atlantic were located in St. Louis.

14–2 Service Framework

The services AMS provides help close the gap between the potential and actual value of technology (Figure 14-3) to clients in our target market. The slope of the potential value line outpaces the actual value line because of the increasing rate of technological change relative to our industry's capacity to actualize its potential. The recent wave of hot new technologies (e.g., GUI, multi-media, pen-based computing, imaging, OOUI, etc.) reinforces this trend and leaves us with a great deal to do with no sign of a let-up any time soon.

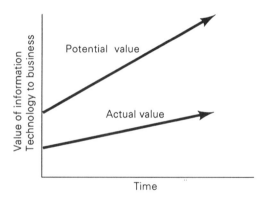

Fig. 14–3
Technology explosion increases potential payoff

One way to think about our work is illustrated by the chart shown in Figure 14-4. We initially engage with a client who is performing at some level over time. In the face of a changing world (economy, competition, customer demands, technology, etc.), our client has a choice. It can continue doing what it is currently doing or it can change. Most of the time, continuing uninterrupted is the preferred solution. After all, if change were introduced in response to every stimulus, we would have constant change or, more likely, chaos.

However, if in the face of change the organization always elects to do only that which it has done in the past, then it will ultimately fail. At some point the forces of change must be reckoned with.

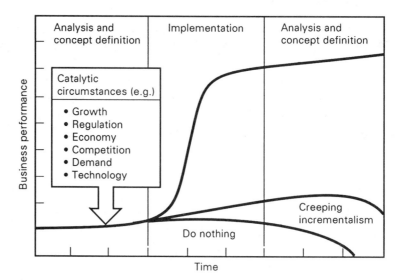

Fig. 14–4

Long-term success requires breakthrough improvements

One option is to change only at the margin. A department of 100 customer service representatives, in the face of growth, increased customer demand, and improved service provided by the competition, might elect to bring on several new service representatives. If the charter, set up, and assignments of the new representatives are more or less the same as that of the original 100, then this might be described as "incremental change." If an organization always changes incrementally, the department of 100 grows to 150, then 300, then 1,000 and beyond—always performing pretty much the same functions in pretty much the same way. Ultimately, this leads to either some form of diseconomy or, worse yet, unchallenged opportunities for competitors to discover ways to perform the same function much more efficiently. Organizations that always change only incrementally may suffer from "creeping incrementalism."

Another alternative is to seek breakthrough improvements through a more substantial change initiative. There are many ways to achieve breakthrough improvements in performance. An organization can reorganize, it can change incentive structures, it can change work flows or processes, and it can even alter the way it thinks about the work being performed. It can also introduce new technology. In reality, it is often the case that many of these options work together in evolving to a new future. For example, a credit and collections operation might introduce new statistical methods, expert systems, and a workstation-based network architecture to change from an age-based to a risk-based approach to managing its receivables. This involves new systems, new procedures, new incentives, new work flows, and even an entirely new way of thinking about the business. This defines a major evolution in the business from one level of performance and way of working to another. AMS is most comfortable serving clients when technology is one of the primary driving change elements. On the other hand, we believe that while the drive to the future involves technology, it is much more than just adding a system to an existing business. The evolution is in the business itself.

To accomplish this evolution requires a clear articulation of the business as it will operate in the future, empowered by technology. We call this description the **business system concept** definition. The description and the process by which it evolves are part of a proprietary methodology whose key component parts are

- clear statement of business objectives and the value of achieving them
- proliferation of options considered, to:
    - ensure a richer final solution by ultimately arriving at a blend of viable options, not just "one or the other," and
    - avoid a selling mode which tends to hard-drive to one preset solution in favor of a participatory planned-change process, which will drive the entire organization to achieve the best possible solution
- A model of the future that evolves, top down, along three dimensions:
    - process,
    - data, and
    - architecture

Once the concept is manifest, we calculate the value of achieving the envisioned future to determine whether it is worth the time, cost, and risk for our client to actualize it. If so, we drive to achieve the concept. If not, we opt for no change or incremental change instead, as appropriate.

In achieving the vision of the future, it is essential that there be a single-client individual empowered by the organization to make timely decisions concerning the systems functionality and future mode of use in the production environment. This person must be able to work comfortably with the entire organization to set direction, align constituents, and motivate the organization to achieve the vision. This individual is our primary client and the gateway by which our services are powerfully introduced for exploitation by the entire organization.

AMS is life cycle-oriented. That is, we like to build things, not just conceive them or talk about them. Once we understand our client's business, our objective is to determine how to use information technology to maximally advance their level of performance. We then assign a team of people to work with our client to actualize the potential. Given the ever-surging capacity of technology available to us and the number of organizations with the scale and orientation to work with us in this framework, we are confident that our services will be in high demand for quite some time.

The CIO's Perspective: Delivering IT Productivity

Michael Zucchini is an executive vice president and chief information officer of Fleet Financial Group, a $48 billion financial services company with over 1,300 offices in the United States. He is responsible for all data processing activities of the Corporation and its subsidiaries, and bank operations of the eight subsidiary banks. In addition, he supervises three non-bank processing subsidiaries—Fleet Mortgage Corp., Columbia, South Carolina (a mortgage banking subsidiary servicing more than $56 billion of mortgage loans with 104 offices in 42 states), AFSA Data Corp., Long Beach, California (the nation's largest third-party student loan processor); Fleet/Norstar Business Data, Newington, Connecticut (insurance processing).

Mr. Zucchini, 45, came to Fleet in August 1987 from General Re Corporation, Stamford, Connecticut, where he was a senior executive since 1974, serving most recently as president, chief executive officer and director of General Re Services Corp.

The holder of a patent for his 1986 invention of a computer terminal outlet that makes mainframe computer terminals portable, Mr. Zucchini also developed an exclusive strategic computer system, known as Confer, while at General Re. He was the 1987 recipient of The Achievement in Managing Information Technology Award, granted by the Carnegie-Mellon Graduate School of Industrial Administration. In 1990, Mr. Zucchini was identified by *Fortune* magazine as an "Executive on the Rise."

A graduate of Pace University, New York, with a bachelor's and master's degree in business administration, Mr. Zucchini was awarded the Certified Data Processor (CDP) designation in 1982. He served as a member of the President's Private Sector Survey on Cost Control, a task force created by President Reagan in 1982 to recommend ways of controlling the cost of operating the federal government. In 1989, Mr. Zucchini was the subject of a Harvard Business School case study which focused on the role of a Chief Information Officer. He is also currently a member of the Board of Directors of Rhode Island Hospital.

In communicating the perspective of the CIO, Michael Zucchini chooses to focus on the financial services industry and to frame his insights in the context of practical, day-to-day reality in the banking business, where the role of the CIO has become critical in the age of consolidation. Today, the successful CIO is no longer a reactive provider of support services, but a proactive leader who needs to think strategically and function at a high level in the organization. Michael exemplifies this role and brings us his keen insight in this chapter. Enjoy IT.

15–1   Introduction

Information is a vital strategic resource in the financial services industry. The accuracy, consistency, and timeliness with which it is managed and delivered are the critical factors determining the quality of our products and services. In banking, the data center and the back office represent the operational heart of the company, encompassing no less than the full range of business functions that industrial corporations carry out at their product development labs, on their factory floors, in their warehouses, and through their physical delivery channels. For bankers, product lines are not merely shaped and supplemented by information, they are composed of information. How successfully we manage and deliver these information-intensive products to our customers determines our business success.

So it's not surprising that the information technology (IT) infrastructure—the staff, automated systems, communications media, and facilities that collectively represent a corporation's ability to manage its information resources—has become an increasingly important focus of attention in our industry. This is particularly true among banks which are merging their operations with those of other institutions.

At the larger American banks, the process of consolidation both defines the CIO's most productive role and provides the best opportunity to achieve maximal business advantage from IT. We will see even more of this consolidating trend in the American banking business in coming years. As banks consolidate, their management is faced with hard choices in deciding how to deal with redundancy and duplication of resources and functions, particularly for those elements concerned with information management.

So my approach in this chapter is to deal in real-world terms with the key challenges in information management facing my own industry, with a dual focus on the consolidations that are reshaping the operation of banks nationwide and on my own experience at Fleet Financial Group.

At Fleet, where we have grown by a factor of four (mostly through mergers and acquisitions) since 1987, we have viewed consolidation as the platform for far-reaching changes in our IT infrastructure. It has provided the opportunity for substantial re-engineering, by which I mean centralizing IT and back office operations, integrating appropriate new technologies, and standardizing our systems and software company-wide, even though state and federal regulation requires that we maintain separate legal banks in each of the six states in which we operate.

American banking is an industry in transition (many would say in crisis). For those institutions that leverage its potential boldly and intelligently, IT can be the key to new levels of success. The CIO is the central player in this new environment, and the re-engineering of the IT infrastructure is his or her most vital tool. This chapter attempts to explain these new realities both in their industry context and in terms of my day-to-day role as a CIO.

15–2   Why IT Has Assumed a Strategic Role in American Banking

By the mid-1970's, new market forces had taken hold in the financial services industry that would transform American banking. For the next decade and more, unique competitive pressures fueled a spirit of expansionism, especially among the larger banks. These forces would prod them into new, and arguably less secure, areas of growth.

What prompted this change in direction by a historically conservative segment of the business community? For one thing, other companies, opportunistic and unregulated, began to mount serious challenges to banks in traditional banking product areas. Competitors like Fidelity Investments offered money market instruments to the public; finance companies expanded their share of the consumer lending market; and large corporations discovered the advantages, as they then perceived them, of going directly to the market with debt instruments.

What resulted was a diversion of revenues previously regarded as native to the banking industry by competitors free of legal restrictions on their operations. No single one of these unregulated companies was offering a slate of services as broad as a bank's, but among them there were enough making loans or taking deposits to constitute a collective challenge to practically every aspect of the banking business among both corporate and individual customers.

Partly because of this accelerating erosion in their traditional base with both large and small borrowers, banks began to venture into less conservative lending sectors. Industry-wide, the exposure of banks in commercial real estate and highly leveraged transactions (HLT's) grew rapidly, as did loans to Third World countries. Still, early on, all these new ventures looked promising and potentially profitable to bankers.

At the same time, banks became larger by stepping up their acquisition activity, expanding the franchise through almost exclusively friendly takeovers of smaller competitors. For many, this expansionist phase both narrowed the field in the struggle for a shrinking domestic market and boosted revenues substantially. All too often, however, the expense of sustaining this growth offset most of the revenue gain, and real productivity improved only marginally. In short, the benefits of these boom years rarely reached the bottom line.

Even before these years of expansion, the role played by information technology (IT) and its specialists in the bank organization was less than strategic. As far back as the 1960's, bank management had tended to view data processing departments with patronizing tolerance. Profits were high; computers were necessary tools in processing the volumes of transactions that supported those margins; and DP specialists drove the computers. But beyond that grudging acceptance of its number-crunching utility, the discipline was little understood and even less appreciated by the high-profile executives responsible for sustaining their banks' health and profitability.

For the most part, managers of bank DP functions were regarded more as supportive functionaries than contributing members of an institution's executive team. The potential of the information management function to contribute to the success of the business at a higher level went unacknowledged. IT professionals, in response, tended to be reactive administrators, answering management's express needs, but rarely seizing opportunities to introduce the kind of value-added contributions their technologies could produce. This was the state of the information function in the banking business well into the 1980's.

Then, as the business began to show signs of faltering later in the decade, American banks shifted into an expansive merger phase, an era of extend-the-franchise acquisitions. At the same time, these new business initiatives, not to mention the industry crisis itself, were exposing the deficiencies in the way information was managed in the banking business, particularly in IT's inability to respond to the new strategic information requirements occasioned by the crisis. Information reporting tools devised to present volume-oriented and undifferentiated institution-wide data proved deficient at identifying the relative contributions of a given bank's products and services to the bottom line. Executive information systems that served well in the good times, when every service offering was making money, were virtually useless at separating the winners from the losers in the banking product suite.

IT departments, prompted by newly-defined information needs from above, scrambled to adjust. In the process they began to explore new proactive roles in contributing to their institution's core business. Bank executives, for their part, came around as well, with a growing appreciation for the value of the information resource in strategic management. Senior executives (in leading banks at least) were beginning to pay attention to their business technology experts, elevating many to the position of CIO, a tacit acknowledgment of the importance of the information resource in corporate management.

Today the crisis in banking persists, but the era of heady expansionism has been replaced by a phase of almost obligatory consolidation.[1] While banks are merging as frequently as before, now it's for reasons of fiscal health: They want the functional synergies and economies of scale that consolidated operations seem to promise. More often than not, today's mergers and acquisitions represent attempts to restore solidity and security to the bank's business foundation, rather than expand the franchise and stake out new territory.

Yet the same competitive pressures, particularly from non-banking entities, continue to shrink banking's slice of the financial services pie. Bankers still face the competitive disadvantages imposed by regulations, which limit the range of products and services they can offer, while simultaneously mandating a high degree of redundancy in their operations. American banks today are laboring under increasing overhead

---

1. See John W. Milligan "Love in a Cold Climate" (*Institutional Investor*, February 1991: 37-40), for an analysis of recent M&A activity in the banking industry. Simon Brady and Caren Chesler-Marsh, in "The Madness of Mergers" (*Euromoney*, September 1991: 66-80), present a thorough, if somewhat negative, overview of the trend. At the end of this chapter other articles are cited that discuss key aspects, pro and con, of consolidation in today's banking environment.

burdens which are exacerbated in turn by the current slow-growth business environment.

The result: The leading banks are looking to undertake sensible acquisitions that can help achieve economies of scale. In this context the consolidation of banking resources stands out as an indispensable tool in a bank's evolution to address new business and economic realities. By some interpretations, mine included, it stands as the key to survival in a changing industry.

Where do these efforts to consolidate the resources of merging banks focus? Almost invariably on their diverse computer systems, facilities, product lines, and back office functions. In today's banking operations, each of these elements depends heavily on information technology and, therefore, directly involves the bank's IT department and CIO.

15–3   What Can Consolidation Achieve?

Mergers are a given in today's banking environment. Increasing numbers of banks are joining forces to meet competitive challenges more efficiently. My own institution, Fleet Financial Group, is a good example. In 1988 Fleet, based in Providence, Rhode Island, merged with Norstar Bancorp of Albany, New York, to become Fleet/Norstar.[2] Over the next two years, we acquired several smaller banks in Maine, Connecticut, and New Hampshire. In 1991, we bid on and won the right to acquire the failed Bank of New England. Today we operate under the Fleet Financial name.

Throughout this period we have focused on the advantages we could realize by consolidating the operations of these individual banks as we absorbed them into a multi-bank holding company. For Fleet, that initiative has meant eliminating redundant operations and resources, primarily in IT, back office, and branch operations. This process, however, is not as straightforward as it might seem. Federal and state regulations demand that a separate legal identity be established and maintained for each state in which a bank conducts deposit-taking operations. In other words, there must be at least one legal bank for each state throughout a banking corporation's franchise. In our case, that means six legal banks across our six-state region.

2. For an objective discussion of the business and organizational issues related to the Fleet-Norstar merger, see Professor Jane Linder's, "Fleet/Norstar Services Corporation: Getting the Best of Both Worlds" (Harvard Business School Case Study: 1989).

But even though federal regulation prohibits interstate branching, we have found considerable room within these strictures to consolidate functions among separate legal banks in different states. For instance, we centralized all our mainframe and technical support operations (serving 800 branches of our separate legal banks across six states) at a single data center (from a pre-consolidation total of 14), and reduced our regional check processing operation centers from 21 to four. This resource consolidation has produced three primary benefits for Fleet.

1   **It has reduced expenses.** From the time our consolidation began with the Fleet-Norstar merger through our absorption of the Bank of New England, completed in the third quarter of 1992, we have realized an annual operating savings of more than $140 million, which represents a 40% reduction in costs.

2   **It has improved the quality and consistency of our banking services** (a factor of increasing competitive importance in the industry).

3   **It has increased our capability for product innovation and refinements in service delivery,** answering customer needs in all our legal banks with unified products, distribution provisions, and management information systems.

Common products also make sense from the standpoint of market responsiveness. There is no technical impediment to allowing for market-specific variations in product offerings within this common structure. A unified deposit system, for example, can be fine-tuned to answer state-by-state, or even locally prevalent, conditions without sacrificing economy-of-scale and commonality.

The central fact behind all the progress Fleet has made is that technology has provided the main impetus in consolidation. The cost and product benefits that we have achieved emerge directly from the technical steps we have taken to maximize the advantages we gain in combining the supporting operations of separate banks.

15–4   The Re-Engineering of the Bank's Technology Infrastructures Is the Key to a Successful Consolidation

Even within the context of federal restrictions on interstate bank operations, there is a range of consolidating approaches focusing on technology and back office operations that multi-bank holding companies can employ to significant advantage.

For one, we can now re-engineer a bank's information (and, to a great extent, back office) infrastructure on a platform of common software and services.[3] This step allows the organization to

1   combine multiple data centers or back office operations centers into fewer locations, in most cases a single location for each function;

2   reduce systems and programming personnel and bank operations staff; and

3   retool core processes and operations to support common software and procedures, as well as a consistent, company-wide set of common products.

Moreover, concrete steps to ensure product consistency can establish the foundation for consolidating additional corporate functions. For instance, accounting and marketing personnel can serve multiple banks, even across state lines, without violating legal restrictions on interstate operations.

Perhaps the most important element in our approach to re-engineering is establishing a base of common software supporting the same product set in all legal banks within a multi-bank holding company. As new banks are acquired, it's not a complex undertaking to retool their infrastructures to mesh with the standard corporate approach. The immediate results are improved quality and consistency and a faster delivery time of common banking products to the customers of the acquired bank. In addition, we achieved significant cost reductions, usually running between 30% and 85% of the acquired institution's previous expenses.

The technology arena is the center of business activity in the modern bank, and the technical infrastructure of a banking company in many ways parallels the engineering and manufacturing components of the industrial corporation. To survive, American banking needs to con-

3. In "The New Industrial Engineering: Information Technology and Business Process Redesign" (*Sloan Management Review*, Summer 1990: 11-27), Thomas H. Davenport and James E. Short discuss the key tenets of IT re-engineering in detail. "The Wiring of Wall Street" (*The Economist*, February 22, 1992: 69-70) outlines the results of applying the re-engineering approach in a non-banking segment of the financial services industry.

centrate its brightest people on IT, the financial services equivalent to the factory floor of our automotive companies. Just as Ford, GM, and Chrysler have focused increasing attention over the last decade on engineering and manufacturing to ensure product quality and responsiveness to the customer, banking should look carefully at the ways its IT infrastructure can improve the product development and delivery cycle for its customers.

At Fleet we are implementing these factory-floor innovations, and that committed focus on IT as a central strategic tool has made a substantial difference in our bottom line and the quality of our banking products. Technology—some of it newly emerging, the rest creatively applied— is the enabling factor in our consolidations.

Many commentators have not paid sufficient attention to this point in evaluating the industry's consolidation. Two analysts at the Federal Reserve Bank, for instance, recently published a paper raising questions about the fiscal advantages achieved by institutions that consolidated banking operations in the mid-to-late 1980's. Similar conclusions were presented in a subsequent Harvard study.[4]

Both studies are substantially correct in their overviews, given their concentration on banking activities, but neither deals with the banks where relatively recent technical innovations are making large-scale data center consolidations possible. The Harvard researchers, in fact, have since taken note of the fiscal and technology management achievements at some of the most successful consolidators, Fleet included.[5]

Emerging technologies have made a big difference. For example, until the last few years, the limited data-carrying capacity of conventional telephone lines, the traditional medium for data communications, constrained our ability to consolidate multiple sites to a single site. Now, with the availability of high-throughput T1 links, the fast, long-distance hookups on which a single-site consolidation depends are practical and cost-effective. Other data communications technologies and advanced system architectures have made it possible to bridge multiple application

4. John H. Boyd and Graham L. Stanley, "Investigating the Banking Consolidation Trend." (*Quarterly Review*, The federal Reserve Bank of Minneapolis, 1991: Volume 15 Number 2: 3-15). Jane C. Linder and Dwight B. Crane, *Bank Mergers: Integration and Profitability* (Working Paper 91-038, Harvard Business School, 1992).

5. Jane Linder and Dwight Crane, "Making Bank Mergers Pay Off" (*American Banker*, July 22, 1992: 4).

systems and adopt advanced branch communication tools. These innovations allow the consolidated site to service geographically dispersed banks through remote communications.

Here's an example of how advanced technologies can introduce capabilities that make a bank more competitive in its market. Our bank offers a consolidated account product, called FleetOne, that we could not provide without the advanced technical capabilities that we have applied in our re-engineering process. FleetOne exemplifies how product and service innovations can be technology-based. This service offering shows, in a monthly statement, balances and other activity data for all a given customer's accounts with Fleet. These accounts include one or more checking accounts, savings, CD's, IRA's, credit lines, and even credit cards issued by Fleet. FleetOne's monthly statement also reports on active loans: mortgages, automobile and boat loans, etc. It even tracks stock trades through our discount brokerage in New York.

Clearly this comprehensive reporting advantage requires sophisticated interfaces with the many application systems that maintain the data on activity in a wide range of accounts. Some of these systems, in fact, are not even under our operational control. For example, we use a third-party specialty firm to handle our credit card processing and another to manage transaction data on stocks in our customers' brokerage accounts. In effect, the interface technology we have implemented makes the "ownership" of each contributing system irrelevant. One fact is certain, however, without this automated platform to roll up current information from a multitude of systems, assembling a single, accurate, consolidated statement for each customer each month would either prove impossible or prohibitively expensive.

There's still another advantage to the re-engineered reporting function behind FleetOne, and it applies every time we bring another bank into the Fleet infrastructure. The new bank can offer this innovative and technology-driven product within a few months of its acquisition because, like all of the automated systems that support Fleet products, it is standardized and available on our corporate-wide common software.

FleetOne is one among many products that make Fleet more competitive in its markets by providing advanced customer service and convenience. The real strategic edge here originates in the standardized technology platform on which FleetOne operates, and that platform is the direct outcome of our initiative to re-engineer the bank's IT infrastructure as we have consolidated operations. That's the important point in this example: Consolidation brings the opportunity to re-engineer IT functions in support of corporate and strategic goals—even when that means a redirection of resources that conflicts with accepted bank practice or time-honored local approaches.

15–5   Consolidating and Re-Engineering the Infrastructure: Selected Cases

Our wire transfer operation provides another instructive example of how even self-contained bank functions can benefit significantly from re-engineering. Each of the banks in our company had traditionally maintained its own wire transfer facility. In each case, it was a small operation, with a staff of seven to ten employees, including managers. There were 56 employees supporting this function throughout our multiple legal banks.

We re-engineered this operation based on the premise that none of its core functions actually needed separate facilities in each bank—nor were there legal or regulatory requirements mandating it. By consolidating wire transfer operations at a central facility, we were able to reduce staff by more than half and, perhaps more importantly, to focus on substantial quality improvements on several fronts. In the first place, our staff consolidation, and the personnel savings it represented, made it possible to recruit a highly qualified manager at a level of compensation that was not practical when the company operated more than a half-dozen, small autonomous wire transfer centers. For obvious reasons, this outcome in itself was a quality advantage.

We also installed an improved wire transfer application system; again a direct effect of eliminating seven other physical wire transfer facilities. The new system offered measurably better service in IT terms and it also provided for dedicated terminals in the offices of our primary customers. Because clients could initiate their own wire transfers without the intervention of Fleet personnel, they saw the new arrangement as a convenient innovation and as evidence of Fleet's respect for their value as customers. At the same time, the arrangement relieved our staff of the responsibility for authenticating client requests for transfers; system-mediated security features handled this task whenever clients logged on.

Several other improvements resulted from the wire transfer consolidation. We developed a standardized set of practices and procedures to support the re-engineered operation, and we were able to train the staff thoroughly. The consolidated facility also made it possible for our audit department to review operations frequently, a practical impossibility under the old decentralized configuration.

A key feature of the wire transfer consolidation was the commingling, for processing purposes, of transactions originating in different legal banks. It bears repeating that, in the banking industry, any technology consolidation across state lines will entail processing transactions from multiple banks. Obviously, handling this mixed transaction stream is not a remarkable technical feat, given available technologies. At the Federal Reserve Bank, however, our wire transfer consolidation raised a few eyebrows.

Each branch of the Fed is charged with regulating wire transfer activity within its territory. When Fleet consolidated its wire transfer operations, however, we were handling transfers originating in two separate Fed regions, New York and Boston, and doing it at a center in Providence, Rhode Island. Fed officials acknowledged that no regulations precluded the consolidation, but they had no standards and practices in place to deal with Fleet's effective invalidation of traditional boundaries between regions. Ultimately we worked with the Fed in Boston to help develop new procedures governing consolidated operations like ours.

Wire transfer is a relatively minor function from the standpoint of the IT resources it involves. Yet, to our knowledge, no bank had ever consolidated the function across state lines and across Fed regions. Thanks to cooperation and support from both the Boston and New York Federal Reserve Banks, we were able to achieve significant business advantages by consolidating and re-engineering the way we handled this operation. The results were significant: We reduced our expenses, improved quality, and enhanced our products and services substantially. Focusing the same tactics on more far-reaching and complex bank operations yields even more impressive returns.

There were no obvious constraints on bringing all our independent wire transfer operations into a single center and re-engineering them as a unified process. The same is true of bank data center operations. With today's technology, our multiple legal banks, with their total of more than 800 branches, can share a single data center, employ common software, and leverage the resulting economies of scale to achieve substantial product and service improvements for our customers.

The approach we used in the wire transfer consolidation, and the information management philosophy behind it, applies just as aptly here. Under the old approach to multi-bank, multi-state data processing, you would find at least one separate data center for each legal bank. Each center's staff would support its own computers and unique applications software and procedures. Moreover, this operational diversity was usually reflected in each bank's range of products and services and, particularly, in the infrastructure through which the institution would manage, define, and deliver its offerings.

The Consolidation of Data Centers

We concluded that our IT infrastructure could serve our strategic needs best if it were centered in a single consolidated facility. To achieve this objective we needed to eliminate the previously-independent data centers and redefine IT operations in a company-wide infrastructure, without regard to geographic boundaries between states. Our decision was to consolidate the data center operations of our autonomous, legal banks into the existing Norstar center in Albany, New York.

The immediate outcome of this kind of consolidation is financial. You reduce costs because you have eliminated facilities and staff expenses. There are no savings from computer hardware per se; the cumulative level of processing power necessary at a centralized facility is comparable to that of the total of the separate centers operating on their own. The meaningful expense reductions come on the personnel side. Instead of multiple data center managers, the company needs only one; and overall staff requirements continue to diminish proportionally down the line, from operators and tape librarians to schedulers and technical services programmers. In many ways it's a classic economy-of-scale multiplier.

The common software central to the operation of a consolidated data center also means that you employ fewer systems and programming personnel. Over the years we have eliminated ten independent systems and programming units in favor of a consolidated program support unit for our common software.

Here's how common software and its concomitant savings make this staff consolidation possible. In a mid-sized bank there are usually about 50 application systems, each supported by a programming team. In an organization composed of seven legal banks, each with its own unique applications that can mean 350 separate systems company-wide.

In our case, the consolidation of operations at a single center and the adoption of common software at all our legal banks cut that figure back to 50.

Similar economies are possible in other bank operations. In fact, as I pointed out earlier, we have saved the corporation more than $140 million through our consolidation initiatives at Fleet.

Yet the important lesson in this kind of IT consolidation is not merely that you cut costs, but that you reduce the scope and complexity of the company's entire IT operation. The first result is substantial cost savings, but the other outcomes are equally important in business terms.

Commonality in IT Resources Means Increased Consistency and Quality

By reducing scope and complexity, I mean standardizing IT operations and the products and services they support. That inevitably means higher product quality. By centralizing its IT infrastructure, management can re-engineer processes and product offerings and focus on developing the right practices and procedures to support the re-engineering, all at a fraction of the cost it would consume under a decentralized IT and back office infrastructure.

This approach builds quality into the operation. With a single deposit system handling all the company's legal banks—as opposed to a handful of "native" systems cobbled together—the programming team can home in on and correct problems expeditiously. Programming improvements and alterations to delivery systems take hold on a company-wide basis; there's no patching or retrofitting of enhancements one-by-one with independent and inconsistently engineered systems in each legal bank.

The advantages we gain through technology-driven consolidation are the best arguments possible for the importance of both IT and the CIO in financial services management. Information management and transaction processing are at the core of the banking business. At Fleet we have consolidated and re-engineered this function, yielding substantial savings, a standardized operating environment, and higher quality and responsiveness in our products and services. That record is the best answer to the commentators who maintain that IT is not a strategic function in the management of a large corporation.

The quality outcomes of consolidation programs and the potential competitive advantages they represent cannot be overstated. In addition to our data centers and our wire transfer operation, we have consolidated several other multi-bank back office functions, including trust, credit card, consumer loan, and customer service. This latter operation in particular provides an instructive example of consolidation's quality dividend.

We centralized our customer service function in Utica, New York, cutting staff by 30%. We were able to introduce automated response units to handle incoming calls on our "800-number" telephone lines. For calls that are straightforward, factual inquiries, such as balance questions (73% of the activity), our audio response systems automatically provide the answers. No staff member is involved in the interaction. Now we need fewer staff members and have been able to invest in upgrading and training our operators. And, of course, we have introduced common software and common procedures. We were also able to set up an independent quality survey to evaluate customer satisfaction with our mixed use of voice menus and human operators. That survey, run on a random sample each quarter, has validated the strategy we have implemented in the customer service center.

Check Processing: The Exception Case in Consolidation

There is one core function in the banking infrastructure that cannot be consolidated into a single operations center if, as in the case of Fleet, the multi-bank company has substantial geographical reach. Check processing is geographically constrained not because of government regulation nor because the systems technologies are deficient, but because most of the checks themselves have to be collected from local branches, processed, and physically transported to the regional check processing facility (a Federal Reserve operation) by a daily deadline. If you miss the deadline, you lose the funds availability represented by the checks.

Because of Fleet's significant geographic span, we could not establish a single operations center to process check transactions. It would be impossible to gather the checks from the branches and process them quickly enough to allow their efficient transportation to the local clearing houses by the deadline. But we could consolidate to four regional operations centers and place them optimally, based on careful evaluation of the drive-time requirements in moving checks from the branches to an operations center, processing them there, and getting them to the nearest clearing house by the deadline.

Even so, we achieved impressive savings, consolidating from a total of 21 check processing centers to our current four. As in all our consolidation initiatives, we introduced substantive quality improvements based on commonality in IT resources. Moreover, it allowed us to bring in large-scale imaging systems and consequent improvements in customer service. These systems were too expensive for installation in 21 widely dispersed centers. Placed in four centers, however, these systems will function cost-effectively.

There is a parallel to this economy-of-scale benefit on the personnel side. The personnel savings we generate can underwrite a smaller, but more highly qualified staff. We can afford to hire the best people at competitive salaries, which in turn ensures the high quality of the services we offer.

From the standpoint of human resource management, that's the positive and uplifting element in technology-driven consolidations: You can upgrade the quality of key people at operations centers. On the downside, of course, are the far-reaching staff reductions that consolidation occasions.

15–6   Human Resource Management Is a Core Responsibility of the CIO in the Era of Technology-Inspired Reductions in Force

Releasing staff is a painful reality in a consolidating corporation, and it is a management responsibility that has to be conducted with honesty, empathy, and tact. During our ongoing consolidation of information technology and bank operations at Fleet, we have reduced staff by more than 3,100 employees, drawn mostly from consolidated data center and back office operations.

As a company, we are emerging from this consolidation in a far more healthy and competitive state, but we are not insensitive to the human dimension of our re-engineering process. I'm addressing it here because it is directly relevant to the function of the CIO. IT is a strategic area at Fleet, and the CIO's management responsibilities don't end with centralizing facilities and streamlining operations. We expend a great deal of energy and resources in minimizing the adverse effects associated with personnel reductions.

For example, I regard it as my responsibility to explain the company's strategy directly to the staff of operating units that we plan to eliminate. We offer a reasonable range of benefits—

severance, outplacement support, counseling, "stay" bonuses to remain with the company through the shutdown date, etc.— but we have found that a direct explanation of our approach and the timetable we plan to use also helps the staff involved to deal with the situation.

During our recent effort at the Bank of New England, for example, I explained our strategy to more than 3,000 employees directly affected by the changes we are introducing, addressing individual units as large as 400 people. We have frequently given groups lead-times as long as eighteen months and we have never experienced willful processing disruptions at units slated to be consolidated. The key element is an honest and non-patronizing explanation of the company's business strategy. There are never "political" motives behind that strategy or behind our selection of one center for consolidation over the others, making my job one of honestly explaining the business rationale behind the decision.

Our management responsibility in these situations also encompasses the need to respond to circumstances we did not foresee in our planning. For example, we had scheduled a large center in one state for closing and the center in an adjacent state to shut down some three months later. About two months before the scheduled closing of the first center, however, we learned that another bank was planning to open an operations center very near the one that we had slated to close second. The other bank's establishment of its new center coincided with the closing of our first center, not the one nearby, which would continue to function for some months after the competitor's center was fully staffed and operating.

We saw this as a creative opportunity to reshuffle our schedule of projected closings and enable staff at the second center to sign on with our competitor. We rearranged our plans with much scrambling, shutting down the second center first and freeing its staff to join our competitor's operation. They worked at our center until the shutdown date, collected their severance and "stay" bonuses, and more than half of them reported for work at the new center within a week after our closing date.

Obviously our success in this case stemmed from a fortunate coincidence. Still, we think we have handled the sometimes painful human resource dimension entailed in today's information management responsibility with care and concern. Consolidations make adjustments in staffing necessary. We would be shirking our responsibility as senior managers if we did not take action on these opportunities for substantial expense reductions. Yet many bank executives, I suspect, are hesitating to conduct full-scale consolidations because of this unpleasant concomitant to the job.

15–7   The Barriers to Successful Consolidation

Not too long ago, banks were small-scale institutions, well-rooted in their communities and led by civic-minded local notables. Even though many of today's banks are much larger, super-regional if not national or international in scope, the old culture persists in most quarters. Many bankers resist the tough cost-cutting decisions that they need to make to ensure their institutions' competitive health, and that infrastructure consolidation makes possible. Banking also has a long tradition of friendly mergers undertaken with implicit attention to preserving the management status quo and territorial prerogatives. Rarely have banks merged with a serious intent to maximize their true synergies and eliminate redundancies.

There is also a misconception in some quarters that a standard infrastructure and standard software make a bank's products less responsive to local market needs. This is not true: Current technology fully supports tailored product options within the context of standardized application systems.

And of course local managers often quite naturally resist initiatives that they perceive as threatening to their influence and that of their staffs. When they think that jobs are at stake, they resist all the more.

For these reasons, among others, it's no surprise that some bank executives opt to avoid the tough decisions by turning over their IT operations in whole or in part to third-party vendors. This outsourcing phenomenon is attracting widespread attention in the trade media, and many banks now undergoing mergers are engaging outsourcers to take over their technology operations. I have commented in detail on the outsourcing phenomenon elsewhere.[6] But in brief, I tend to view a large company's outsourcing of all or a major portion of IT as an abrogation of management responsibility. Surprisingly, not even all CIO's share my view of the outsourcing option.

6. Peter F. DiGiammarino and Michael R. Zucchini. "The Four-S Outsourcing Model: How Issues of Scale, Speciality, Sale, and Surrender Figure in the Banker's Decision to Outsource" (*Perspectives on Outsourcing*, The American Bankers Association: 1992). *Selected Readings* lists several potentially helpful articles on the outsourcing phenomenon that have appeared in academic, trade, and general business periodicals.

Essentially, the multi-bank holding company that outsources its IT functions (except for select scale or specialty areas like credit card and student loan processing) renders them irrelevant as strategic assets. The advantages to the outsourcing bank are financial; in the best case, the outsourcer has better economies of scale and passes some of its savings back to the contracting bank. Most large banks, however, could achieve higher cost reductions by consolidating on their own.

Why don't they? In many cases their executives prefer to take a diminished financial return if they can avoid the complications of running IT or avoid the personnel cutbacks often associated with consolidations. Instead they transfer (surrender) their IT staff to the outsourcer. In other cases, bank management simply surrenders IT operations in a tacit admission that it cannot run IT effectively.

Still another motive for outsourcing is the financial "quick fix" that results when a bank unloads non-earning assets from its balance sheet by turning them over to an outsourcer, or decides to take short-term expense reductions, forgoing longer-term, more substantive savings.

The current regulatory and legislative environment represents still another barrier to effective consolidation, mainly by imposing burdens on the ability of multi-bank companies to compete and to consolidate obviously redundant interstate operations. No other enterprise within the borders of a given state is required to operate substantially independently of its parent company and affiliates and to accommodate a separate board, management team, and operational infrastructure.

Fleet, for example, operates some 800 branches spread over six contiguous states. In terms of land mass, our operating territory makes up less than two-thirds the area of California, a state that is home, for example, to a single legal bank with more than 1,400 branches.

Yet current regulations require us to operate a minimum of six wholly separate banks—one per state—each with its own independent board, president, and management team, under separate financial, legal, and regulatory reporting requirements. Each of our six host states, moreover, imposes additional and varying regulations on our operations. And our customers suffer as well. For example, they are not permitted to make deposits at our branches from our own out-of-state banks.

In short, because of restrictive banking regulations, banks that conduct operations in several states have to accept redundancies in staffing and facilities that banks of comparable size, but with operations confined within a single state's borders, do not.

Legislators defend these restrictions by pointing to their responsibility to help maintain safety and soundness in banking institutions. But safety and soundness, it seems, are more likely to emerge from stronger, more efficient bank operations. Consolidation and re-engineering foster these objectives. In effect, although the goals of legislators and those of bank management are wholly complementary, these restrictions impede our ability to take maximal advantage of consolidation initiatives that involve separate legal banks in different states.

15–8   A New Role for the CIO

The banking CIO is in a unique position to lead in the industry's evolution. Because nearly all banking products and services are mediated by systems technology, the re-engineering process becomes a strategic initiative and the continuing management of the institution's information resources becomes a vital strategic function. The banks that devote appropriate attention to this discipline are likely to emerge as the most competitive and the most responsive to changing conditions through the 1990's and beyond. It falls to the CIO to marshal these resources and lead the re-engineering process. There's no place in today's banking environment for reactive management.

To contribute effectively, the CIO has to command prestige and real influence in the multi-bank holding company. He/she has to exercise proactive leadership, continually exploring new avenues to apply technology that advances the bank's continued growth and success. All too often, corporate technology managers view their role as one of providing advice only when that advice is solicited, not unlike the relationship between doctor and patient or lawyer and client. That model is inappropriate in the current business environment.

Given the cultural elements I outlined in the previous section, CIO's in the financial services sector should expect to encounter some resistance from other senior managers, some of whom will feel that their turf is being invaded or their prerogatives usurped. Today's CIO needs to be persistent: We often have to re-educate as well as re-engineer.

As we defined our consolidation and re-engineering strategy at Fleet, we were aware that the key managers whose support we needed were the senior technical executives in the independent bank data centers that we wanted to consolidate. At the same time we knew that many would react to our plans, naturally enough, out of the impulse to preserve their operations and their own positions, not to mention those of their staffs. Even though our objective from the outset was the consolidation of IT resources, we approached this consensus-building stage with no preconceptions about which data centers would go and which would become the single-site facility.

In other words, we had delineated a consolidation and re-engineering strategy, but had not worked out the specific details of its application at our existing facilities. We used this element as an asset, setting aside several days for an exercise in which our data center managers would collaborate in building a hypothetical model of how a multi-bank holding company (comparable in size to Fleet and with branches in the same places) should construct an IT infrastructure for its banking business. The ground rules precluded any special pleading for existing site-specific advantages. Freed of their parochial attachments, our technology managers together created the model we employ today: a single-site consolidated data center with common software and products. That initial model yielded a set of working technical and environmental requirements that we used to evaluate the relative merits of each of our existing centers to house the consolidated facility.

IT and the CIO Can Make Vital Contributions to American Business in the 1990's

The discipline of automated information management is relatively young, and its strategic potential in business is only now beginning to be explored. From its origins in the 1950's well into the 1970's, the management of the IT function in business revolved around the struggle to automate previously manual operations, to perform straightforward, often high-volume, transaction processing. By the mid-1970's IT had begun to expand into the realm of management information handling, essentially reporting to management the data relevant to running the enterprise. The elaboration of decision support systems in the 1980's extended this natural evolution. Still, all these developments were largely reactive and supportive to what were regarded as the more important, mainline functions of a business. IT was a new management discipline forced to play catch-up in a mature organizational environment.

Today IT has achieved a degree of maturity in its own right and has begun to exert strategic influence in the businesses in which it is properly applied. The chief information officer, of course, is the central figure in this evolving strategic dimension. The performance of CIO's will increasingly be judged by how effectively they guide the information technology of their enterprises into leading rather than ancillary roles.

I have used the banking industry and its IT operations to illustrate the new demands and the exciting potential of the discipline, but the core realities that I have addressed apply just as strongly in all sectors of American business. Right now CIO's in all industries are faced with the same challenges and opportunities.

First, they must provide creative guidance in re-engineering the processes central to their businesses. That's a daunting responsibility in its own right, akin to shooting at hundreds of shifting targets. And the increasingly rapid evolution of systems and communications technologies adds other, even more complex dimensions to the task. To contribute strategically, the CIO needs to be attuned to the potential of new technologies, many of them not yet routinely applied in business, and then integrate them appropriately into complicated operations undergoing re-engineering.

The human resource issue is also increasingly important in the CIO's job. As the driving force behind the resource consolidations that technology makes possible, he or she has the unenviable job of presiding over sometimes extensive reductions in force. Owning up to that responsibility is essential. It's not a task to be taken lightly or passed off to subordinates or a corporate human resource unit. It demands forthrightness with and respect for good people who, through no fault of their own, find themselves in the wrong place at the wrong time.

The job of the CIO in today's business environment demands more proactive leadership than perhaps any other factor. More and more CIO's are taking their places on the senior executive teams of corporations. Once there, the CIO has to lead the way, and create the space for technology to advance corporate goals at the highest levels.

15–9   Selected Readings

Bank Mergers, Consolidations, and Related Topics

Berger, A. N. and Humphrey, D. B., "The Dominance of Inefficiencies over Scale and Product Mix Economies in Banking," *Finance and Economics Discussion Series* 59, Board of Governors of the Federal Reserve System; 1990.

Clark, J.A., "Economies of Scale and Scope at Depository Financial Institutions: A Review of the Literature." *Economic Review* 73, The Federal Reserve Bank of Kansas City; September/October 1988: 16-33.

Humphrey, David B., "Why Do Estimates of Bank Scale Economies Differ?" *Economic Review* 76. The Federal Reserve Bank of Richmond; September/October 1990: 27-50.

Katz, Norman "The Unfolding Trends in Bank Consolidation." *The Bankers Magazine*. January/February 1992: 12-16.

Norman, James R., "Megamergers: A Solution to the Banking Crisis?" *Forbes*. September 17, 1990: 36-38.

O'Sullivan, Brendan and Whitehead, Brian "Realizing I/S Savings in Consolidating DP and Operations Centers." *Chief Information Officer Journal*. Winter 1991: 5-9.

Watt, James B., "Bank Reform: Is Bigger Necessarily Better?" *The Bankers Magazine*. January/February 1992: 22-27.

Zucchini, Michael R., "Fleet/Norstar Cashes in on Centralizing I/S for Its Northeast Banking Institutions." *Chief Information Officer Journal*. Spring 1990: 15-17.

Re-engineering and the IT Infrastructure

Davenport, Thomas H., Hammer, Michael, and Metsisto, Tuano J., "How Executives Can Shape Their Company's Information Systems." *Harvard Business Review*. March 1989: 130-134.

Hammer, Michael "Reengineering Work: Don't Automate, Obliterate." *Harvard Business Review*. July 1990: 104-112.

King, Julia "Re-Engineering: Rip It Up!" *Computerworld*. July 15, 1991: 55-57.

Wilder, Clinton "Time to Make Hard Changes." *Computerworld*. December 16, 1991: 77.

The Outsourcing Phenomenon

The American Bankers' Association 1992. *Perspectives on Outsourcing*.

Apte, Uday "Global Outsourcing of Information Systems and Processing Services." *The Information Society*. 1990; Volume 7: 287-303.

Barthel, Matt "Industry Asks If Outsourcing Really Pays Off." *American Banker*. August 21, 1991: 1.

Caldwell, Bruce "Feds Alarmed by Bank Outsourcing Practices." *Information Week*. January 6, 1992: 13.

Crone, Richard K., "Negotiating an Outsourcing Agreement." *Bank Management*. March 1992: 59-62.

McPartlin, John P., "Is the O-Word Becoming a No-No?" *Information Week*. May 1992: 73.

O'Heney, Sheila "Outsourcing Solutions to the DP Puzzle." *Bankers Monthly*. July 1991: 27-31.

Schwartz, Julie "Ordering Out for IS." *CIO*. February 1992: 18.

The Implications of Downsizing for Human Resource Management

Lunt, Penny "Banks Soften the Blow of Layoffs." *ABA Banking Journal*. March 1991: 59-61.
Overman, Stephenie "The Layoff Legacy." *HR Magazine*. August 1991: 29-32.
Zucchini, Michael R., "The Real Art of Letting People Go." *American Banker*. December 5, 1991: 4.

Information as a Strategic Corporate Resource

Clemons, Eric K., "Competitive and Strategic Value of Information Technology." *Journal of Management Information Systems*. Volume 7, number 2. Fall 1990: 35-43.
Nolan, Richard L. "The Strategic Potential of Information Technology." *Financial Executive*. July 1991: 25-27.
Scott Morton, Michael S. ed. *The Corporation of the 1990s: Information Technology and Organizational Transformation*. Oxford University Press, 1991.

Putting IT All Together
Before It Falls Apart

Stuart E. Madnick is the John Norris Maguire Professor of Information Technology and the Leaders for Manufacturing Professor of Management Science at MIT Sloan School of Management. He is also an affiliate member of the MIT Laboratory for Computer Science, member of the Research Advisory Committee of the MIT International Financial Services Research Center, and member of the Executive Committee of the MIT Center for Information Systems Research.

His current research interests include connectivity among disparate distributed information systems, database technology, and software project management. He is the author or co-author of over 150 books, articles, and reports on these subjects, including the textbook *Operating Systems* (McGraw-Hill) and the recent book *Software Project Dynamics: An Integrated Approach* (Prentice Hall).

He has been active in industry, making significant contributions as one of the key designers of projects such as IBM's VM/370 operating system and Lockheed's DIALOG information retrieval system. He has also been the founder or co-founder of five high-tech firms and currently runs Langley Castle Hotel in England.

We have presented trends and perspectives in the IT industry. In this concluding chapter, Professor Stuart Madnick identifies critical trends in business and their relationship to some of the important new developments in the IT industry. Exciting new opportunities are made possible by exploiting the convergence of these trends around the issue of increased connectivity among systems. Enjoy IT.

16-1   The Double Threats: Business and IT Challenges

Most businesses, large and small, around the world are facing twin crises in both the business environment and information technology. How they respond to these crises will determine the winners and the losers.

The external signs of the business crises can be seen in the media on almost a daily basis. Companies that have never experienced an annual loss in their entire history, often going back 25, 50, or even 100 years, are experiencing first-time losses. Furthermore, for companies that have seen both good times and bad times, the losses that they are experiencing are often at all-time records, where the losses of a single year may dwarf the total profits of the previous decade.

What is even more disturbing is that much of this is happening not in the face of complacency, but often in sincere efforts to improve. Unfortunately, 10% improvements in cost reduction or quality are of cold comfort if your competition has improved by 20%. Incremental improvements, though always desired and beneficial, are no longer enough. For many organizations, dramatic, often even radical, changes are needed!

For a long time there has been an academic debate over whether organizations will be willing or able to make major changes unless confronted by imminent crisis. This issue is becoming an increasingly moot point for most organizations because the crisis is now here. You can think of these business symptoms as the "wake up call" for many organizations. If your organization has not received this "call" yet, it is highly likely that it is on the list to be called.

In a similar manner, the IT field is also being challenged. Not only are many of the key computer companies suffering financially, but the general mood of much of the public has turned skeptical. This is evidenced by dramatic reductions in the number of students concentrating in computer science or IT and by surveys of executive attitudes towards IT which indicate a dissatisfaction with the amount of gains realized.

These issues can be summarized by a typical criticism that IT in many organizations is not being effectively used and directed in ways that benefit that organization—there has been a disconnect. In some organizations, the "wake-up call" to the IT groups is being delivered with a "2-by-4" through radical reorganization, replacement of key IT executives, and by outsourcing.

Although such shake-ups do gain immediate attention, the long-term solution to both the business and IT challenges lies in understanding the forces affecting both and how they can be made to converge in a positive way. That is the goal of this chapter.

16–2   Key Business Forces

Four business forces will, for many organizations, shape their destiny in the 1990's. The first of these forces is the rapidly increasing growth in *globalization*, whereby the scope and presence of organizations are expanding beyond their traditional geographic boundaries. In the case of current multinational firms, the entire corporation and all of its subsidiaries are being increasingly coordinated to provide maximum impact, such as in manufacturing and supply activities, as well as in marketing and distribution. The inverse effect in the form of *worldwide competition* is also on the rise. This means that the number of competitors one must face in each marketplace and geographic region has increased by the entry of corporations that are expanding through their globalization activities. This puts increased pressure on the established organizations in these marketplaces and, in many cases, changes the entire nature of the competition.

In order to seize the opportunity of globalization and withstand the impact of worldwide competition, corporations are seeking ever increasing levels of *productivity* improvement. These productivity requirements take many forms. They may involve better coordinated manufacturing and purchasing so as to make maximum effectiveness in economies of scale and production, local efficiencies of labor force, and efficient purchasing and warehousing of components. Furthermore, by increasing the responsiveness to market trends and the requirements of customers, they are intended to gain sales volume and minimize wasted energy.

Attaining such improvements in productivity would be a significant challenge under normal circumstances, but the process is made significantly more complex by the increasingly *volatile environment*. This volatile environment emerges not only from the business forces described above, but also through various governmental, sociological, and legal changes. As one example, the various steps being taken to form a boundary-free European community represent a major change to the business map of the world, with implications both for business in Europe and businesses dealing with Europe, as well as rippling effects throughout the world.

As a result of various governmental and legal actions encouraging deregulation and privatization, as well as desires for corporations to rapidly accelerate their globalization efforts, massive mergers, acquisitions, and divestitures are taking place. Thus, at the same time that one is attempting to coordinate for maximum efficiency the various plans and resources of a corporation, the status of these resources is rapidly changing. Thus, if a division is sold off or divested, it is necessary to adapt both marketing and manufacturing activities to replace any capabilities that were being provided by those facilities. On the other hand, if other organizations or divisions are acquired, it is desired to assimilate these facilities as rapidly as possible into the total environment, eliminate unnecessary redundancies and duplication, and produce as efficient a marketing and production capability as possible. In a highly stable environment, traditional approaches to optimization and productivity improvements can be used. But, in this highly volatile and somewhat unpredictable environment, novel approaches to attaining high levels of productivity must be pursued.

In almost every major industry, these business forces can be evident and, in many cases, are fairly advanced even at this time. Independent from these forces, there are various developments occurring in information technology that have a strong bearing upon the situation.

16–3   Key IT Opportunities

Various continuing IT trends can clearly be identified. Advancement in both cost reductions and performance improvements in information technology is almost taken for granted based upon four decades of this process. As one colleague noted, although this progress seems continuous, in fact whenever a factor-of-ten improvement in cost and/or performance occurs, major discontinuities usually follow. The rapid infusion of personal computer technology throughout society in recent years is clearly one example, as is the current acceleration of local area networks (LAN's). There are many explanations for discontinuities, but in general they revolve around the fact that a 10% improvement merely allows existing applications and uses to be done somewhat more effectively or economically. A factor-of-ten change usually enables whole categories of applications to emerge that did not previously exist.

Although these advances in the individual components of information technology are quite important, an even more significant impact will occur as a result of new information technology architectures (i.e., new ways to organize and interconnect these components). Three particular trends in this direction can be identified: extensive communications networks, accessible distributive databases, and enhanced human interface workstations.

The development of high-performance, high-reliability, *comprehensive communication networks,* both intra-organizationally and inter-organizationally, is occurring at a rapid pace. At the same time, both hardware and software technologies are evolving in ways that make it possible to maintain extensive amounts of information on line, and to be able to access this information in conjunction with the communication networks from almost any location through *accessible distributed databases.* Furthermore, the increased capability of advanced personal computers and workstations, are providing many improvements in *ease of use* enabling people to work with these systems with much less formal training, yet be able to accomplish much more complex tasks. In fact, such enhancement in the human interface has been one of the many important aspects, besides the reductions in costs, which have enabled personal computers to be absorbed into our society at such a rapid rate.

16–4 Convergence of Business and IT Trends: Increased Connectivity

At the intersection of 1990's business forces and 1990's information technology opportunities lies the need and ability to provide increased and more flexible connectivity as depicted in Figure 16-1.

There have been dramatic increases in efforts to establish much more efficient and tightly coupled *inter-organizational business relationships.* A major thrust is to increase productivity, reduce cost, and improve service by providing highly automated end-to-end electronic connectivity. In the most idealized case, all of the processes from the entry of an order at the customer site, through its processing at the manufacturer's site, and on to the request for replenishment of necessary supplies, will be handled through direct electronic connections among customers and suppliers, with minimal manual intervention or paperwork.

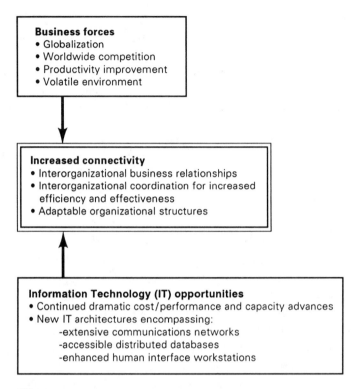

Fig 16-1
Advances in IT provide opportunities for dramatically increased connectivity, enabling new forms of inter-organizational relationships and enhanced group productivity.

In addition to these "electronic," arms-length transactions, there is an increasing emergence of "virtual corporations." This often occurs as the byproduct of the agreement among two or more corporations to pool their resources for the purpose of pursuing a particular business opportunity. In some cases, divisions or groups from sometimes hundreds or even thousands of separate corporations are essentially working together as departments within a virtual corporation in pursuit of the design and manufacturing of a product or service (especially for large military projects, e.g., B-1 bomber). This type of activity is being seen at an increasing rate as corporations strive to take advantage of manufacturing economies and expertise available in other organizations or particular cost advantages of labor and raw materials. In these situations it is desirable to set up an efficient management structure and information flow comparable to that which would be expected in a large, mature organization; but it is necessary to establish this infrastructure on a dramatically accelerated time scale.

Looking within a single corporation, we find various similar forces at work, driving for more *intra-organizational coordination* for increased efficiency and effectiveness. Due to corporate culture or the past limitations of information technology, many corporations have run as loosely coupled mini-corporations, each running autonomously from its siblings. Although this often simplifies the management structure, it incurs various inefficiencies. For example, the designers are often removed from the concerns and needs of the manufacturing and purchasing groups. This has led some organizations to strive to develop task forces that consist of members from design, manufacturing, and purchasing that work together as a group on new products. Furthermore, in looking at the traditional regional separation or product separation within corporations, opportunities can exist to take advantage of the entire corporation's resources, such as by pooling purchasing activities to gain greater economies of scale or by pooling warehousing and distribution capabilities so as to accomplish higher utilization and reduced costs.

As a by-product of these inter- and intra-organizational needs, we must also add forces identified as part of the volatile environment of the 1990's. Significant adjustments to an organization may need to occur on rapidly accelerated timetables, leading to the need to develop approaches to support *highly adaptable organizational structures*. It is not uncommon to read about an organization that has switched from being structured based on regional divisions to being organized along product lines. At the same time, another corporation, often in the same industry, is undergoing the exact reverse reorganization. Furthermore, in this environment of acquisitions and divestitures, it is not uncommon to find two large corporations merging to form a mega-corporation and spinning off various smaller divisions, either to operate as autonomous corporations or to be absorbed into other corporations. There is a need to be able to rapidly restructure organizations in response to these changes and to provide all of the necessary support in terms of the information technology infrastructure. This is being made possible, to varying degrees, through the developments currently underway in information technology.

16-5   New IT Requirements

There are many examples of IT already being used to provide increased connectivity noted in the preceding chapters. But, this is not always easy, especially for the situations that need connectivity most critically—large, diverse and inter-organizational or intra-organizational.

Two of the new IT challenges involve the *interpretation* and the *quality* of the information that is being exchanged. Within a single organization, close proximity to the information's source and its traditional uses allows one to develop an understanding of the information's meaning and quality. This is usually an informal process that is rarely documented. When information is exchanged with other organizations, the receivers may not be able to immediately realize any peculiarity in the interpretation (e.g., all distances for routes within the USA are in miles, but those in Canada are measured in kilometers) and, if realized, special procedures may be needed to convert the information into a form compatible with the information systems of the receiver's organization (e.g., all distances are in miles).

Similarly, although we would like all the information that we use to be perfect, the reality is that there are often deficiencies in areas such as accuracy, completeness, and timeliness. Realizing these deficiencies allows us to use the information in appropriate ways.

There is on-going research to address these new requirements such as the data quality efforts described in Chapter 10 and the Context Interchange System Laboratory (CISL) project at MIT, as well as related research at other organizations.

16-6   Conclusions: IT Is in Your Hands

The key message of this chapter is that in the face of severe business challenges, there is significant good news to look forward to from IT. The advances that have occurred and that are forecast provide for improvement through dramatic reductions in cost and improvement in speed, performance, and functionality of such magnitude as to provide opportunities that have not been identified at this time. This is similar to the way the advances in telephone technology made possible new ways to run organizations that were not foreseen at the time telephone technology was first introduced.

Some of the most important IT developments involve vastly improved and more convenient human interface to the systems, the ability to support the cognitive activities of the users, and the ability to access distributed information and use data semantics to gain a more compatible and comprehensive view across the entire organization.

It is important to realize that most of these benefits are not self-applying. Attention and action on the part of general management are critical. Consider the analogy of giving a power saw to a tradition-bound lumberjack. The lumberjack picks up this saw with a groan and attempts to move the saw back and forth in a cutting motion, complaining about how difficult it is because the power saw is so heavy and because the teeth on the chain keep moving. The problem is that nobody explained that there is an ON switch that would enable the power saw to perform the cutting motion itself. In a similar vein, merely "dumping" new IT into an organization does not necessarily mean that it will be used in a productive manner. This chapter is an attempt to highlight the location of the ON switch on your IT opportunities that would turn your organization into a power organization.

16–7   Bibliography

Dertuzos, M., "Building the Information Marketplace," *Technology Review.* January 1991.

Gupta, A. and Madnick, S.E., "A Taxonomy for Classifying Commercial Approaches to Information Integration in Heterogeneous Environment," *IEEE Data Engineering.* June 1990, pp. 28-33.

Madnick, S. E. "The Information Technology Platform," *The Corporation of the 1990's: Information Technology and Organizational Transformation,* edited by Michael S. Scott Morton, Oxford University Press, 1990, pp. 27-60.

Madnick, S.E., Siegel, M., and Wang, R. Y., "The Composite Information Systems Laboratory (CISL) Project at MIT," *IEEE Data Engineering.* June 1990, pp. 10-15.

Quiddington, P., "Cruising Along the Information Highway," *MIT Management.* Spring 1992, pp. 29-32.

Siegel, M. and Madnick, S.E., "A Metadata Approach to Resolving Semantic Conflicts," *Proceedings of the International Conference on Very Large Data Bases.* Barcelona, Spain; September 1991.

Wang, R.Y. and Madnick, S.E., "A Polygen Model for Heterogeneous Database Systems: The Source Tagging Perspective," *Proceedings of the VLDB Conference.* Brisbane, Australia; August 1990, pp. 519-538.

Glossary

Stacey Schussel-Griffin is the managing editor of *Schussel's Downsizing Journal.* Prior to her work at Digital Consulting, Inc., Griffin graduated cum laude from Wellesley College (B.A., economics, computer science). Griffin did an extensive amount of her undergraduate work at MIT (including 15.565). Future plans include returning to graduate school for an M.B.A.

The IT industry, like many others, has created a bewildering array of terms and concepts. A glossary of basic terms and concepts is available in Peter Keen's new book, *Every Manager's Guide to IT,* which is published by Harvard Business School Press (1991). Here in this glossary, Stacey Schussel-Griffin focuses on more advanced terms used in this book. Enjoy IT.

ADE application development environment.

ANSI American National Standards Institure. Works to develop and propagate computing standards.

array An N x M x Q matrix of data. Arrays are normally considered to be either two-dimensional (N x M) or 3-dimensional (N x M x Q), but there is no limit to the number of dimensions an array can have.

automatic locking In order to present consistent database views, a DBMS has to be able to hold the values of various fields constant for the entire duration of an update. In order to prevent another program from coming in and reading and writing against a field that is being updated, the DBMS needs to be able to "lock" the data until the update is complete.

back-end Data server; where data for a DBMS is stored.

batch unloading The process of taking a database, or a major portion of it, and rewriting or reformatting it to a new, external source.

BLOB's Binary large objects. A phrase that has been attributed to James Starkey, formerly of Interbase Software (now part of Borland), to describe a field type in a database that can store straight binary data that can, at any time, be converted by a custom macro.

caching The process that reduces object retrieval time by retaining an object in program memory after it has been accessed by the program for the first time.

CASE Computer-aided software engineering; software designed to run on computers to help developers create new software.

CICS Customer information control system. An IBM product that is an on-line, transaction processing monitor.

CIO Chief information officer. Person responsible for overseeing all computer systems and MIS personnel.

client/server An architecture where all of the applications are distributed across client machines (usually PC's) only, and the database(s) is located only on a "server" (can be anything from a 386 PC to a VAX mainframe).

clustering The ability to group together physical copies of objects in persistent memory.

COBOL A third generation compiler language that was popular for writing applications.

commit roll-back logic The process of committing an action means that the DBMS insures that all of the files affected by a transaction are properly updated before the transaction is committed. If one of the files is corrupted or can not be updated, then none of the updates in the transaction are processed.

component object databases (CODB) Systems with the added features of extensiblity and flexibility above and beyond DOB's.

concurrency management When changes are being made to a distributed database system, the database must be changed in a manner such that all users receive consistent data.

CPU Central processing unit, the processor chip(s) that is responsible for processing and storing all information.

database computer A computer (any type or style of hardware) that is dedicated to storing and managing data.

data dictionary A repository of data definition, or metadata. Normally concerned with the usage and meanings of the data types stored in the database.

data modeling The process of creating a graphical model to represent the meaning and relationships among various data elements in a database.

database creation Creation has many phases which include both the logical design of the database which is done by a human (a DBA), and the actual, physical creation of the database environment which involves the use of specific database programs or commands within the SQL language.

database engine This refers to the heart of the DBMS product. This is the software that is resident during run-time and provides the essential DBMS services such as record locking, concurrency control, creation of the log, and prioritizing input messages.

database management system (DBMS) The array of software which allows the creation and management of on-line databases. Such databases are normally available to multiple users concurrently and offer levels of data integrity against corruption. A DBMS controls, organizes, and dictates all access to the database.

database semantics Semantics refers to the meaning of constructs within the database.

databases of objects (DOB) Systems designed with more sophisticated database features above and beyond PLE's.

DATACOM A DBMS. Computer Associates currently owns that was built prior to relational systems, and therefore, is not based on SQL.

DB2 The premier IBM relational DBMS (RDBMS). It has been available on the market since the early 1980's and runs in the IBM mainframe MVS environment.

DBA Database administrator. Person responsible for overseeing a company's DBMS, database, and all technical database issues.

deadlock detection Part of concurrency management; the ability of the application to detect when a lock has been placed on the database for updates to occur. This becomes an issue in the deadly embrace problem: where two running applications have each placed a lock on the data the other needs to successfully complete the update. The DBMS must be able to recognize the occurrence of such a deadly embrace, and rollback.

design repository Where system information is stored for future application maintenance and enhancement.

distributed access Network-based computing where access from one computer is allowed to a database file stored at a remote location.

distributed database A database that has been distributed over several physical locations, rather than being physically located on one machine.

distributed lock manager When a DBMS needs a lock to be placed on a block of data, that request is sent to the distributed lock manager that, in turn, locates the data and handles the modifications and security.

downsizing A paradigm shift occurring in the IS industry where IT departments are removing applications from mainframes and minicomputers and rebuilding them on smaller machines like PC's, usually in a network configuration.

encapsulation An OO approach which involves packaging data and functions together with an object. This is how a OODBMS delivers data independence.

entity Can be either an abstract concept or concrete thing and can usually be represented as a noun. An entity is the most fundamental part of the ER methodology.

entity-relationship approach ER approach, a methodology first proposed by Dr. Peter Chen that is the standard for designing databases.

entity-relationship diagram Graphical representations of entities, relationships, and attributes. There are given, standard conventions for the representation of each of these parts of the diagram.

event notifiers A facility for a portion of the database to notify an external program that a particular event within the DBMS has occurred.

fault tolerant A computing environment where failure can be tolerated and the system can continue to perform. Usually this involves disk mirroring where there are two or more copies of the database which execute the same events simultaneously. When a failure occurs, all surviving machines (with identical copies of the data) can continue to process jobs while the down machine is fixed. Using this type of system limits the amount of user down time.

front-end The user's software interface with a computer system. Historically, this has meant a character-oriented interface but recently, most typically, this has meant some sort of GUI.

4GL's Fourth generation languages, these are application development languages that came on the scene after traditional compiler languages such as COBOL and FORTRAN (third generation languages). The first generation consisted of machine languages, and the second generation categorizes assembler languages.

gateways A combination of software on a client and a server which allows client software access to a database located on the server. Usually these databases are foreign (not from the same vendor) to the client software.

graphical user interface (GUI) The new style of user interface which employs menus and icons for application-user interaction. GUI's were popularized early on by the Apple Macintosh, and more recently, by Microsoft's Windows environment.

I-CASE Integrated CASE, refers to a system into front-end CASE (design) through and with back-end CASE (code generation).

IDMS A DBMS Computer Associates currently owns that was built prior to relational systems, and therefore, is not based on SQL.

IMS The premier IBM DBMS from the 1970's. A hierarchically structured system with a reputation for speed, reliability, and lack of user-friendliness.

information engineering A set of data and process models in combination with business models.

INGRES-STAR One of the first relational DBMS systems, developed by RTI (now the INGRES division of ASK Computers).

inheritance Objects in a hierarchy can inherit data and methods from superior objects in the same hierarchy.

integrity Refers to the general facility within a DBMS that can automatically be performed to insure a high quality of data. Specific types of integrity include referential integrity where the DBMS will check foreign tables where data is referenced so that when a primary table is updated, the correct corresponding updates will be made.

ISO International Standardization Organization, a group that endorses various industry standards, with special attention for communication standards.

JOIN An SQL function which merges relations on a common domain.

kernel Usually refers to the central, controlling element within a piece of software. For a DBMS or operating systems, the kernel is normally RAM resident at all times (not paged onto disks or part of virtual memory).

life cycle The various phases, stages, and tasks in the development of an application.

local area network (LAN) A group of computers (all within a close physical proximity) that are linked together for communication and sharing data through cables.

logging The creation of a disk or tape file of transactions that have occurred against a database.

loosely coupled An architecture where a bus is used for communication between processors of which each has its own memory.

LU6.2 Logical Unit Type 6.2. An IBM LAN communications protocol.

microprocessors Computers operating with only one processor (most common example - any IBM PC or clone). The most popular microprocessor chips are from Intel's 80x86 line (e.g. 286, 386, 486).

middleware Computational software that sits between the front-end and the back-end. Is not necessary for all applications.

minicomputers Historically this term referred to 16-bit word length machines or small, 32-bit word machines. Used for on-line, real-time, or time-sharing. The term "minicomputer" does not retain much meaning in the modern context of computing.

massive parallel processing system (MPP) Machines with large amounts (1,000) of processors running concurrently.

multi-threaded The ability of a single copy of software to maintain concurrent, open, multiple transactions.

object identity The ability to distinguish objects without using any of the objects' attributes.

object library Where copies of all objects in a system are stored and indexed.

OLTP On-line transaction processing.

object-oriented (OO) A collection of data and methods (procedures that can be done to the data) that satisfy the requirements for inheritance, encapsulation, and polymorphism.

OODBMS Object oriented database management system.

painting This refers to Windows application development environments (Window 4GL's) in which programmers can "paint" new applications using pull-down menus and icons, rather than actually writing code.

persistence A program's ability to allow object definitions to exist outside the programs in which they were created.

persistent language environment (PLE) Allows access to and storage for objects from within a given language environment.

persistent memory Where objects with persistence are stored.

polling Used to divide CPU time between dumb terminals. The CPU, sequentially, asks each terminal if it is ready to send a command or information to the CPU for processing.

polymorphism When the same method is applicable to different objects.

query optimizer The intelligent software in a RDBMS that takes SQL queries and determines the physical file search path necessary to satisfy the query.

RDA Remote data access. See distributed access for definition.

RDBMS Relational database management system.

real-time Events that occur real-time give immediate, or very quick, responses to queries.

recovering The ability to restore the database with the proper handling of transactions that were in the midst of being processed when a system down occurred.

relationship The association between two or more entities.

remote procedure call (RPC) A set of instructions stored in the database that can be called from a remote program and will be executed.

repository A DBMS embedded within CASE applications and tools that stores information about objects.

RISC Reduced instruction set computing, refers to the practice of encoding silicon chips with a reduced instruction set instead of the more typical complex level set. Examples include SUN SPARC and MIPS R4000.

robustness Refers to environments rich in functionality especially as it relates to professional data processing security and integrity issues. In other words, the word is not normally used to describe user-friendliness or other high level features.

security The safety of the database (both the data as well as the actual machine) which can be controlled both physically and digitally. Data can be secured through controlled user access.

software engineering Refers to the design and development of applications (software).

SQL A database access language, written in the 1970's by IBM, that has become the standard for relational databases.

SQL Extended Extensions to the SQL language to handle transaction processing and/or other features. Normally, individual vendor projects are several years ahead of standards. Therefore, most vendors are able to offer extensions to the basic SQL.

SQL query A request sent to the database for information, written in SQL.

storage manager (SM) Handles the physical copy of an object, including layout in both program and persistent memory and transfer to and from persistent memory.

stored procedure Procedures stored in with the database that can be accessed by programs running on clients.

super-servers Minicomputer-style hardware, built to run as servers in a client/server DBMS environment. These machines are marketed by most hardware vendors, and are built with common semi-conductors such as the Intel 80486 or SUN SPARC.

symmetric multi-processing (SMP) A computer system with several processors operating with one, single, common memory. An operating system such as UNIX needs to be provided to allow for the distribution of tasks across multiple processors.

table-level locking When an update needs to be done to a row in a table, the entire table is locked.

TCP/IP Transmission Control Protocol/Internet Protocol, a LAN communications protocol that is most commonly available within the UNIX environment.

tightly coupled An architecture where a bus(es) is used for communication between multiple processors that share the same memory.

TPC Transaction Processing Council, a group that has set several, important database benchmarking standards.

triggers Written in SQL Extended, they are small SQL programs stored in the DBMS. They are automatically executed whenever a transaction updates the table.

two-phase commits Process used to insure concurrency management for databases. This allows transaction transparency.

visual information access (VIA) On-line, on-screen DBMS reports.

VSAM An IDM file management system, lower in functionality than a full database management system.

Windows 4GL's A new class of projects that are called Windows 4GL's to indicate that they are newer and more modern than languages like COBOL, C, or FORTRAN. The Windows name describes the fact that these languages are used within GUI environments such as Microsoft's Windows, OSF's Motif, or IBM's Presentation Manager. Windows 4GL's typically work in a painting environment and generate applications which generally run in GUI environments. Examples include Powersoft's PowerBuilder, INGRES's Windows 4GL, Microsoft's Visual Basic, and Revelation Technologies' Open Insight.

workstations   Single-user computer systems that usually run UNIX, typically for engineering applications, and are powered by RISC chips. Workstations are usually three to four times as powerful as PC's. They also have larger monitors than PC's with one million pixel or better resolution.

Index

A

Academic journals, 10
Accessible distributed databases, 283
Active data dictionary, 76-77
Ada, 134
AD/Cycle (IBM), 88, 89, 110
ADEs, *See* Applications development
    environments (ADEs)
Advantage/Mantis (Cincom), 108
ADW (KnowledgeWare), 86, 87, 105, 108
Aggregated entity types, 21-22, 23
AI Corp., 7
Aldus Corporation, 232, 234
Amdahl, 7, 122
    Huron, 107
American Airlines, Sabre airline
    reservation system, 6-7
American banking:
  CIO role in, 256-57
  consolidation, 265-74
    advantages of, 268-69
    barriers to, 272-74
    check processing, 269-70
    of data centers, 267-68
    era of, 259-60
    purpose of, 260-65
  data communications technologies,
    263-64
  DP functions, managers of, 258
  IT role in, 257-65
  re-engineering of technology
    infrastructures, 261-65, 268, 270
American Management Systems (AMS),
    8, 155, 161, 241-54
  core competencies, 246-47
  business development, 247

    business/technology analysis,
      246
  complex business systems
    development/implementation, 246
  complex reusable applications
    systems
    development/support/
      implementation, 246-47
  market segments, 247-50
  client accessibility, 247, 249
  client culture/location/language, 247,
    250
  client size, 247, 248-49
  client technology preferences/
    orientations,
    247, 250
  industry/business function, 247, 249-
    50
  service framework, 251-54
American National Standards Institute
  (ANSI), ER model, 27-28
America's IT industry, 2-4
  report card, 3
  See also Information technology (IT)
    industry
Ami Pro (Lotus), 227
AMS, *See* American Management
    Systems (AMS)
Andersen Consulting, Foundation, 105,
    107
Andrews, Tim, 11, 63
Applications development environments
  (ADEs), 89, 90, 97, 104, 110
Applications development technology:
  alternative strategies/vendor
    classes, 100-112

forces affecting, 90-100
See also CASE
Applied Data Research, 56, 83
APS (Intersolv), 108
APT Workbench (Sybase), 109
Ashton-Tate, 230, 231, 234, 235
ASK/INGRES, 27, 58, 229
    Intelligent Database, 58
    Windows 4GL, 45
Asymmetrix, Toolbook, 172
AT&T, 8
Attributed entity-relationship (ER)
    diagram, 18
Attributes, 17-18

B
Bachman Information Systems, 6, 87
Bachman Workbench, 24, 25
    Analyst, Designer, and DBA, 107
Banking, *See* American banking
Bank Systems & Technology, 207
Banyan, 233
Bar charts, creating in VIA tool, 174
Barron's, 4
Batch unloading, 48
BLOB data types, 54-55
Block level locking, 149-50
BMC, 7
Boehm, Barry, 99
Borland International, 4, 7, 10, 58,
    227, 230, 231, 234, 235
    dBase IV, Server Edition, 45
    Interbase, 58
    Object Vision, 45, 172
    Paradox, 45, 64
    Quattro Pro, 231
Boston Globe, The, 5
Bottom-up approach, to enterprise
    model development, 23
Britton-Lee, 42, 118
Bulkeley, Bill, 199
Business:
    connectivity, increases in, 283-85
    and IT challenges, 280-81
    IT value chain and, 6-7

key forces in, 281-82
key IT opportunities, 282-83
new IT requirements, 286
Business process automation (BPA), 96-
    97
Business system concept definition, 253
Byte magazine, 4, 9

C
C++, 28, 64, 65, 94, 107, 154, 159
Caching, 69-70
Cadre Technologies, Teamwork, 107
Cardinality, 16-17
CASE*Designer/CASE*Generator
    (Oracle),105, 108
CASE, 11, 83-115, 159
    alternative strategies/vendor
        classes, 100-112
    bottom-up revolution/top-down
        evolution, 111-12
    model-prototype-build
        approaches, 103-10
    prototype-and-build approach,
        100-102
    benefits/pitfalls of, 88-90
    data-oriented techniques, 87
    development organization self-
        assessment/road map, 112-15
    forces affecting, 90-100
        client/server architecture and
            GUIs, 90-92
        iterative life cycle (process)
            models, 98-100
        multiple platforms, 94
        new application types, 96-98
        next-generation CASE, 95-96
        object-oriented technology, 92-
            94
    history of, 86-88
    lower CASE tools, 87, 100
    problems addressed by, 84-85
    process-oriented techniques, 87
    repository, 88
    system development methodologies
        vs., 85-88
    toolsets, evaluation of, 106-10

upper CASE tools, 86, 87, 101, 103-4
Ca SuperCalc, 231
CC:Mail (Lotus), 227
CDC, 7
CDD Plus, 88
Central Point Software, 234
Central processing unit (CPU), 134
CGI, 88
    Pacbase/Paclan/PacReverse, 107-8
Channel Computing, Forest & Trees, 45
Chen ER-Modeler, 24, 25-27
Chen, Peter P.S., 11, 13-14
Chief information officer (CIO), 2, 6
    IT industry perspective, 255-78
    new role for, 274-76
    See also American banking
Cincom, 56
    Advantage/Mantis, 108
Cisco, 8
Client/server computing, 228-40
    defined, 90-92
    market share analysis, 230-35
        desktop publishing, 229, 234
        drawing, 229, 235
        file managers, 229, 235
        integrated products, 229, 234
        languages, 229, 232
        PC database management, 229, 231, 233
        presentation graphics, 229, 232
        project managers, 229, 235
        spreadsheets, 229, 230-31, 233
        utilities, 229, 234
        word processing, 229, 230
Client/server database computing, 38-39, 41-46, 55-61
    background on, 41
    benefits of, 38-39, 56-57
        cost savings, 38
        faster application development, 39
        GUI interfaces, 39
        interoperability with desktop, 39
        robustness, 38-39

scalability, 38
client, 43
distributed database computing compared to, 41
functionality of, 41
functions handled by, 45
hardware choices, 57
history of, 42-43
network, 44
performance, 57-61
server, 44-45
software transaction capabilities, 59
SQL, 38-46
    benefits of using, 45-46
Clustering, 69-70
CM-5, 135
CODBs, See Component object databases (CODBs)
Codd, E. F., 117, 118-19
Cognos, Power Play, 175
Cohesion, DEC (Digital Equipment Corporation), 88, 110
Comdex, 9
Communications services, 8
Compaq, 60
Component object databases (CODBs)., 65, 71-75
    advantages of, 71-72
    component class libraries, 72
    PLEs/DOBs compared to, 72
    storage manager (SM), 72-75
Component-of relationship, 20
Comprehensive communication networks, 283
Computer-aided software engineering, See CASE
Computer Associates, 7, 40, 58, 83, 235
    Datacom, 40, 58
    IDMS database management system, 31
    IDMS/R, 40, 58
Computerland, 6
Computer press:
    functional publications, 207-8
    industry-specific publications, 207

technology-specific publications, 208
Computer Reseller News, 207
Computers in Libraries, 207
Computerworld, 4, 8, 9
  audience, 209-10
    direct reader contact, 209-10
    focus groups, 209
    readership studies, 209
    surveys, 210
  beats, 210-11
  on IT industry coverage, 201-16
    advertisers' influence, 215
    computer press, 207-8
    "gee whiz" attitude toward
      high technology, 214-16
    understanding gap, 203-6
  news reporting:
    bad news vs. good news, 212
    company size, 212
    decisions, 211-13
    exclusivity, 212-13
    fundamentals of, 213-14
    relevancy, 212
    timeliness, 212
  staff, 211
Concurrency management, 45
Concurrent, 60
Conference proceedings, 10
Consistent user interface, next-
  generation CASE, 95
Consultants, 241-54
  service framework, 251-54
  target market, 242-50
    general market, 243-47
    market segments, 247-50
Contextual ER model, 33
Cooperative Solutions, Ellipse, 45
Copy transparency, distributed DBMS,
  47-48, 51
Corel, 235
Corporate Computing magazine, 9
Cost savings, client/server computing,
  38
Cray Computer/Cray Research, 7, 123
CSC–Arts and Letters, 235
Cullinet, 56

Cursors, distributed database
  computing and, 54

D
Daisys (S-Cubed), 108
Data access locks, 143-44
Data audibility, providing, 196
Database computers, 117-31
  background/motivation, 118
  centralized data repository,
    connectivity options for,
    121-22
  characteristics, 122-24
  heterogeneous platforms, sharing
    data across, 121
  micro-processor revolution, 120-21
  NCR 3600/3700, 131
  RDBM, 119-20
  relational database architecture,
    recognition of, 118-19
  Teradata DBC/1012, 122, 124-30
    access module processors
      (AMPs)/disk storage
      units (DSUs), 124, 126-29
    architecture of, 124-30
    changes in, 129
    communication processors
      (COPs), 124, 125-26
    FALLBACK/availability, 130
    interface processors (IFPs),
      124, 125
    scalability/linearity, 129-30
Database creation, 45
Database engine, 46
Database instances, 143
Database management systems (DBMS),
  92
  ER-related, 28
Databases of objects (DOBs), 65, 70-71
  defined, 70
  PLEs compared to, 70-71
Datacom (Computer Associates), 40, 58
DATA data types, 54
Data definitions, standardizing, 196
Data Ease, 45, 231
Datamation magazine, 9

Data modeling, 87
Data product value chain, 185-86
Data quality:
    analysis of, 188-89
    continuous data quality
        improvement,
        institutionalizing, 195
    data quality management,
        operationalizing, 195-96
    data quality responsibility within
        IS, establishing, 191-93
    data quality vision, articulating,
        191
    importance of, 32-33
    improvement of, 189
    managerial impacts of, 181-83
        customer service, 182
        managerial support, 182-83
        productivity, 183
    managing, 190-96
    measurement of, 187-88
    new data quality skills, teaching,
        194-95
    project/system managers, educating,
        193
    social impacts of, 180-83
    See also Total data quality
        management (TDQM)
Data Systems Life Cycle, 184-85
dbase, 64
dBase IV, Server Edition (Borland
    International), 45
Deadlock protection/resolution, 45
Deadlocks, 150
DEC (Digital Equipment Corporation), 7,
    58, 60, 61, 88, 122, 229, 236
    Cohesion, 88, 110
    DEC Professional, 208
    Rdb/ACMS, 58
    Rdb RDBMS, 52, 56, 237
    VAX, 57, 237
Decision-support systems (DDS), 96, 142
DEC World, 9
Deft (Sybase), 109
Design repository, object-based
    systems, and, 160-61

Detailed entity-relationship (ER)
    diagram, 18
Development-support tools, next-
    generation CASE, 95
Development tools, next-generation
    CASE, 95
DiGiammarino, Peter, 199, 241-42
Digital Consulting, Inc., 9
Digital News, 208
Disk mirroring, 54
Distributed database computing, 38-41,
    46-55
    advanced capabilities, 52-55
        application-specific functions,
            55
        BLOB data types, 54-55
        cursors, 54
        disk mirroring, 54
        event alerters, 55
        extended data types, 54
        gateways, 52
        multi-dimensional arrays, 55
        multi-threaded architecture, 53
        relational integrity, 52-53
        remote procedure calls (RPCs),
            54
        symmetric multi-processing, 53
        triggers, 53
    basic requirements, 47-48, 51
        copy transparency, 47-48, 51
        fragmentation transparency, 48,
            51
        local DBMS transparency, 48, 51
        location transparency, 47, 51
        performance transparency, 47, 51
        schema change transparency, 48, 51
        transaction transparency, 48, 51
    client/server database computing
        compared to, 39-40
    functionality of, 46-47
    history of, 40-41
    IBM's phased implementation steps,
        48-49
        distributed tables, 49
        extracts, 48
        replicates, 49

snapshots, 48-49
market for, 40-41
problems associated with
    technology, 61-62
server DBMS compared to, 56
software optimizers, 49-50
two-phase commit protocol, 51-52
Distributed lock manager, 148
Distributed tables, 49
Downsizing, 38, 41, 155
Dunkle, John, 7

E
Easel, 7
Economic perspective, of data quality,
    189-90
EDS, 8
Egghead Discount Software, 8
Ellipse (Cooperative Solutions), 45
Enable, 234
Encapsulation, 31, 32, 73
Enterprise model development,
    pragmatic skills in, 23
Entity hierarchy, 19-20, 29
Entity-relationship approach, 13-36
    aggregated entity types, 21-22, 23
    attributes, 17-18
    component-of relationship, 20
    directions of, 28-33
        entity lattice, 29-30
        entity-relationship vs. object-
            orientation, 30-32
        quality/contextual ER model, 32-33
        time dimension extensions, 29
    enterprise model development,
        pragmatic skills in, 23
    entities:
        defined, 14
        weak, 19
    entity-relationship (ER) diagrams, 14
        detailed/attributed, 18
        variants of, 18
    ER-related software tools, 24-28
    gerund entity type, 22
    ISA relationship, 19-20
    relationships, 15

relationship types, 15-17
values/value types, 17-18
Entity supertypes, 29
Epstein, Robert, 42-43
ER-related software tools, 24-28
    CASE tools, 24-27
    database management systems
        (DBMSs), 28
    repository systems, 27-28
Event alerters, 55
Excelerator (Index Technology), 86
Excelerator (Intersolv), 24
Excel (Microsoft), 231
Existing corporate data, certifying,
    195-96
External data sources, certifying, 196
Extracts, 48

F
Federal Computer Week, 207
Fifth Generation, 234
Fine-grain locking, 148-49
First Publisher (Spinnaker), 234
Fleet/Norstar Financial Group, 256-75
Focus (Information Builders), 45
Forecasting, middleware and, 172
Forest & Trees (Channel Computing), 45
Fortune, 4
Foundation (Andersen Consulting), 105,
    107
FoxBase, 64
Fox Software, 10, 231
Fragmentation transparency,
    distributed DBMS, 48, 51
Friend, David, 12, 165, 166, 180
Front-end GUIs, 169, 172-75
    categories of, 172
        friendly SQL interfaces, 172,
            175
        general-purpose Windows
            development tools, 172-
            73, 174
        Visual Information Access
            tools, 172
Functional publications, 207-8

G

Gartner Group, 83
  reports, 9
Gates, Bill, 10, 204
Gateways, 49, 52
GEM, 235
Gerund entity type, 22
Gillin, Paul, 199, 201
Goldman Sachs' reports, 9
Graphic user interface (GUI), 4, 77,
  89, 90, 92, 94, 226
  client/server computing, 38-39
Grochow, Jerrold, 12, 153
GTE, 8
Gupta Technologies, 118
  Quest, 45
  SQLBase, 58
  SQL Windows, 43, 45
Gupta, Umang, 43

H

Hewlett-Packard, 7
  Softbench, 110
Highly adaptable organizational
  structures, 285
HPS (Seer), 109
Huron (Amdahl), 107
Hyatt Hotels, client/server system, 58
Hypercube, 135

I

IBM, 4, 6, 7, 50, 56, 58, 60, 61, 88,
  122, 131, 226, 233
  AD/Cycle, 88, 89, 110
  -Apple agreement, 213-14
    Pink operating system, 228
  DB2, 31, 43, 48, 52, 56, 122, 129
  Display Write, 230
  ER language prototype, 28
  IMS, 52
  OS/2, 53, 57, 61
  OS/2EE, 43, 58
  Repository Manager (RM/MVS), 28, 88
  software laboratories, 40
  SQL/400, 43
  SQL/DS, 43

I-CASE vendors, 104-5
IDMS, 120
IEF (Information Engineering Facility),
  24, 25
IEW/ADW (Information Engineering
  Workbench/Advanced Development
  Workbench), 24, 25
IEW (KnowledgeWare), 86, 87
IMAGE data types, 54
IMS, 56, 120
Index Technology, Excelerator, 86
Industry reports, 9-10
Industry-specific publications, 207
Infoalliance (Software Publishing
  Corp.), 45
Information Builders, 7
  Focus, 45
Information Engineering Facility (IEF),
  Texas Instruments, 86, 87, 105,
  110, 111
Information Resource Dictionary System
  (IRDS), 27
Information Resources, Inc. (IRI), 185
Information systems (IS) managers, 6
Information technology (IT) industry,
  1-12
  America's IT industry, 2-4
  CIO's perspective on, 255-78
  consultant's perspective on, 241-54
  information overload, 8-10
    expert advice, 9
    literature searches, 9-10
  investor's perspective on, 221-40
  IT intermediaries, 6
  IT value chain, firms in, 6-7
  market segments of
    products/services, 7-8
  media's perspective on, 201-20
    Computerworld, 201-16
    Wall Street Journal, The, 217-
      20
  participants in, 4-6
    investors, 6
    media, 4-5
Information technology (IT)
  infrastructure, 256

Informix Corp., 7, 27, 43, 58, 60, 229, 234
   Informix 4GL, 45
   Informix Online, 58
   Personal Access, 45
Infoweek, 9
Infoworld, 207
Ingres Division, ASK Computers, 27, 229
INGRES-STAR, 40
Inheritance, 31-32, 77-79
Inspection and data entry, 194
Integrated CASE vendors, *See* I-CASE vendors
Intel Warp, 135
Interleaf, 234
Internal data, controlling, 196
Internet worm, 206
Inter-organizational business relationships, 283
Intersolv:
   APS, 108
   Excelerator, 24, 108
Intra-organizational coordination, 285
Investors:
   and IT industry, 6, 221-40
      client/server computing, 228-40
      mainframe/minicomputer software vendors, 225
      new product introductions, 225
      PC software trends, 226-28
      securities analyst role, 222
      software/computer service company stocks, 223-26
      technological discontinuities risk, 224
IPSC, 135
ISA relationship, 19-20, 25
Iterative life cycle (process) models, need for CASE to support, 98-100

J
JYACC, JAM, 43

K
Kendall Square Research, 4, 118, 131
Kilgore, Bernerd, 218

KnowledgeWare:
   ADW, 86, 87, 105, 108
   IEW, 86, 87
Kon, Henry B., 12, 179

L
LAN Manager, 61
LightShip (Pilot), 172
LMBS, System Engineer, 108
Local area networks (LANs), 39, 41, 54, 57, 92, 121, 124
Local DBMS transparency, distributed DBMS, 48, 51
Location transparency, distributed DBMS, 47, 51
Logging and recovering, 45
Loosely coupled processing, 138, 139
Los Angeles Times, The, 5
Lotus Development Corporation, 230, 232, 234
   Ami Pro, 227
   CC:Mail, 227
   Notebook, 45, 227
   1-2-3, 231
   1-2-3 for Windows, 221
LU6.2, 44

M
Macworld, 208
Madnick, Stuart, 200, 279
Maestro II (Softlab), 109
Magazines, for literature search, 9
Management technologies, next-generation CASE, 95
Managing Automation, 207
Mandatory relationship, 17
Market segments of products/services, 7-8
Massively parallel processing (MPP), 133-52
   architecture, 138-40
   database applicability, 140-44
   definition of, 134
   high performance, roadblocks to, 136-38
   need for, 134-35

MCI, 8
Media, and IT industry, 5-6
Meiko, 135
Michelangelo virus hysteria, 206
Microfocus, 232
Micrografx, 232, 235
Micro Rim, 231
Microsoft Corporation, 6, 10, 58, 204-
    5, 210, 226-28, 230, 232, 234,
    235
    Excel, 231
    Gates, Bill, 10, 204-5
    SQL Server, 58
    Visual Basic, 45, 172-73
    Windows, 27, 43, 46, 57, 226-27,
        233
        Windows NT, 46, 53, 57, 61
Middleware:
    forecasting and, 172
    speed and, 171
    VIA systems and, 169-72
MIPS, 61
Model-prototype-build approaches, 103-
    10
    with multiple vendors' tools, 103-4
    with multiple vendors' tools but
        single vendor's ADE
        framework, 110
    with single-vendor's ADE and tools,
        104-10
Morris, Robert Tappan, 206
Multi-dimensional arrays, 55
Multi-platform implementations, 54
Multiple inheritance, 31-32
Multi-threaded architecture, 53

N
Nantucket, 231
Natural (Software AG), 109
NCR, 117, 118
nCUBE, 118, 123, 133-34
    Oracle for (case study), 144, 146-
        52
nCUBE-1, 135
nCUBE-2, 135, 139-40, 142, 151
Netware, 57, 58

Netware SQL, 8, 58
Network services, 8
Network World, 207
Networld, 9
Newspapers, company/product news, 9
New York Times, The, 5, 63, 203
Next-generation CASE, 95-96
Norton/Symantec, 234
Notebook (Lotus), 45, 227
Novell, 233
    Netware SQL, 8, 58

O
Oates, Ed, 12, 133
Object databases (ODBs), 63-82
    approaches, 75-81
        component integration, 76-77
        inheritance/registration, 77-79
        single-level
            stores/seamlessness, 79-
            81
    background of, 64-65
    product categories, 65-75
        component object databases
            (CODBs), 65, 71-75
        databases of objects (DOBs),
            65, 70-71
        persistent language environments
            (PLEs), 65-70
Object hierarchy, 31
Object identity, maintaining, 66-68
Object-orientation (OO):
    defined, 30-31
    encapsulation, 31, 32
    entity-relationship vs., 30-32
    inheritance, 31-32
    polymorphism, 31, 32
    technologies, 92-94
Object-oriented database management
    systems (OODBMS), 4
Object-oriented programming languages
    (OOPLs), 64, 68, 79
Object Vision (Borland International),
    45, 172
On-line transaction processing (OLTP),
    96, 131

On-screen reporting systems, *See*
   Visual information access (VIA)
   systems
ONTOS DB, 71, 77-78
Open Insight (Revelation Technologies,
   45
Open Look, 43
Optional relationship, 17
Oracle, 4, 7, 43, 50, 58, 60, 88, 118,
   131, 134, 135, 138, 141, 144,
   170, 229
   CASE*Designer and CASE*Generator,
      105, 108
   for *n*CUBE, 144, 146-52
   Oracle Card, 45
   Oracle Server, 58, 146-48
   Oracle SQL Forms, 45, 108
Organizational perspective, of data
   quality, 190
OS/2, 53, 57, 61
Ovation Technologies, 204

P
Pacbase (CGI), 24, 107-8
Paclan (CGI), 107-8
Pacreverse (CGI), 107-8
Paper-based reporting systems, 168
   problem with, 168-69
   VIA systems compared to, 169
Paradox (Borland International), 45, 64
PC Magazine, 208
PC software trends, 226-28
PC Week, 4, 9
PC World, 208
Performance transparency, distributed
   DBMS, 47, 51
Peripherals, 8
Persistent language environments
   (PLEs), 65-70
   caching, 69-70
   clustering, 69-70
   development of, reason for, 65-66
   DOBs compared to, 70-71
   efficient transfer of objects, 68-
      70

object identity, maintaining, 66-68
   primary function of, 65
Personal Access (Informix), 45
Picturetel, 6
Pilot, LightShip, 172
Pink operating system, 228
Pioneer Software, Q + E, 45, 175
Plant, Norman, 157
Polymorphism, 31, 32
PowerBuilder (Powersoft), 43, 45, 111
Power Play (Cognos), 175
Predict CASE (Software AG), 109
Process control, 194
Pro File (Software Publishing Corp.),
   235
Progress Software, 58
PROMOD, 24
Proteon, 8
Prototype-and-build approach, 111-12
Pyramid, 60, 236

Q
Q & A (Symantec), 235
Q + E (Pioneer Software), 45, 175
Quality ER model, 32-33
Quantum, 8
Quattro Pro (Borland International),
   231
Quest (Gupta Technologies), 45

R
Rabinowitz, David, 12, 117-18
Registration model, 77-79
Relational database management system
   (RDBMS), 229, 237-39
Relational integrity, 52-53
Relationships, 15-17
   mandatory, 17
   optional, 17
Relationship types, 15-17
   cardinality, 16-17
Release 1.O, 4
Remote procedure calls (RPCs), 54, 55
Replicates, 49
Report writers, *See* Paper-based
   reporting systems

Repository, 27-28, 33, 88
  design repository for object
    technology, 160-61
  next-generation CASE, 95-96
Repository Manager (RM/MVS), 28, 88
Revelation Technologies, Open Insight,
  45
Rin, Adam, 11-12, 83
Robustness, client/server computing,
  38-39
Rossotti, Charles, 199, 241-42
Row level locking, 150
R-Star project, 40
Rudin, Kenneth, 12, 133

S
Sapiens, 107, 109
Scalability, client/server computing,
  38
Schema change transparency,
  distributed DBMS, 48, 51
Schussel, George, 11, 37, 38
S-Cubed, Daisys, 108
Seagate, 8
Seamless environment, 79-81
Seer Technology, HPS, 105, 109
Sequent Computers, 7, 57, 60, 137, 236
Sequoia, 7
Sharebase, 118
Sherlund, Rick, 199, 221, 222
Simultaneously accessible data, 121-22
Single-level stores, 79
Slate, 7
Smalltalk, 64, 65, 94, 154, 159, 160
Snapshots, 48-49
Softbench (Hewlett-Packard), 110
Softlab, Maestro II, 109
Software AG, 56
  Predict CASE/Natural, 109
Software engineering, 156
  defined, 156
  for object technology, 157-62
    design repository, 160-61
    documentation, 158
    estimating methods, 161
    life cycle, 157-58

    methods/techniques, 158
    tools/languages, 159-60
    training/education, 161-62
Software Magazine, 9, 207
Software Publishing Corp., 230, 232,
  235
  Infoalliance, 45
  Pro File, 235
Spinnaker, First Publisher, 234
SPX/IPX, 44
SQLBase (Gupta Technologies), 58
SQL Server (Microsoft), 58
SQL (structured query language), 38-46,
  79, 92, 119, 124
  benefits of using, 45-46
SQL Windows (Gupta Technologies), 43,
  45
Storage Technology, 8
Strategic business systems:
  defined, 155
  object technology and, 152-64
  portfolio, 156
  See also Software engineering
Subsystems, 8
Sun Microsystems, 7, 61, 122, 229
Sunworld, 208
Sybase, 4, 6, 7, 25, 27, 43, 58, 60,
  64, 118, 131, 229
  Deft/APT Workbench, 109
  SQL Server, 58
Symantec, 234, 235
  Q & A, 235
Symmetric multi-processing (SMP), 53,
  146-48
System integration tools, 4
Systems design, 195
Systems development methodology,
  defined, 85-86

T
Table-level locking, 149
Tandem, 7
TCP/IP, 44, 124, 148
Teamwork (Cadre Technology), 107
Technology perspective, of data
  quality, 190

Technology-specific publications, 208
Teradata, 4, 118, 131
Teradata DBC/1012, 122, 124-30
  access module processors
    (AMPs)/disk storage units
    (DSUs), 124, 126-29
  architecture of, 124-30
  changes in, 129
  communication processors (COPs),
    124, 125-26
  FALLBACK/availability, 130
  interface processors (IFPs), 124, 125
  scalability/linearity, 129-30
  YNET intelligent bus interconnect
    (YNET), 125-26
Tesler's Law of Conservation, 68
Texas Instruments, 88, 105
  Information Engineering Facility
    (IEF), 86, 87, 105, 110, 111
TEXT data types, 54
3Com, 233
Tightly coupled systems, 137
Toolbook (Asymmetrix), 172
Top-down approach, to enterprise model
  development, 23
Tops, 233
Total data quality management (TDQM),
  1, 179-98
  data product value chain, 185-86
  Data Systems Life Cycle, 184-85
  framework for, 186-90
    continuous measurement/analysis/
      improvement, 187-89
    economic/technical/organizational
      perspectives, 189-90
    interrelated dimensions, 186
  managerial impacts of data quality,
    181-83
    customer service, 182
    managerial support, 182-83
    productivity, 183
  social impacts of data quality,
    180-83
  See also Data quality
Transaction-oriented database system
  software, 142-44

ultra-high performance
    applications and, 144-46
Transaction Processing Council:
  benchmark standards proposed by,
    138
  client/server performance tests, 58
Transaction transparency, distributed
    DBMS, 48, 51
Two-phase commit protocol, 51-52

U
Uniface, 43, 45
Unisys, 7
  DBMS, 27
U.S. IT industry, See America's IT
    industry
UNIX, 53, 57, 61, 107, 131, 137, 229,
    233
USA Today, 203

V
Values/value types, 17-18
VAX, 57, 237
Ventura Publisher (Xerox Corporation),
    234
Virtual corporations, increase in, 284-
    85
Visual Basic (Microsoft), 45, 172-73
Visual information access (VIA)
    systems, 165-77
  defined, 167-68
  pillars of, 169-70
    back-end database server, 169,
      175-77
    front-end GUI, 169, 172-75
    middleware, 169-72
VMS, 53
VSAM, 52, 120, 122

W
Wall Street Journal, The, 4, 9, 180-81,
    199, 203, 213
  on IT industry coverage, 217-20
    basic editorial direction, 218-
      19

      guideline for news worthiness,
         219-20
      Marketplace section, 220
      OTC Focus section, 220
      What's News columns, 219
      Who's News pages, 220
Wang, Richard Y., 1, 179
Weak entities, 19
Wellfleet, 8
Wide-area networks (WANs), 121
Windows 4GL's, 43, 45
Windows, 27, 43, 46, 57, 226-27, 233
   Windows NT, 46, 53, 57, 61
Wirfs-Brock, Rebecca, 157
WordPerfect, 227, 230
Word Star, 230

X
XDB Systems Inc., 43, 58
   XDB-Server, 58
Xenix, 233

Y
Yao, Bing, 43

Z
Zortech/Symantec, 232
Zucchini, Michael, 199, 255, 256